Individualizing
instruction

Individualizing instruction

C. M. CHARLES

Professor of Education, San Diego State University,
San Diego, California

SECOND EDITION

with **127** illustrations

The C. V. Mosby Company

ST. LOUIS • TORONTO • LONDON   1980

Cover photograph by Gerald S. Upham

SECOND EDITION

Copyright © 1980 by The C. V. Mosby Company

Previous edition copyrighted 1976

Printed in the United States of America

The C. V. Mosby Company
11830 Westline Industrial Drive, St. Louis, Missouri 63141

Library of Congress Cataloging in Publication Data

Charles, C   M
    Individualizing instruction.

    Bibliography: p.
    Includes index.
    1.   Individualized instruction.   I.   Title.
LB1031.C47   1980   371.39′4   79-26645
ISBN 0-8016-0974-7

GW/VH/VH   9   8   7   6   5   4   3   2   1   02/B/242

Let us build our lives
as works of art.

Preface

Individualized instruction — retrospect and prospect

The first edition of *Individualizing Instruction* appeared in 1976. Since that time, several important trends, some mandated, others emerging naturally, have appeared on the educational scene. Almost all of them have had implications for individualized instruction.

Foremost among the trends has been a *growing disenchantment* with public education. Historically, American public education received extensive local and national support. It was valued as the ladder to success, as the fire beneath the melting pot—the prime democratizing agent for American society. In recent years, the enchantment has faded. Highly emotional issues such as busing and other means toward desegregation arose. Beleaguered taxpayers began to balk at blindly supporting schools as well as other public agencies. The clamor arose again for *accountability in education*, for measures of *cost-effectiveness*. Lawsuits were filed against schools by parents of high school graduates who remained illiterate. This prompted a movement toward establishment of basic competencies as requirements for graduation from high school. The require-

ment of basic competencies, in turn, necessitated a return to the "basics" in education, taught in semi-individualized formats.

Accountability in teaching was the natural child of accountability in education. Teachers, being most directly in charge of learning, were called on to produce significant and specific learning gains in each and every student. This thrust focused attention on the individual student rather than on the class as a whole.

On the heels of accountability came a resurgence of *parental concern*. At one time parents trusted schools and teachers to do what was best for their children. Nowadays that trust, while certainly not gone completely, is jaded. Parents are monitoring their children's progress more closely than ever before.

To summarize these points, public confidence in education has diminished. Tax revenue for school construction, teacher salaries, and program expansion has shrunk. Schools have had to cut back on spending. Teacher salaries have not kept pace with inflation. Supply budgets have been trimmed. Music and athletic programs have been curtailed.

Extras, such as field trips, have vanished from many school systems. At the same time, the public is calling for accountability. Teachers and schools are expected to produce learning across the board, at a rate considered commensurate with expenditures of money.

But this general disenchantment is not the only trend affecting education and individualized instruction. Far from it. At least three other major trends have exerted growing influence on the formats by which learning is made available to students. Those trends are (1) the back to basics movement, (2) desegregation and multicultural education, and (3) the mainstreaming of handicapped students into regular classrooms. A fourth movement, based on research rather than politics, has shown new stirrings, too. That movement has to do with learning styles. A clearinghouse for research and development in this area has been established at St. John's University in New York.

The *back to basics movement* has come partly in response to fiscal and educational accountability and partly as a perennial swing of the pendulum between "frills" and "basics." First, money has become tight. Decisions thus have had to be made about what portions of the educational program would receive strong support and what portions would have their support reduced. Basics have been winning out in that struggle. Second, a continual ebb and flow occurs in education as regards control vs. freedom, knowledge learning vs. values learning, and the pursuit of individual interest vs. education for the common good. The natural flow in the last few years has turned more strongly toward basics.

This back to basics movement strongly suggests individualized instruction. Minimum standards, for example, are stated for everyone. Individuals are at different points in reaching those standards. Individually planned programs facilitate student progress toward the goals and furnish graphic evidence of progress. Since diagnosis of needs and prescription of activities are useful in such programs, individualized diagnostic-prescriptive instruction is a most useful teaching method.

A second movement, that of *desegregation and multicultural education,* also strongly suggests individualized instruction. Integration increases the span of abilities, aptitudes, interests, values, and achievement within given classes. As commonality is reduced, individual diagnosis, instruction, attention, and evaluation must be increased.

A third movement, *mainstreaming handicapped students*, does more than suggest individualized instruction. It has legal force behind it. Public Law 94-142, The Education of All Handicapped Children Act of 1975, stipulates that all handicapped children, ages 3 to 21 years, be identified and educated at public expense. This education is to be provided in the "least restrictive environment," which according to the law is to be the regular classroom, under the direction of the regular teacher, unless the child cannot function successfully in that setting. Exceptions can be made only by agreement of parents and special educators, and written justification for the exception must be made.

Public Law 94-142 also states that an "individualized education program" (IEP) must be prepared annually for each handicapped child. This IEP must state specific goals, objectives, instructional activities, and evaluation procedures for the student. This approach is, ipso facto, individualized instruction, which is named specifically in various parts of the law. The individualized approach called for in Public Law 94-142 is highly structured. It emphasizes diagnosis of needs and careful prescription of learning activities. This approach is synonymous with diagnostic-prescriptive teaching (DPT). The techniques for teaching through this method are discussed in detail in this book.

A fourth movement slowly picking up momentum is concerned with *individual learning styles*. In this approach, attempts are made to identify differences and characteristics in student learning styles and to adjust teaching methods and materials to those styles. While still more a whisper than a movement compared to the other three movements, it is based on a solid foundation of research. It is not unlike individualized instruction fifteen or twenty years ago. It is persistent; it is growing. New success stories appear regularly. It will be a force to consider in the future.

These newer movements in education have been accompanied by waxing and waning in other educational matters. Especially noticeable have been the trends involving commercial programs and materials, open and alternative education, affective education, diagnostic-prescriptive teaching, and the use of classroom learning centers.

Commercial programs and materials show simultaneous growth and decline. Materials for individualizing instruction have appeared in ever increasing numbers. There are more kits on a wider variety of topics than ever before. Duplicator materials for individualizing instruction have increased as well.

Declining in popularity are the large-scale packaged programs such as *Individually Guided Education* (IGE), *Individually Prescribed Instruction* (IPI), and *Program for Learning in Accordance with Needs* (PLAN). That is not to say that these programs have disappeared. Quite the contrary. IGE in particular is used in a large number of schools in the United States. Problems with implementation, however, combined with criticisms of its overall effectiveness have dampened the enthusiasm it enjoyed earlier.

Interest in *open education and alternative schools* has also declined. National concerns

over cost-effectiveness have combined with a back to basics frame of mind to nip the bloom from open education. (Don't confuse open education with open space. Open education is a style of teaching that permits much student choice and latitude. Open space is a type of building that doesn't have walls to separate different classes.) Many teachers still allow student choice in learning activities, but the choices have become more limited, the activities more structured, and the time devoted to them shorter.

Alternative schools still exist for students who do not benefit adequately from traditional schools. Their effectiveness has been questioned strongly, and the movement, while not dead, is in remission.

Affective education is still considered very important. It is approached rather differently than it was in the middle 1970's. At that time values clarification, morals development, and self image enhancement received much attention.

Values clarification is a technique that has flowered and borne seed. The bloom is gone, but its vestiges have been incorporated into many teachers' ongoing teaching styles.

Morals development has never really taken wing. The public usually drags its feet, or even girds for battle, when schools move openly into the realm of morality.

Self image continues to receive wide attention in research and classroom practice. The trend has moved away from using special exercises for self image enhancement. Many authorities now advocate success, responsibility, and the practice of good manners as the best routes to strong self-image. They believe teachers should concentrate on student achievement in regular curricular topics, together with responsibility and behaving in accord with the Golden Rule.

Diagnostic-prescriptive teaching (DPT), meanwhile, has grown by leaps and bounds. Already well established when the first edition of *Individualizing Instruction* was written, DPT now pervades almost every aspect of teaching.

This growth has come from several sources, most of them mentioned earlier. One of them is the resurging interest in the basics. DPT is especially well attuned to teaching fundamental material in logical, sequential order. A second source is the widespread establishment of minimal competencies, not only for graduation from high school but as target goals in many subject areas at all grade levels. A third source is the attention currently given to teacher accountability and to program cost-effectiveness. A fourth is the nationwide implementation of Public Law 94-142 for educating handicapped children. As described earlier, this law requires "individualized education programs" for each handicapped student to include specific objectives, instructional activities, and measures of evaluation—elements perfectly suited to diagnostic-prescriptive teaching.

Classroom learning centers have become more popular during the past few years, but they have tended to become smaller, simpler in design, and more easily stored and set up. They have moved steadily upward from their primary grade beginnings, entering general use in upper elementary grades, and making their appearance in junior high and high school classrooms. A trend seems to have developed that hybridizes learning centers with bulletin boards. The result is a wall-mounted display with materials and work space provided on a table beneath. This type of learning center requires less preparation, takes up less space, and is more easily managed than the larger, free-standing centers.

These realities and trends have somewhat changed the overall picture of individualizing instruction. Still, individualization has grown significantly from its own natural roots.

Individual differences in abilities, interests, tempos, learning styles, and so forth remain with us as always. Constant, too, is the educational philosophy of teaching to individual students, to take them where they are and then as far as they can go, to encourage the development of special abilities, and to press the pursuit of special interests.

Knowledge, skills, and techniques for individualizing instruction have continued their gains. Formerly, many people talked about individualized instruction, but few knew how to provide it. The majority of teachers now know how to individualize instruction, at least to some degree. They are comfortable with the idea and capable of implementing it.

Individualized instruction continues as a major vector in teaching. It still carries the banner of learning with efficiency, personal meaning, and growth of the individual self. Its importance transcends financial and political upheavals, undiminished so long as concern for the individual remains. The special skills and techniques it requires are there for the learning. It is the purpose of this book to bring them into easy reach of every teacher.

C. M. Charles

Contents

PART III

STEPS TO INDIVIDUALIZATION

PART IV

MODELS FOR INDIVIDUALIZING

PART V

INDIVIDUALIZATION—POWER AND PROMISE

I

THE GREAT DIVERSITY

*explaining some of what we
know about how people differ, and why,
and what those differences imply
for teaching, through*

1

How different we are

2

Human growth, learning, and personality

1

How different we are

trees, forests, and teaching

Who ever sees a tree in a forest? Who ever takes the time to know the one among the thousands? A tree is a tree. It is like all others. It has roots, trunk, bark, limbs, twigs, and leaves. That's about all you need to know about trees. Or is it? That depends. If you want to grow a tree, nourish it, train it, make it vital, help it to flower, help it to bear fruit, make its branches strong, make its leaves glisten, you must know more. Of course trees grow without our care. With it, though, they grow much better.

Knowing what to do to help trees grow is a complicated business. But it is simple when it comes to knowing what to do to help young people grow. Take our students in school (*please*, some would say). Their parents, their teachers, society, everyone wants them to grow strong, flower beautifully, calmly withstand every storm. The students want the same thing, only they don't know how to make it happen. We are not completely sure either. But don't be fooled. We do know a great deal about the young. We know much more than we put into practice, and that's a fact.

Teachers are very, very good at teaching

groups, at teaching mythical average students who presumably have the same intellects, the same abilities, the same personalities, the same interests, the same backgrounds, the same motives, the same this, and the same that. Teachers are not so good at teaching individuals, at teaching persons who are unique—distinct from each other in very important ways. Don't get the wrong idea. Teachers know that students are individuals. They would love to teach them as individuals. Many try extremely hard to do just that. Most of them aren't successful, at least not as successful as they want to be, and not, in truth, as successful as they could be.

Teachers find it difficult to teach individuals for three reasons. The *first* reason is that while students are all unique individuals, they are also very much alike. When you put them together in a large group, as we do in school classrooms, they become like forests that mesh the characteristics of individual trees. When you are looking at a group of thirty-five eighth graders, it is easy to see them as a group. It is hard to see them as thirty-five separate individuals.

The *second* reason is that even when teachers are able to see the students as individuals and are aware of their unique abilities, personalities, and so forth, they don't know how to teach each person individually. For over fifty years authorities have admonished teachers to recognize individual differences and adapt instruction to them. But few, indeed, were the authorities who ever said just how that could be done. No one made up sets of materials to fit all the differences. No one showed how to assess, quickly and accurately, all those unique traits toward which teachers were to adapt instruction.

A *third* reason is that even if teachers saw students as individuals, identified all their unique traits, and had the materials and strategies to teach them, how could they ever manage instruction? Suppose a class of students has thirty different ability levels, thirty different personalities, thirty different motivation levels, and thirty different styles of learning. Look at the combinations and permutations! Thirty to the fourth power gives 810,000 combinations to keep in mind. Even if you could identify the combinations, you still have to plan, provide materials, provide activities, give feedback, evaluate, and keep records for thirty individuals. The mere thought of it is mind-boggling. It drives teachers back to the lecture podium.

We had better take a moment here to catch our breaths. This book is supposed to inspire and instruct you, not turn you off to the idea of individualization. The chapters that follow will tell you how to individualize instruction, accurately and easily, with fewer tears than peeling an onion.

AWARENESS OF INDIVIDUALS

The first step you must take is to truly begin thinking of students as individuals. Later we will note some of the findings about human growth and development that point to the uniqueness of each person. But just reading those facts, figures, and conjectures

doesn't do the job. Somehow you must learn to focus on individuals, apart from others, yet in relation to them. If you already have that inclination, fantastic. If not, you must start concentrating on the individual rather than on the crowd.

Sometimes, awareness of individuals erupts in unexpected places. It happened to Arthur Maxwell when he took Mark, his 14-year-old son to enroll in high school. Maxwell tells of the event with special interest. He had been a university professor of American history for almost twenty years. Thousands of students had sat in his lecture halls. Rarely had he known one of them by name. He did his best to make the lectures interesting, informative, and provocative. He tried to make his examinations demanding but fair. His graduate seminars, with only twelve students, were not greatly different from his lectures. He talked, required students to report on reading he assigned, required them to write on assigned topics, and had them all write extensive essay examinations.

That routine began to change after he took Mark to enroll in Carson High School. He went with Mark reluctantly, only because his wife insisted. He believed that high school students should go through registration on their own. The instructions were simple enough. Anybody could follow them. "You keep holding their hands, you'll do it forever." He was disgruntled.

But his wife insisted. Mark was sick to his stomach with nervousness, very insecure, and much in need of his father. Maxwell asked, "Mark, do you want me to go with you?"

"Yes," Mark replied. Maxwell read the look in his son's eyes, and he knew he had better go.

Maxwell gave his morning lecture, then returned home to pick up Mark, who was waiting with his packet of materials. He saw that Mark wasn't wearing his glasses. "Where are your glasses, Mark?" he asked.

"In my pocket." The outline of the frames showed through the pocket of the jeans.

"Why are they there? Did you break the temple again?"

"No. I just took 'em off. I'm putting them back on." Mark retrieved the glasses with brown plastic frames and put them in place.

They drove to Carson High School, parked, and started toward the entrance. Mark walked a few feet behind Maxwell. "Walk beside me, Mark," Maxwell said, and Mark pulled alongside. They came to a bend in the walk. Mark cut across the grass, just a few feet away, but the shortcut put him in front. He didn't look back or speak.

Maxwell, saw, with a twinge of hurt, that Mark, his buddy, his special pal, his own kid who needed and wanted him there, didn't want to appear to be with him. Maxwell let Mark walk ahead of him into the auditorium. They sat in adjacent seats. Mark seemed nervous.

Maxwell was uncomfortable, too. The auditorium was filled with lively ninth graders. They yelled back and forth. Some crossed and recrossed between the seats and the stage, en promenade, trying their best to look cool or cute or whatever it took to be noticed. Mostly the kids seemed to be in groups of three to six. Remarks—cool, semi–smart aleck, sarcastic—came from all sides, about anything and everything. Maxwell scanned the audience. He spotted only three or four adults among the hundreds of adolescents. Am I uneasy for Mark or for having these kids look at me? he wondered. Why does my kid need his dad when all these others don't?

No one spoke to Mark, nor did he take notice of anyone else until suddenly he said, "There's Kenny." He pointed across the room to a boy in a yellow shirt. Kenny had spotted Mark, too. Talking to someone next to him, Kenny pointed across to Mark and waved. Mark looked away. After a moment,

he looked back at Kenny and waved for him to come over. Kenny waved for Mark to come to him. While they were motioning to each other, the principal took the stage and everyone quieted down.

After the introductions, welcomes, reassurances, and directions, Maxwell and Mark filed out with the throng toward the registration area. Kenny was waiting for them. He and Mark began to talk. Kenny talked incessantly. Mark commented once in a while. Often he would look at Maxwell after one of Kenny's observations, with a look of immense humor in his eyes. Maxwell would raise one eyebrow ever so slightly, and Mark would burst out laughing. Kenny hardly noticed, but kept on talking without addressing his remarks to anyone in particular.

They got in line behind a group of three girls and two boys who were caught in the ecstacy of flirtation. Every ten seconds one of the boys would say something and a girl would respond with an indignant blow to the shoulder. "You're awful," she would shriek. They would laugh and repeat the lines.

Maxwell raised his eyebrow and looked at Mark, who had yet to taste that sweet play. Mark's glasses were off. Maxwell mouthed his question so no one would hear, "Where are your glasses?"

"Here," Mark said, pointing to his pocket. "Don't want rain on them." No sooner had he spoken than Maxwell noticed tiny drops falling from the overcast sky. "Yeah, Buddy," Maxwell said. Mark grinned and protested. "Really. It's not what you think." He seemed pleased that the mist was falling.

They worked their way past a senior boy. He was checking to see that everyone had their forms filled out before they entered the registration area. He also methodically checked out the freshman girls, provided they had a certain look in their eye, as to appearance and feel of back and waist. How unerring he was. His scrutiny unfailingly brought tosses of hair and smiles from corners of eyes. Maxwell, now in front of Mark, threw him off, but just for an instant, when the heated young eyes turned abruptly on his 45-year-old face. "You—er—ah—," the senior stammered. Maxwell pointed to Mark who duly presented his papers for checking. Was that a glimmer of admiration in Mark's eye? Cleared by the adolescent lech, Maxwell, Mark, and Kenny proceeded into the registration area. Maxwell looked over the printed instructions. Mark's class schedule was among the papers. Maxwell looked at it, really for the first time.

1. *Basic mathematics.* That was remedial math, Maxwell knew. Other ninth graders were taking Algebra 1 and even geometry. Mark, at 14, still made errors in simple addition and subtraction. Rarely did he ever get a "word problem" right. He didn't know fractions well, didn't really get the idea of decimals, and couldn't estimate accurately in long division. Percentage was foreign to him. His failure to learn arithmetic had driven his mother to distraction. She worked long and hard, but she didn't get much help from his teachers, who always gave him work beyond his capability.

2. *Honors English.* What a contradiction, Maxwell thought. Mark read widely, far above average, composed eloquently, spelled well though sometimes inventively. He used both the school and the public libraries, searched them for topics that interested him, usually had four or five books checked out. His compositions showed an uncommon ability to turn phrases in delightful ways. He made plays on words and ideas that you wouldn't expect.

3. *Social studies.* This would be a conglomerate of history and geography with a little civics thrown in. Mark would excel in geography, especially in anything involving maps. They held a fascination for him. He always grabbed the map when the National

Geographic arrived, poured over it, memorized it. You named countries of the world, he would tell you exactly where they were located. You named cities in the United States, he would point to their exact location on a blank map. It was extraordinary, more amazing really than that Mark could repeat the significant dialogue, word for word, from any *Get Smart* or *Gomer Pyle* episode you named. How is it possible, Maxwell wondered so often, that Mark can do those things yet still be unsure of basic facts in addition and subtraction? The human mind is ever a mystery.

4. *Physical education.* Team sports. Flag football. Volleyball. Basketball. Softball. They could be fun for Mark, if the teacher made things right and didn't let students be cruel to each other. They could be awful if not. Little buddy Mark, Maxwell mused. Never played a game of real football, but thinks he wants to. Wants one of those letterman's jackets with a bright red C on it. Five-feet-four, 120 pounds, weak eyes, slow of foot. "Football's not for you, Mark," Maxwell explained. "You have to be very big and strong. If you aren't, you have to be very fast and very, very tough. You 100 pounds too small and 5 seconds too slow."

"Maybe I'll try out for the baseball team," Mark replied.

Oh Mark. Don't you know you never played little league because you were in real danger? Don't you remember that the ball would go over your glove and hit you in the face? "Well you might give that a try," Maxwell said.

Individual sports, Maxwell thought, would be right for Mark, if he ever had the chance. He could hit a golf ball long and straight. He could swim, not competitively, but well. He would like archery. He would dedicate himself to weight training, to build his body. But in team sports he was bound to be at the bottom of the barrel, the last one chosen, the one everybody yelled at.

5. *Spanish.* A chance for excellence. Everyone in the family except Mark spoke Spanish. Maxwell fluently. Flo, Mark's older sister, fluently. Mark's mother, adequately. Mark had already taken a year of Spanish, but he would not yet speak a single phrase outside the classroom. How do you get the timid to speak? How do you get them to be secure and proud of their new ability?

The mist turned into a light rain. Registration tables were hurriedly pulled into the gymnasium. Everyone went inside to get out of the rain. Lines formed at each table. Immediately the air was hot, heavy, moist. Yelling and laughing built an incredible din. Maxwell, standing near the front of the line with Mark and Kenny to buy student body cards, found the noise and heat intolerable. He wrote out a check for Mark and told him that he would be waiting outside under the overhang until Mark bought his card.

Maxwell went outside. The rain had almost stopped. He looked at the pool area, set up for competitive swimming and diving. He stood around. When Mark didn't come for him, he went back inside.

He scanned the lines and did a double-take. Mark and Kenny were still in line, but farther back than they were when he left. He pushed in alongside them. "Mark," he said with an edge to his voice, "what's going on? You should have been through by now."

"They've been crowding in up ahead."

"Good grief. Why did you let them?"

"I can't keep them from it."

"Yes you can, damn it. Tell 'em not to."

Maxwell knew Mark wouldn't say any-thing. He stood near the head of the line. A couple of students came up, spotted friends, and started edging in. Maxwell frowned at them and shook his head. They went to the back. Sweating and buffeted by the noise, Maxwell stood guard until Mark got his student card. He helped the boys through two more lines. They got their locker numbers and paid for their yearbooks. They went into the main building and located lockers, classrooms, staircases, and lunch area. Maxwell felt like he'd been through the wringer. "Remember how to do all this, Mark. You'll have to do it by yourself next year."

Driving home, Maxwell reassured Mark about the bus stops and schedules. Mark talked on, excitedly. His glasses were back in place. He looked more grown up and acted it. He seemed confident. Mark talked, but Maxwell wasn't listening. Driving through the rain, he reflected more and more on the students he had seen, on what he had noticed as an observer instead of a teacher. What an extraordinary range of personalities, some so brash and outgoing, some so timid. How different they had been in physical development, some of them little boys and girls, some of them looking like adults. What a variety of ploys they had used to draw attention to themselves or to divert it.

"How different we are, one from the other," he murmured.

"What?" Mark asked.

"Nothing, Buddy. I was just thinking." His thoughts held on Mark for a while. Bit by bit they shifted to the students in his graduate seminars. How remarkably different we are, he mused, one from the other.

2

Human growth, learning, and personality

Professor Maxwell had his eyes opened when he took his son Mark to enroll in ninth grade. His mind for years had dwelt on the sameness of human beings. Of course he recognized differences. People came in different sizes, colors, and proportions. Some were aggressive, some submissive. But their sameness, to Maxwell, was what made all institutions possible. After all, how could you have education if some people were horses, some lizards, and some amoebas? How could you have law or religion or politics if all people didn't have the same great needs, aspirations, and views of the world?

That notion of sameness was correct, of course. We humans are, indeed, very much alike. At the same time, though, we are very different from each other. Maxwell's experience with Mark at Carson High School helped focus that insight for him.

How can we be very alike and very different at the same time? The answer is that we are basically alike in the wider aspects of appearance, needs, intellectual capabilities, physical abilities, social inclinations, and so forth. That is, aside from injuries or birth defects we are made of the same kinds of bones, muscles, organs, and nervous tissue. These similar parts are put together in similar ways. We can easily tell the difference between any human and any horse.

The same is true for our psychological needs. We all have physical needs, needs for safety, needs for love and belonging, needs to develop ourselves and to experience aesthetic beauty. We all have the ability to form concepts, think rationally, and look ahead to the future. We all (almost all) seek out the company of other humans.

Our *myriad differences* occur within these wide aspects that are the same for everyone. No two faces or bodies are exactly the same, even for identical twins. Our metabolisms and growth rates vary greatly. Some of us are robust, others weak. The ways we seek to meet our common needs vary, and our social behaviors vary accordingly. Sometimes we are unable to meet one or another of our basic needs, and our behavior reflects frustration, hostility, or resignation. While we all can think rationally, there are considerable variations in our ability to use abstractions. Even our thought processes flow along different lines, some highly analytical and others more global and intuitive.

It is these differences, these very important differences within our sameness, that call for different approaches in teaching. If these differences did not exist, we could teach everyone in the same way, at the same speed, on the same topics, with the same materials. But you know from your own experience in school that students are not equally intelligent, that they don't have the same interests, and that they don't all respond to instruction in the same way.

The purposes of this book are first to direct attention to those differences that play powerful roles in learning and responding to schooling and second to provide practical, accurate advice on how to attend to those differences. The point is to make it possible for each and every student to profit from schooling to the fullest. That profiting to the fullest is the *ideal* toward which we strive. We are far from being able to reach this ideal, as matters now stand in education. We can, however, come much closer than we could a few years ago.

In later chapters you will see some of the effective teaching strategies and materials that have been developed in recent years. First, however, we will review findings about human growth, learning, and personality that have special significance for teaching and learning in the school setting. The review will be presented in sections on (1) physical development, (2) intellectual development, (3) modes of learning, (4) personality development, including social and emotional aspects, (5) special aptitudes, (6) exceptionality, and (7) levels and ranges of school achievement. The chapter ends with three instructional principles that are closely related to the points presented in the seven sections.

PHYSICAL DEVELOPMENT

The most noticeable source of differences among students is physical development. We can so easily see the remarkable differences in size, strength, speed, and coordination.

Yet these differences, great as they are, have less significance for teaching than do the other areas of difference we will examine.

You can see how schools have made accommodations for physical differences. The chairs, tables, and desks are made to the appropriate size and shape. Materials are matched to coordination and visual acuity. Games involve mostly large muscle activities at first, adding fine muscle control as students get older.

Physical growth patterns produce few problems needing special attention until students reach junior high school. At that point, two phenomena come into play. The first is the onset of puberty, which brings with it profound body changes. These changes produce an emotional effect that has strong bearing on learning and in-school behavior. Students are uncertain about what is happening to them. They become insecure. They may become moody and withdrawn for a time or wildly outgoing and eager to experiment. They often vacillate between the two states. Their minds are filled with more fantasy than fact about the adult world they are approaching. They are part babies and part adults, and their behavior shows both.

The second phenomenon concerns athletic skills. The die is usually cast in junior high school. A few individuals will show exceptional athletic ability. They are channeled into interscholastic athletics, the most fantastic programs for "gifted" students our schools have ever produced. They will enjoy the finest equipment, instruction, and opportunity. Unfortunately, the number who can make the grade is small indeed. Because special programs await them, their special talent has little significance for instruction in other areas of the curriculum.

INTELLECTUAL DEVELOPMENT

Differences among students in intellectual development are every bit as great as differences in physical development. They are much more difficult to detect, but they have great implications for instruction. We can see why this is so if we review the three major theories of intellectual development, each of which has a history of research to support it.

The IQ concept

IQ stands for intelligence quotient. One's IQ indicates the level of intellect as compared with others of the same age. The average IQ is 100. Individuals in the 120's and 130's are considered very bright, those in the 160's and higher are considered geniuses. Those in the 70's and lower are considered to have degrees of mental retardation.

The IQ concept generally rests on a two-factor theory of intelligence—the general ability of *abstract thought* and a group of *several special abilities* such as memory, spatial relationships, analogies, and problem solving. This notion suggests that all individuals grow in the same way intellectually, much as a balloon grows when air is blown into it. More advanced students have larger vocabularies, are better readers, can handle abstractions better, and are superior in solving problems. Less advanced students are considered to have the same abilities, but to a lesser degree. Most of the intelligence tests used today are based on this two-factor theory. There are two other theories, however, that are equally plausible and that have far greater implications for teaching.

The growth through stages concept

Work by the great Swiss psychologist Jean Piaget has shown strong evidence that the intellect does not grow like an expanding balloon. Rather, it is seen to grow through stages. One moves through these growth stages in a manner analogous to climbing steps. At each level, or stage, there are certain intellectual functions that one can perform. Equally important, there are functions

that one simply cannot perform, regardless of how much instruction and exhortation are given. Piaget has identified three stages of intellectual growth that are especially important to teachers.

The first of these stages, the *intuitive thought stage*, is usually in operation while the child is between 4 and 7 years of age. In this stage, thought occurs mainly in the form of mental pictures combined with intuitions, or hunches. What we think of as adult rational thought is not possible. Piaget found that children at this level are poor at remembering rules and following directions. They fabricate a great deal and have few feelings of guilt about anything. They are highly imitative. Most important, perhaps, is that their concept of numbers is poor. While they can memorize addition and subtraction facts, they cannot perform number operations with understanding.

The second stage is that of *concrete operations*. The average person enters this stage at approximately 7 years of age. This stage shows great new abilities. Students are now able to conceptualize numbers and number operations. They can use rational thought as long as it does not involve abstract ideas, which they are still unable to use. The thought processes they use involve the visualization of real, concrete objects—hence the name concrete operations.

Usually by 11 years of age, students begin to move into the stage of *formal operations*. In this stage, they understand highly abstract ideas, such as love, honesty, and loyalty. They can think about ideas—think about thought—which was not possible earlier. They are able to do adult-type reasoning, following the "forms" of deductive and inductive thought, thus the name formal operations. This stage is usually reached fully by 15 years of age.

Piaget found that all individuals pass through the same stages in the same order, but not at the same rate. Some move faster, some more slowly. For that reason it is important for teachers to identify the stages at which individual students are functioning. That knowledge tells them what they can and cannot expect from the students, as well as the kinds of instructional activities and materials that will be most beneficial.

The cells in the cube concept

Recently a new concept of the intellect has been postulated. J. P. Guilford, using factor analysis, has suggested that the intellect is comprised of the interactions of *mental inputs, operations,* and *outputs.*

Guilford calls the inputs *contents,* which can be figural, symbolic, semantic, or behavioral in nature. The mind can perform five different functions, or *operations,* on these input contents. The five operations are cognition, memory, convergent production, divergent production, and evaluation. The results of these operations performed on contents are called *products.* Guilford identified six categories of products—units, classes, relations, systems, transformations, and implications.

These three facets can be represented as a cube. The four contents make up one face, the five operations a second, and the six products a third. The interaction of contents, operations, and products can produce 120 combinations. Guilford sees each of these 120 combinations as cells within the cube. In this theory the intellect is comprised of these 120 cells.

This theory holds that the intellect grows largely from learned behavior and that everyone can improve their intellectual abilities through suitable activities. If research continues to support this notion, the implications for instruction will be far-reaching.

Mary Meeker has followed Guilford's work. She is researching means of identifying cells that are weak for any given individual and devising prescribed instructional activities for strengthening the weak cells.

MODES OF LEARNING

For centuries teachers taught as if students learned best through *listening* to what more learned people said. In the last hundred years books have become available to students, followed recently by great quantities and varieties of printed materials. With their advent, teachers taught as if students learned best through listening to and *reading* what more learned people wrote. Today most teachers still teach that way, with activities added to allow students to practice using information acquired through listening and reading.

Teaching methodology, however, is lagging many years behind what we know about learning. We know, for example, that at least 75% of all we learn is acquired through observation and imitation. We do, of course, learn through listening, and we learn through reading. But the vast majority of our social behavior is learned through watching and imitating other people. The implications of that fact are tremendous. Some day perhaps we will pay serious attention to them. Teaching through example will become more than simply a good idea.

We also know that people learn through trial and error, though that process usually involves many trials and mountains of errors. Trial and error is basic in what we refer to as "experience is the best teacher" and "the school of hard knocks."

We know that people can learn through pure reasoning, using deductive and inductive logic to "figure things out." We know that people learn through association, for example, the word *libretto* with the book of lyrics sung in operas. We also know that people learn through sorting and reorganizing information, a process that goes on continually in our heads.

We know that people use different senses in learning, that they can and should use different intellectual processes (making relationships, analyzing, and so forth instead of always memorizing), and that they have their own preferred styles of learning. For example, some people learn better through talking than reading. Some learn better through observing media and real objects. Some learn better by working with their hands. Some prefer to work alone, others with a partner, others in larger groups. Some like structure and close direction. Others prefer latitude and the chance to use their own ideas.

Yet most of us continue to teach in the good old-fashioned way—read, lecture, test. Not that it's bad. It's very good for some things. But there are other ways of teaching that open up additional learning opportunities for students. We should use some of them, too. In short, we should provide instruction that allows students to use different means of learning, using a variety of materials within a variety of activities.

PERSONALITY

Personality is the sum total of one's behaviors, emotions, and aspirations. It is the total self. It is not correct to say that Susan or John has a lot of personality. We all have more or less the same amount. Some personalities seem happy, outgoing, and confident; others shy, withdrawn, and anxious.

Psychologists believe that we learn the major part of our personalities. That is, we learn to be smiling, fearful, talkative, quiet, and so forth. Some evidence, especially from studies of identical twins raised apart, points to a genetic factor that influences personality. The preponderance of opinion, however, holds to personality as learned behavior.

Interesting and provocative theories have been put forth to explain personality development. Notable examples come from the works of Erik Erikson, Abraham Maslow, and Sigmund Freud.

Erikson's theory

Erikson, a Dane who immigrated to the United States in 1931, theorizes that personality develops through eight stages. Each stage includes a major conflict. Successful resolution of the conflict permits healthy growth to continue. Unsuccessful resolution shackles the individual with psychological impediments that make full, healthy functioning impossible. The eight stages are as follows.

Basic trust vs. basic mistrust. This conflict predominates during the first year and a half of a person's life. Whether the child becomes basically trusting or basically distrusting, both of self and others, depends on the quality of mothering, which should combine sensitive care and reliability.

Autonomy vs. shame and doubt. This conflict emerges during the second year of life, usually at about 18 months of age, when we begin to distinguish between ourselves and others. If adults generally approve and encourage the child's behavior, self confidence and self direction grow. If behavior is generally disapproved and punished, the individual may be forever troubled with self doubt and shame.

Initiative vs. guilt. By 3 years of age children are actively exploring and trying out new behaviors. It is natural for them to show much initiative, and they will continue to do so later provided their explorations are encouraged at this stage. If their explorations bring continual punishment and reprimand, however, initiative will be stifled and they will be plagued by a continuing sense of guilt.

Industry vs. inferiority. This is the basic conflict the child must face between 6 and 12 years of age. Children have great new physical and intellectual powers. They are eager to use them. When encouraged to apply them to play or purposeful tasks, a strong sense of industry develops, along with a sense of competence. If one's activities are generally frowned on, the opposite occurs. A gross feeling of inferiority results, one that is very difficult to eradicate later in life.

Identity vs. identity confusion. Between 12 and 18 years of age, individuals move toward becoming independent adults. A search begins for identity. Who am I? What am I? Which models should I emulate? Their struggles will produce much conflict with adults, especially parents. Yet they must be encouraged to develop a sense of who they are, what they can do, what their relations with others can be. Patient, understanding, gently guiding adults help the young find clear identity. Without that identity, they struggle in confusion about their roles and purposes in life.

Intimacy vs. isolation. This is a time when young adults seek intimate relationships with others, relationships that go beyond close acquaintanceship and require significant commitments. Failure to establish such relationships at this stage greatly reduces the chances of ever being able to do so.

Generativity vs. stagnation. Generativity refers to procreation, productivity, and creativity. When unsuccessful in this stage, the individual has great difficulty moving ahead on any front, tending to feel useless, unsuccessful, and personally impoverished.

Ego integrity vs. despair. This is the major conflict of middle age. One thinks the course is run, the game played out. Those feelings lead to general despair. Life seems wasted. Death is feared. Successful ego integrity permits one to look back on life, take satisfaction in it, and continue with the feeling that it has been good and worthwhile.

Freud's theory

Sigmund Freud is called the Father of Psychoanalysis. His theory of personality development is probably the most important theory ever proposed in psychology. Its importance has little to do with whether it is right or wrong. It is important because of the vast amounts of reflection, research, and argument it has stimulated.

Briefly, Freud theorized that personality is comprised of three parts, all working in concert. They are the *id*, the *ego*, and the *superego*. The *id* is the original personality with which we are born. It is totally unconscious, and it always operates on the "pleasure principle." Soon after birth, the *ego* develops. It is conscious, a computer that operates on the "reality principle." It sizes up situations and selects courses of action, without attention to right or wrong, but with recognition of possible consequences of actions. The *superego* develops as the child begins to internalize values. It is moralistic, concerned with right and wrong. It is conscience, and it operates on the conscious level. It struggles against the "bad" desires of the *id*.

Freud also theorized that one's basic personality is fixed very early in life. Key times are the periods of suckling and toilet training. If the infant does not do a sufficient amount of suckling before weaning, he may develop an "oral fixation" and continue through life doing things that bring oral gratification such as chewing gum, smoking, and eating excessively. People with this fixation tend to be gullible. They are usually dependent on others in times of stress, as they were dependent on their mothers for suckling. When aggressive they are argumentative, using sarcasm and biting wit.

Freud believed that children who have unpleasant experiences during toilet training acquire "anal fixations." Their personalities later show behavior characterized as stingy, stubborn, cruel, and destructive.

To the understanding of human beings, as in teaching, one of Freud's contributions is the identification of *defense mechanisms* that all of us use to a greater or lesser degree.

These mechanisms are intended to protect oneself from hurt. They are often counterproductive, however, because they deny, falsify, or distort reality. They function at the unconscious level, and individuals are seldom aware that they are using them. The main defense mechanisms are:

1. *Repression*—blocking traumatic events from the conscious mind. We hold them in the subconscious and cannot recall them at will. This mechanism is rarely of concern to teachers.
2. *Projection*—assigning to other people hurtful defects or shortcomings seen in oneself. Teachers often see this mechanism evidenced in tattling and gossip.
3. *Regression*—returning to behavior that was successful in earlier phases of life, such as crying, pouting, throwing temper tantrums, or showing dependent submissiveness, when threatened.
4. *Displacement*—taking out one's frustration built up against the boss, job, teacher, or bully on someone who won't fight back.
5. *Rationalization*—finding reasons and excuses for every shortcoming, explaining away the problem.
6. *Fantasy*—finding escape in fantasizing and daydreaming when things get too tough.

Also very common are children's behaviors of aggression, lying, cheating, and stealing. From a Freudian point of view, these behaviors are means of defending the self from danger and feelings of inferiority.

Maslow's theory

Freud's theories focus on maladaptive behavior, on the actions of people having trouble coping with life. A more positive theory is that proposed by Abraham Maslow. Maslow believed that a healthy growth motive was the prime thrust in everyone's life. This concept of a basic drive toward healthy growth has attracted much attention, especially among people who work in the helping professions such as teaching, counseling, and social work.

Maslow believed that each of us is in a continual state of "becoming." We are never static. We are always in a process of change. If people are able to behave "normally," that is, able to meet their basic needs, the process of change always takes them in the direction of greater growth, ever toward the "fully functioning" state. To Maslow and to other psychologists of the same persuasion, full functioning is the ideal, the highest level of humanness.

For Maslow, personality development could be explained in light of this basic growth motive. If unthwarted, one could fill all basic human needs. By so doing, the personality reflected security, sense of self worth, confidence, and positive relations with others. If the normal growth process were stifled through inability to fulfill basic needs, the personality reflected less than optimal humanness. One might, because of resignation or frustration, show insecurity, hostility, aggression, deviousness, feeling of inferiority, or lack of self worth.

Maslow hypothesized a series of levels of need, called "Maslow's Hierarchy of Needs," which, from lowest to highest, are aesthetic, self actualization, esteem, love and belonging, safety, and physiological. Maslow believed that all of us have this same basic group of needs. Further, we must continually fill the lower order needs before we can fill the higher order needs. That is, we must have food, water, shelter, and protection from harm before we are much concerned about seeking the esteem of others.

Full functioning requires that one reach the highest levels, that one earn the esteem of others, that one self actualize (be self directing, continually developing, and using potentialities to a high degree) and seek and find beauty in all its forms.

The implications of Maslow's ideas are clear. Schools must endeavor to help students meet needs at all levels. Oftentimes this will be difficult. Schools cannot control what happens to students outside school, nor more than to a moderate degree what happens inside. Persons who are very hungry do not show an abiding interest in aesthetics. Persons who are very fearful can never self actualize.

Because teachers have only moderate opportunity to help students meet their basic needs, the influence we do have should be as efficient as possible. It should be the best we can do, through example, care, and concern.

SPECIAL APTITUDES

An aptitude is a proclivity, an inherent natural ability for something. We all have aptitudes for the entire range of human behavior. Many persons have one or more "special" aptitudes, aptitudes that are so strong they stand apart. We sometimes see manifestations of such aptitudes in music. Most of us can hum "Twinkle, Twinkle, Little Star," but few of us can play concert piano at 6 years of age as Mozart did.

We see persons with special aptitudes of many different types—for math, for mechanics, for gymnastics, for art, and so forth. If one mission of teachers is to help students develop unique talents, we must search out and nurture the unusual abilities that we see in students.

EXCEPTIONALITY

That which falls outside the range of "normal" is by definition "abnormal." Normal technically means average or typical of the majority of people. In common use, however, normal has come to refer to all but the most extreme cases of behavior or appearance. Abnormal, on the other hand, has come to mean undesirable, something to be shunned. For these reasons we have come to use the word "exceptional" instead of abnormal for those individuals who stand apart

from the majority. One may be labeled exceptional by reason of very high or very low intelligence, by reason of special aptitude or low achievement, or by reason of organic, orthopedic, or emotional dysfunctions.

Students identified as exceptional often spend at least part of each day in special classrooms in which the instruction and facilities are specially suited to them. More and more they are also being "mainstreamed." This means they attend regular classes with "normal" students for at least part of the day. When they are mainstreamed, the classroom teacher must provide them the special instruction they require. Today, most schools give special attention to students who are mentally gifted, mentally retarded, educationally handicapped, blind, partially sighted, deaf, hard of hearing, speech impaired, and orthopedically handicapped. Mainstreaming of these students makes individualized instruction not only desirable, but essential.

LEVELS AND RANGES OF ACHIEVEMENT

One of the great illusions under which we teachers operate is that of "grade level." Fifth grade teachers use a complete set of "fifth grade" books. They mourn if all their students don't read up to fifth grade level. They gnash their teeth because some are only at third grade level in math.

Getting everybody to grade level is a fine ideal, but teachers have to work with reality as well as ideals. Don't misunderstand. This is no apology. We can do a great deal to speed slower learners. But the fact is simple: no matter what you do, no matter how well you teach, no matter how many extra hours you give the lower achievers—you will still have a spread of achievement in your grade or class. The spread will be wide. There is nothing you can do about it. In fact, there is sound reason to believe that very good teaching actually serves to increase, rather than decrease, the spread of achievement.

Rather than fight against this spread, teachers should adjust instruction to it. They do that by supplying, so far as they can, instruction that has the right mixture of familiarity and challenge for every student. If you are teaching sophomore English but have students who cannot read the tenth grade books, you have to find things they can read. At the same time, those experiences should improve their reading ability. Similarly, if you are teaching fourth grade but have students who can read at high school level, you need to do something for them besides have them take turns reading from the fourth grade reader.

Regardless of the grade level, be it kindergarten, twelfth grade, or graduate school, you will find widely differing levels of knowledge and ability among the students. In a fourth grade, for example, a typical class of thirty-two students will have a range of reading achievement such as that given in the following:

Grade level	Number of students
1	1
2	3
3	7
4	10
5	7
6	3
7	1

There is a span of seven years for this hypothetical class. Research has shown that the typical span of reading achievement for a class is *four years* at second grade, increasing to *ten years* by eighth grade. The higher the grade level, the fewer students reading at grade level. The same is true for other curriculum areas, such as language, mathematics, science, and physical education. The point is clear. Rather than expect one's students to be "at" grade level, one should expect them *not* to be at grade level. Those who are constitute the minority, not the majority.

PRINCIPLES OF TEACHING

Principles of teaching are ideas and practices that have held true over long periods for learners of all types. Presented here are three such principles that are crucial in teaching individual students.

1. All humans have a natural potential for learning. Some learn faster than others, but all continue to learn throughout life.
2. Humans vary greatly in several ways that affect learning. Among those differences are:
   a. Intellectual development
   b. Background of experiences
   c. Levels of school achievement
   d. Preferred styles of learning
3. Humans learn fastest when instruction, including classroom climate, materials, and activities, is matched to their intellect, background, personality, interests, and preferred styles of learning.

SUMMARY

In this chapter an overview of human growth and development was presented, focusing on the ways people differ. Special attention was given to differences in physical development, intellectual development, modes of learning, personality development, special aptitudes, exceptionality, and ranges of school achievement. A listing of three principles of teaching, especially significant for individualized instruction, concluded the chapter.

II

THE MYSTERIOUS SELF

*exploring some regions, only
partially charted, of the individual
personality; revealing a strong
relationship between self image
and behavior; postulating ways
of strengthening self image; and
suggesting adaptations between teaching
and individual styles of learning,
through*

3

The new humanism

Dear Reader, will you take a few minutes to hear the story of Samuel Morgan?

Sam burst upon the scene (well, you must allow a few exaggerations) as seventh grade teacher in a small town out West. Not *a* seventh grade teacher—*the* seventh grade teacher. There were only enough kids for one. Twenty-nine young scholars fell under his tender care, all craving wisdom but considerate enough not to show it. To outward appearances, in fact, they seemed at first utterly indifferent toward the immense promise of schooling. Not hostile, not antagonistic. Just indifferent. They endured reading and math and geography, figuring that the Louisiana Purchase, dangling participles, and inverting to multiply were natural parts of the misfortune of being young.

It wasn't that they were altogether unmotivated and ignorant. They knew at least a thousand times more than Sam about steers and calves and "'em ole cows out there." They cussed fifty times better, principally because they practiced so much. They could, every boy and girl, ride horseback all day without blistering their tails, and even if they fell off the horse, which they almost never did, they knew how to catch it and get back on. They could tell by the way the thunderheads looked whether it was going to rain hard, hail like the dickens, or just blow sand. They could call chickens, butcher hogs, drive every known brand of tractor, trap quail, and smoke cigarettes on the sly.

Sam brought to this group of youngsters the following things:

Himself (of course)
An undecipherable philosophy of education
A passable grasp of the English, math, and other wisdom of the ages he was supposed to pass along
A disorganized bundle of teaching skills
A vague set of high standards and expectations
A grade book
A lesson plan book left by the teacher before, who had used only 2% of it
Three or four textbooks for each kid
A dictionary, a couple of charts, and a few odds and ends
A level of overconfidence bound to get shot down, which it did

Good ole naive Sam. A preordained failure, right?

In truth, his chances didn't look too good. The kids resembled only slightly the adolescents in the city where he had done his student teaching. They showed up for school looking around, acting sort of scared, the boys in their fresh bowl haircuts with white scalp shining, new Levi's, worn but polished boots; the girls wearing dresses for one of the few times in the year, pigtails with ribbons, and brown oxfords with white socks. When they found Sam wasn't fierce, they took to giggling, showing off, yelling, and acting silly, even (can you believe it?) when Sam was talking, a situation that alternately angered him, left him nonplussed, and threw him into a state of powerless despair. Sam was merely nervous the first day. He literally dreaded the second, and the third, and the fourth, and. . . .

You may be interested to know that Sam didn't give up. He didn't go insane. He didn't take to drink, nor begin beating his adoring wife. As a matter of historical fact, he turned out to be, all in all, pleasingly effective as a teacher, with occasional trials and tribulations to be sure, but also with fleeting moments now and then of wild, wonderful, ecstatic success.

How this happened bears reviewing because it points to some of the things today's "humanists" are urging on us. They are telling us to be concerned with humane-ness, with feeling for others, with values and morality, with well-rounded full development of human potentialities.

Sam Morgan didn't think up a grand scheme loaded with these laudable points for working with his seventh grade charges. It would be nice to say he used them because he had remembered that Rousseau and Pestalozzi and Dewey and Jesus and Confucius and a lot of other smart people thought of them long before. He didn't, though. He learned to work effectively with his kids through an unlikely mixture of perceptiveness, inventiveness, responsiveness, and dumb luck. He also remembered a few favorite things his own teachers had done years before.

Little by little he found that things went better when

Students had a chance to talk about things they especially enjoyed, like the State Fair, the local movie, the ball game, animal pets, hunting trips, and assorted holidays.

He read them stories and books like *Robinson Crusoe, Moby Dick, Nancy Drew, A Tale of Two Cities,* and *David Copperfield.*

They raised tadpoles in an old dishpan until the critters turned into little frogs.

They played math games, had contests, and worked on riddles and puzzles.

They had a bet on whether the hairs of a horse's tail would turn into hair snakes if left in water (you are culturally deprived if you don't know about hair snakes around watering places) and on whether you could suck Coke out of the bottle using a rubber stopper with a piece of glass tubing through it.

They changed poems to make them sound funny, like

"By the rude flood
that arched the bridge,
Their breeze to April's
flag unfurled,
There once the enfarmered
battles stood
And shot the fire
heard 'round the world."

and wrote limericks by the hour and laughed their heads off, like

There was this gal named Alice
Who lived in a creaky old palace
      And rode an old bay
      After steers all day
Til she got callouses on top of her callous.

And wrote a few real letters to real people; a state congressman answered one of them once.

And made a personal history of the early days of their community by asking parents, grandparents, aunts, Old Man Perkins, and really old Miz Cora Blackwell what it was like then, how they traveled, where they got water and food, how they built dugout houses and what a problem the centipedes were in them, and a million and one other fascinating things.

No need to carry on with more of Sam's classroom. You might find other details of his first year interesting enough. But let's leave them for another time and see if we can tell why sour teaching turned sweet in Sam's life.

To put it in a nutshell, Sam Morgan stumbled and fumbled his way into

a concern for his students as people, with their interests, values, and senses of right and wrong.

That concern, growing bit by bit, reshaped and remade Sam's relations to his students. He slowly became more accepting. He saw their ways of thinking, feeling, and doing as just that—ways—not necessarily the best nor the worst, the most correct nor the most incorrect. Just human ways. He learned he could disagree with some of those ways without feeling personally attacked. He worked on changing some of their ways, because he believed strongly they could be better. But instead of haranguing the students, he worked through subtle example, group discussion, and genuine person-to-person talk. Most important of all, he came to know the parents and gain their trust and support.

At the same time, his students began to see Mr. Morgan as a different sort of teacher. They did not fear him, but neither did they scoff behind his back. In many ways they related to him as they did to Jack Donohue, the village "jack"-of-all-trades. If you had a problem, you could talk to Jack about it without getting put down. If you wanted to know how to fix a cracked water pipe, he would show you without fanfare or frills. Jack was a person you could go to when you needed help. He wouldn't lecture you or give you a bad grade. He would just do what he could for you.

In a way Sam slipped into that same kind of role. Not completely, understand, because he couldn't shake off all his teacher-is-right, teacher-demands-respect upbringing. But he did learn to listen better, to talk with, to accept, and to reject kindly when he simply could not accept. He still lost his temper occasionally. He still thought kids should learn

to read and write and cipher. He still thought neatness preferable to sloppiness, industry more valuable than slothfulness, good manners better than boorishness. He kept demanding these things of his students. The demands, though, softened in style. They became more gentle, more persuasive. They became continual expectations, because Sam believed they stressed personal qualities that gave life greater satisfaction.

As you have gathered, these changes in Sam didn't come as full-blown revelations. It would be difficult, if not impossible, to name all the influences that brought them about. There were, however, a few conditions of the community that helped Sam become more than his modest skills might have foretold.

For one thing, the community was quite small, numbering no more than six hundred townfolk with a couple of thousand farmers and ranchers spread out like spokes from the hub. This smallness, like it or not, assured that everybody knew everybody else—their names, their work, what kind of car they had, what their house looked like, who was related to who, what scandalous affairs were going on, and various and sundry skeletons in closets. As a part of this smallness, everybody knew the school teachers by name.

Conversely, every teacher knew, or soon came to know, the parents of most of his students. The school was in reality the center of the community. The plays, the ball games, the spaghetti suppers, the open houses—these were the main entertainment attractions. Parents and nonparents alike turned out for them. Of all these, the high school basketball team most rallied community support and cohesion. The gym was filled for every home game, and on Saturday nights a dance followed, with its inevitable drinking and two or three fights.

Then, too, the community necessarily required volunteer services from able-bodied persons, teachers like Sam included. The fire department was manned entirely by volunteers. When the siren wailed, teachers and grocery clerks and service station mechanics and even some high school boys dropped everything on the spot and raced to the station or the fire, whichever was closest. Sometimes it was only a haystack, providing a welcomed break from routine. Occasionally there would be real tragedies. In his first year, Sam helped remove the charred bodies of Mr. and Mrs. Wilbur Sikes, whose wooden shack had gone up like tinder around them in the driving snow of a gray January afternoon.

It was through activities and services such as these that Sam Morgan was thrust into the real life of the community. He had to know parents since he couldn't avoid them if he wanted to. He had to know the community, the values, the ways of the folk. He had to know the lives of his students. In the city he couldn't recognize half the people on his own block. In the country he was thrown into contact with people who lived miles from town in every direction.

Well, so much for Samuel Morgan. He went to the country to teach for a year, stayed six, and there was taught to be a teacher.

YESTERDAY'S HUMANISM

Samuel Morgan's story shows how he began to relate to students in warmer, more open, and more accepting ways. The circumstances that forced that change took place more than twenty years ago, yet they are pertinent to a current thrust in education called *humanism.*

Presently we will examine the intents and designs of humanism in education. First, though, you should recognize that the term humanism is not a new one. It has been used for a long, long time, with several very different meanings.

To give us perspective, let's note some of those meanings. The fact that they came into

vogue long ago doesn't mean that they have died out altogether. Some, such as classical humanism and scientific humanism, continue in force today. Others have been incorporated into newer conceptions. Here are some of them:

1. *Human beings* are the center of the universe—not deities, not institutions, not governments. It is within humans that we find beauty, truth, nobility, and all the higher qualities of life. Ancient Greek and Roman thinkers, artists, and writers developed this philosophical viewpoint. This humanism put great emphasis on the thought and behavior of human beings, as opposed to gods and the supernatural.

2. *Classical humanism*, emerging during the Renaissance, represented a renewed interest in Greek and Roman thought. In medieval times much emphasis had been placed on the deity, sin, heaven, and hell. At the time of the Renaissance, scholars were rediscovering classical Greek and Roman literature and art. Classical humanism directed itself to Hellenistic thought, on the belief that a study of the classics would liberate the mind. This belief, though not as pervasive as before, persists to the present day. One of its strongest proponents is Robert Maynard Hutchins, whose "great books" programs emphasize western wisdom of the ages. Classical humanism's method stresses scholarly study of the works of history's great thinkers.

3. *The humanities*, as areas of human endeavor, must be studied to give humans the historical, philosophical, and moral underpinnings for competent living. The nonhumanities, such as the natural sciences and the practical arts, do not contain the stuff for developing a sense of value. Thus, scientists although able producers, will not have the sense of right and wrong to enable them to use their power wisely, unless of course they are also versed in the humanities. The hu-

manities emphasis urges deep study into such areas as philosophy, literature, history, art, and music. Its proponents believe it gives perspective and sense of direction in dealing with problems of individuals and societies.

4. *Scientific humanism* takes the position that the methodology of science serves better than any other technique in enabling humans to move into higher realms of existence. This approach emphasizes logical analysis and clear thought. Superstitions and purely emotional behaviors serve only to keep people repressed, tied to old and inefficient ways. The means for breaking out of the confines of the old ways consist of careful, analytically rational thought applied to solving the problems that beset human beings.

5. *Creative thought* will best serve in the search for higher levels of human existence. The most human of all characteristics—the least animal-like—is the ability to think. Of the various kinds of human thought, creative thought occupies the highest level. Schiller, a German philosopher and playwright, popularized the humanism that places emphasis on creative thought as the basis of personal truth, freedom, and dignity. In a sense the individual becomes the source of truth, not merely a seeker after it. Just as beauty is in the eye of the beholder, truth is in the mind of the thinker.

6. *Existential humanism* focuses on the question: Here we are—we exist—so now what do we do? Human existence takes on meaning in relation to the choices one makes. We are responsible for ourselves. We are responsible for our acts. Our lives consist of continual choices among alternatives. We must choose. We cannot look to heaven, nor to society, nor to astrology, nor to any external source to find reason for our existence. We must look to ourselves. We are alone. The life we have is the life we choose from options available.

TODAY'S HUMANISM

Today when people speak of humanism in education, most are referring to something different from any of the humanisms described in the preceding paragraphs. Basically, they are speaking of concern for others, the thread that unites the various concepts drawn together in the most recent of the humanisms. This concern for the welfare of others is certainly not new. It has found prominent places in ethical and religious thought for centuries. As an emphasis in education its origins are vague. It received impetus from Rousseau. Other writers such as Pestalozzi, Montessori, and Dewey stressed it strongly. Just now the idea is attaining its greatest impact ever on school practice. Specifically, the new humanism focuses on enhancement of the total individual person—intellect, emotions, values, morals, feelings—through interpersonal relationships that are warm, open, supportive, facilitative, and nonthreatening.

To see more clearly what the new humanism is all about and how it is influencing education, we will examine (1) humanism's basic concepts, (2) what humanistic schools should do, and (3) what humanistic teachers should do.

Basic concepts

The new humanism stresses the individual in ways never before attempted in education. We have long embraced the concept of individual differences. But the teaching focus was on the group and, in recent years, on democratic group functioning. The individual was subordinate to the group. Now attention comes more directly to the individual. The group still exists, but emphasis is placed on the welfare and growth of the individual. The group simply helps provide some of the conditions for this growth. Aspects of the individual that receive special attention include the following.

Dignity. By the simple reason of being human, every individual has worth. Every individual is judged able and potentially competent. Every individual is important. This belief in the innate value of every single person forms the cornerstone of the new humanism.

Freedom. Full human development occurs only within an atmosphere of freedom. Such freedom includes freedom of choice, freedom to try, freedom to fail, and freedom from abrasive coercion. Curricular freedom is limited only by the range of choices available. Personal freedom is limited only when it infringes on the rights of others.

Values. Every individual has a system of values—those things we consider right and wrong, good and bad, desirable and undesirable. We act on the basis of the values we hold. Ideally, we should be able to recognize and specify the values we hold, so that acts based on them will be rational and considered. That's why the new humanism emphasizes not the imposition of new values but the clarification of values persons already hold.

Morality. Closely related to values, morality concerns beliefs about right and wrong and the disparity between what is and what should be. Education should sensitize people to justice and injustice and help them toward behaving in ways consistent with their moral judgments.

Feelings and emotions. We have, in the past, stressed cool, calm, rational thought as a supreme human quality. Now we are realizing that emotions and feelings are as human and as worthy of attention as rational thought. Education should help people accept their emotions as natural aspects of behavior. Too, it should remind us that everything we do is surrounded by an aura of feeling that strongly influences our inclination to act.

Concern. The feelings we show for the well-being of others are the mark of our humanity.

When we take pains to avoid hurting others, when we speak kindly, when we quietly help, we enlarge ourselves in equal measure. Education should foster this concern. It is a means of bettering the personal conditions of us all.

What schools should do

We have seen that the new humanism thrusts toward dignity, freedom, values, morality, feelings and emotions, and concern for others. Now let's see what the school can do to further those ends.

A first step should be to eliminate practices that are dehumanizing. Combs has identified several such practices.[1] Some of them are:

An atmosphere of distrust instead of trust between teacher and student

Continual emphasis on the "right" answer

The lockstep progression of students, where all go through the same activities at the same pace, in the same period of time

The conformity and boredom that usually accompany the single textbook approach

The shallow teacher-student relationships that result from "objectivity" (the treat 'em all alike attitude) and overcrowded classes

A marking and grading system that produces undesirable competition, odious comparisons, damaging pressure, and an inevitable sense of failure for some students

The implications of Combs' points are clear. Schools must find ways to promote trust among all members of the classroom. This means avoiding activities or evaluation procedures that boost one student at the expense of another. It also means placing emphasis on helping students, while eliminating, to the extent possible, conditions that

---

[1]Combs, A.: An educational imperative: The humane dimension, to nurture humaneness: Commitment for the seventies, Washington, D.C., 1970, Association for Supervision and Curriculum Development Yearbook.

thwart development of personal interests and abilities.

Everyone needs basic skills of communicating, computing, and seeking and processing information. These skills are tools, not ends in themselves. Beyond the fostering of such skills, schools must find ways to help students seek out information that has special importance, relevance, and meaning in their lives. Such information seldom has an absolute right-wrong connotation. It is information to be considered, to be explored, to be talked about. Its range is practically limitless. It can include pervasive concerns in all the traditional humanities, sciences, and practical arts. It can have to do with life-styles. It can have to do with morality, as evidenced through customs of various social, ethnic, and tribal groups. It can have to do with one's striving for something more, something beyond immediate grasp. It can have to do with macramé and leather crafting. Combs believes that the entire thrust of schooling should move in this direction, that is,

From—mere acquisition of factual information
To—discovery of the personal meaning of information[2]

Schools must also find ways to break students out of the lockstep curriculum and time molds into which they are cast. We have said for decades that students differ in many educationally important ways, in abilities, interests, needs, cognitive styles, emotional make-up, and so forth. Schools must begin to do more than merely recognize those differences. They must begin to provide instruction and experiences especially suited to them. This implies the provision of different activities, different topics, and different time schedules for students, over both short and long hauls.

As important as any other consideration is the necessity that schools become helpers, facilitators in the process of every student's educational growth. Much of this task falls to individual teachers, who will have to seek ways to move out of somewhat authoritarian, dominating roles and into the role Rogers calls "facilitating learning." The dimensions of this facilitating role have become specific enough to give guidance to teachers who are ready to change. We will examine some of these dimensions in the next section.

What teachers must do

When you get right down to it, the curriculum is what goes on in the classroom. Regardless of what school policy, curriculum guides, and teachers' manuals say, it's the classroom action that counts. The same can be said for teaching. It's whatever the teacher does in the classroom. Admittedly, these definitions are simplistic. Still, they point to the teacher-student encounter as the essential ingredient in schooling.

What must teachers do, then, inside their classrooms, if they want to move toward more humanistic ways of teaching?

They must give attention to three aspects of teaching behavior. These three aspects, artificially separated since they obviously overlap, are:

Personal behavior, which should be open, genuine, and humane
Curriculum strategies, which should, first, focus on topics and activities of real importance to students; and second should differentiate activities to match them more closely with each student's interests, abilities, needs, pacing, and cognitive style
Teaching strategies, which should emphasize facilitation of learning

The configuration these three aspects of teaching behavior take as they move in more humanistic directions follows.

Personal behavior. Most of us have had teachers who were authoritarian, domineer-

[2]*Ibid.*

ing, cold, and sarcastic. Many such teachers are successful in one respect: they often get students to learn a good deal of information. Students learn because they are afraid of the consequences if they don't. Meanwhile, however, they fear and hate the teacher, dread school, and are inhibited from exploring important personal interests.

Humanistic teachers avoid these traits. They work hard to be open and flexible instead of authoritarian. They try to listen to students, to hear and understand their wishes, preferences, and points of view. They try to change their ways of doing things when they believe change would make students more comfortable, eager, and involved.

Too, these teachers try to relate to students in ways that might be called warm and nonthreatening. "Warm" means that teachers manage smiles and other signs of affection appropriate to the age of their students. They are willing to joke a bit, enjoy a laugh, and pay attention to students' feelings. "Nonthreatening" means that students aren't kept on guard constantly against failing, making a mistake, or saying the wrong thing. Nonthreatening doesn't mean no standards of behavior in the classroom or that any old thing goes. It does mean that the boundary lines are clear, well known to everyone. You don't have to worry about the teacher jumping down your throat over the slightest matter. Cutting sarcasm is forbidden. It is not to be used by teacher or students.

Curriculum strategies. These strategies refer to

1. The topics, activities, and materials selected and made available for students.
2. The adaptations made in these topics, activities, and materials to match them to student differences. Obvious differences include abilities, interests, pace, and cognitive style.

The classroom in which personalized instruction occurs contains a rich variety of in-structional materials. Most of these materials have been selected and provided by the teacher. Their selection depends on the topics and activities deemed desirable for the students. They make possible different kinds of activities within each topic area. If the topic area is addition in elementary mathematics, the materials might include beansticks, counting rods, worksheets, chalkboard, workbooks, math rummy, math bingo, dice games, egg carton games, and so forth. If the topic area is high school creative writing, materials might include samples of various styles of expository writing, selections of descriptive writing, copies of student verse, worksheets on word selection, unfinished stories, stories without beginnings, task cards for exercises in fluency and flexibility, task cards for numerous writing topics, pictures for starting ideas, and so forth.

Selection of topics and materials doesn't depend entirely on the teacher, however. Students, as they get older, play increasingly important roles in identifying areas of interest they want to pursue. In cooperation with the teacher they agree on topics and activities, and together they share responsibility for obtaining necessary materials. For example, if a group of students in an eighth grade class wants to look into motorcycle racing, they might decide to ask riders and mechanics to visit the class. They might obtain a cutaway engine or get an old engine and disassemble it. Putting it back together makes a priceless lesson on internal combustion engines. It can also lead to related topics, like lubricants, electrical systems, and metals and metal work. Students can find a wealth of printed materials on motorcycles and racing. Careful observation, diagramming, and note taking occur as natural parts of such activities.

Humanistic instruction is personalized, that is, made available in a form that best suits each learner. Not all students are interested in the same things. Some read faster, work faster, and learn faster than others. Some can stick with a topic for a long while. Others can't. Some need strong support and encouragement from the teacher. Others prefer to go winging off on their own.

Grouping is also important in personalized instruction. Many topics and activities are best pursued in large groups. Group music, class discussions, and team sports are examples. In other topic areas, such as mathematics and science, most work is best done individually or in small groups. When individualized work is indicated, various clear-cut approaches should be made available to students. These approaches vary in their degree of structure, the size of work segments, the activities used, and time allocations for each. Some can be open in nature, where students select the topic and proceed to work on it. Others can be assigned, with definite objectives to be attained through completion of specified tasks. You will find detailed descriptions of several such approaches in later chapters.

Teaching strategies. Carl Rogers has urged, perhaps more strongly than anyone else, that teachers stop "teaching" and start "facilitating." He makes the point that "self-initiated learning" aids personal growth and is more lasting and valuable than information transmitted by the teacher. The kind of learning Rogers refers to holds these essential qualities:

1. It involves the total person, physical, emotional, and mental.
2. Its direction comes from within the student.
3. It makes a difference in the behavior and attitudes of the student.
4. It is evaluated by the learner, not the teacher, thus fostering independence, creativity, and self reliance.[3]

The teacher holds the key to this kind of learning, making or breaking it according to the teaching functions employed.

Guidelines for facilitating learning include the following:

1. Facilitators help draw out and clarify what students want to do.
2. They help organize the experiences students have identified and help provide a wide range of learning activities and materials.
3. They serve as flexible resources, to be utilized by members of the class.
4. They establish accepting classroom climates.
5. They behave as participant learners—as members of the group.
6. They take initiative in sharing their own feelings and thoughts with the group.
7. They recognize and accept their limitations.[4]

Rogers' work gives us one of the clearest descriptions of the humanistic teacher's role. However, his scheme for facilitating learning need not be embraced religiously as the be-all and end-all of humanistic teaching. Indeed, many students may require—at least they do actively seek—more structure and sense of direction than implied in Rogers' self-initiated learning. You will find, too, that students usually won't select activities often enough in basic skill areas of mathematics, language, and reading. Much practice is required to develop these tools properly. Without such development, students' potentialities will be limited.

Concern for the individual, for his preferences and capabilities, tells us to keep eyes and ears alert. We seek out students' interests, likes, and dislikes. We listen. We try to be genuine persons. We remain flexible. We try our best to help. We try to make learning enjoyable. That is what humanistic teaching is all about.

[3] Rogers, C.: The facilitation of significant learning, In Siegel, L., editor: Instruction: Some contemporary viewpoints, New York, 1967, Intext Educational Publishers.

[4] Rogers, C.: Freedom to learn, Columbus, 1969, Charles E. Merrill Publishing Co.

AND WHAT OF BEHAVIORISM?

This chapter may seem a strange place to write of behaviorism. Most people see humanism and behaviorism as direct opposites, archenemies, the good and the evil. Precisely because of that attitude, we must look for a moment at behaviorism.

Behaviorism held a preeminent position during psychology's early years. Psychologists thought if they were to make a science of psychology, they would have to limit its sources of information to behavior that could be directly observed. Thus, when it came to your study, say, of me, you would know me only by what I did—by my gestures, expressions, words, movements, and so on. You couldn't know my feelings because you couldn't observe them directly. Of course I could tell you what they were. But as a scientist you would mistrust my descriptions. You would believe only what you could see with your own eyes.

Many psychologists still firmly believe that observable behavior—not covert feelings, emotions, dreams, and mysterious mental processes—furnish the only valid factual information for psychology. Others disagree, among them Rogers, Maslow, Combs, and Kelley, all referred to in this book. They think feelings, emotions, attitudes, and values make up the truly human parts of our natures. They believe that these topics, instead of being minimized, should be emphasized, because they explain human behavior far better than observable acts. That, you see, is the fundamental difference between humanism and behaviorism as schools of thought in psychology.

But when teachers and educational psychologists talk about humanism and behaviorism—usually to ridicule the absurdity of one or the other—their remarks center mainly about two spin-offs from behaviorism. These spin-offs are:

Behavioral objectives
and
Behavior modification

Behaviorists believe strongly in the value of each. Humanists detest both. The disagreements over these two ideas have so divided humanists and behaviorists that each sees nothing good in anything the other does.

What are the arguments? Take behavioral objectives. Some people (I guess you're automatically a behaviorist if you are one of them) think behavioral objectives help a good deal in teaching and evaluating. They think if you state objectives that specify

The act to be performed,
The conditions under which the act is to be performed, and
The criteria of acceptable performance

you can give tremendous guidance to learners and teachers alike. What you do is avoid such vague, unobservable (though laudable) objectives as appreciate, learn, understand, enjoy, and know. You choose instead verbs that represent observable acts. Thus, you would *not* say in your instructional objectives:

The students will know and understand the works of Hemingway."

You would say, instead:

"The students will be able to name five works by Hemingway and prepare a short written summary of each, identifying the main characters and the conflict situations. Maximum time allowed will be one hour. Acceptable performance will be 80% correct, in the judgment of the instructor."

Other people (you're automatically a humanist if you are one of them) think that behavioral objectives are worse than useless. They believe these objectives force students into one single direction, putting a damper on their interests and a ceiling on their possibilities.

Instead of objectives, they say, you should concentrate on the experience. That is, you should provide students the richest experiences possible, with many avenues to explore. You encourage and help, but you let them go where, as far, and as fast as they want. You do not evaluate their work. That is for them to do.

The other argument between humanists and behaviorists concerns behavior modification. This is a technique that uses principles of reinforcement to shape student behavior in directions the teacher thinks desirable. What you do is reward students when they do things you want them to do. Rewards can vary from smiles to kind words to gum drops to privileges to play money to coin of the realm. You give students these things immediately after they do what you want them to do, and they will tend to keep repeating the desired behavior. There is no denying that behavior modification works.

But it is abhorrent to humanists. They see it as a petty way of getting students to do things contrary to their natural inclinations. They see it as a way of buying students off, to get them to be quiet and to conform. Instead, humanists provide rich experiences to motivate learners. They use good instructional materials to bring involvement natural-ly. They provide broad opportunities for students to involve themselves. They stress warm, open personal relations. These conditions all reduce disruptive behaviors that come from boredom and frustration. Behavior modification, they say, is nothing but a patch-up for poor teaching.

This either-or polarity is unfortunate. Both humanism (facilitating type) and behaviorism (objectives and modification type) make real contributions to the art of teaching.

Some learners are eager, have a sense of direction, and want to work at school tasks. Others need encouragement and guidance. Some learners have respect for others and do not produce conflict in the classroom. Others have different temperaments, emotions, or whatever; disruption and conflict follow in their wake. Behavior modification can make their presence much more tolerable for the other members of the class.

Again, when we want to personalize instruction, we want to relate well and warmly with students. We want to be ever considerate of their interests, attitudes, and feelings. We want to arrange learning experiences that bring success, enjoyment, and productivity. We need to find and use all teaching techniques that further these ends. It doesn't matter from where the techniques come.

4

The power of self image

A great deal has been said and written in recent years about self image—its nature and how it relates to mental health and school achievement. Despite these contributions, it is safe to say that most teachers have not been effectively informed on what constitutes self image, how it is investigated, and what determines whether a student has a good or a poor one. The intent in this chapter is to provide that information.

WHAT IS SELF IMAGE?

Put very simply, self image is the totality of

1. What one believes to be true about oneself
2. The value one places on those beliefs, individually and collectively

What we believe to be true about ourselves comes from our perceptions of what we do and what we are like, relative to others, and from feedback others give us. All of us perceive a great many things about ourselves. We perceive aspects of our physical beings, such as size, strength, speed, coordination, and appearance. We perceive character traits, such as dependability, courage, willingness, and personal relations. We have perceptions about the degree to which we are accepted by others, including people in general, people with whom we have close personal relations, and people who hold positions of power over us. We have notions about our ability to perform, whether it be performance in general or performance on specific tasks. We perceive ourselves as relatively successful or unsuccessful, and our efforts as recognized or not recognized. The perception categories mentioned here are but a few of the many that are important in our lives, and each of the categories is a composite of numerous specific impressions.

The second part of self image has to do with the value we place on whatever qualities we do perceive—that is, with whether we consider them to be poor, mediocre, or good. This part indicates how we feel about ourselves. This feeling determines whether we have a good, positive self image, or a poor, negative self image. Our feelings about the qualities we perceive in ourselves seldom take the form of extreme conscious pleasure or displeasure. They are more like a general satisfaction or a general dissatisfaction with the trait. These satisfactions and dissatisfactions determine whether, and to what extent, we are able to accept ourselves.

Self image is not a single factor that can be expressed with numerical or verbal precision, as ".70" or "in the sixth stanine," for example. It consists of numerous discrete perception-evaluations. Some of these perception-evaluations assume great importance to us. Others assume little. This degree of importance depends in large measure on the value attached to the perceived trait by other significant people—people who are important in our lives. For example, size and strength might be very important factors in the overall self image of a fourth grade boy, whereas being a good conversationalist might be relatively inconsequential. But these two factors might well be reversed in importance when that boy becomes an adult.

This illustration simply shows that when we look for discrete factors that have importance in overall self images, we find little consistency. Important factors vary from person to person, time to time, place to place. But if we reduce discrete factors into certain kinds of categories, then those categories seem to be fairly stable for different people in different places and times. For example, the strength factor and the conversation factor might both be fit into a category of "ability to do"—to do things important in life.

Presently we will take note of some of the broad categories that seem to be present generally within self image. First, though, let us look briefly at some of the ways investigators have attempted to identify and measure self image.

HOW IS SELF IMAGE EXPLORED?

The assessment of self image presumes that individuals do in fact hold value-opinions about themselves and that the most important of these value-opinions have to do with traits and conditions one considers crucial in life, such as ability to function and acceptance by others. Examples of personal traits that are generally valued in most societies are ability, attractiveness, and dependability. Examples of conditions generally valued are acceptance, recognition, and security. Personal introspection, as well as work by trained analysts, confirms the existence of value-opinions and shows that value-opinions about certain personal traits and conditions have compelling importance in peoples' lives—compelling because they influence to such a degree the way people behave in stress situations as well as in ordinary purposeful and serendipitous activities. It is convenient to refer to the totality of these value-opinions as "self image."

Procedures used in investigating the factors that make up self image have been guided by four different aims. One of these aims has been to identify what individuals believe about themselves. A second has been to try to determine the accuracy of those beliefs. This is usually done by comparing an individual's perceptions of himself with those made by another person, such as a teacher or psychologist. A third has been to try to decide what value an individual places on beliefs he holds about himself, regardless of whether they are accurate. And a fourth has been to identify undesirable or maladaptive behaviors that might signal negative opinions of the self.

Information gained through the third and fourth aims serve teachers best because they tell whether a student has a good or a poor self image. As far as mental health is concerned, it is not overly important that students—especially younger ones—have extremely accurate self perceptions. What is important is that the students have relatively positive feelings about themselves. This positive outlook helps them function more adequately and be more accepting of themselves and others.

Information concerning students' feelings about themselves is important to teachers in their attempts to improve self image. There are various ways of obtaining this information. One method simply involves asking students personally what they think about themselves overall and what they think of specific traits and conditions. Using language appropriate to the age of the student, you can ask questions such as: Do you feel happy (secure) in school, or do you feel unhappy (anxious, insecure)? Do you think you are fairly successful in your school work (good in reading, math, and so on)? Do you feel other people like you? Do they recognize your accomplishments? How do you feel about your physical appearance? If you use this procedure, you must of course use language suitable for the student with whom you are talking. You would ask the questions of a first grade student in a very different way than you would a high school student.

This method can be quite successful in yielding information if personal trust exists between teacher and student. Like all other methods, however, it has certain limitations. Students may not feel free to reveal their feelings openly. They may give responses they think you want to hear, what their parents would like them to say, or what their ideal selves would desire. They may not be able to put their feelings into words accurately, so that difficult interpretation is required. Still, talking directly with students is one of the best ways to begin finding out what they think of themselves.

Another method is the projective technique often used by therapists and psychometrists. Students are shown pictures or given verbal descriptions of people and events, then asked to explain or tell about the picture or event. Their descriptions are often projections of their own traits and conditions, and thus they describe perceptions and beliefs about themselves. This procedure also helps bring out poor self images that would not otherwise be voiced since few of us willingly tell others if we see ourselves as hateful, aggressive, weak, irresponsible, or unpopular. But to use this technique properly, one must have special training. Also, considerable time is required. Since teachers seldom have

either the training or the necessary time, projective techniques are rarely used in exploring normal students' self images.

A third technique, one widely used, involves the administration of self reporting scales that students can fill out easily and quickly. Students are asked to respond orally or with check marks to items designed to provide information about what they think about themselves. One example of such a rating scale is the "How I See Myself" scale developed by Gordon.[1] On this scale students are asked to judge themselves on forty different items, which cluster into several different factors, such as body build, academic adequacy, appearance, and self control. Fig. 1 shows a reproduction of Gordon's "How I See Myself," Elementary Form.

Another example of a rating scale is the "Self Concept Scale" developed by Sears.[2] This scale consists of one hundred items. Examples of items are "Being good at sports" and "Being willing to help others." Students indicate on each item how they compare themselves with other students in the class, whether they are satisfied with their status, and whether they think they are making improvement.

Sears was also instrumental in the development of another scale used in research at the Stanford Center for Research and Development in Teaching.[3] This scale consists of forty-eight items distributed across nine categories, and it is accompanied by a score sheet that shows students' numerical scores in each of the categories. The scale is shown in Fig. 2, the score sheet on p. 36.

---

[1] Gordon, I.: Studying the child in school, New York, 1966, John Wiley & Sons, Inc.
[2] Sears, P., and Sherman, V.: In pursuit of self-esteem, San Francisco, 1964, Wadsworth Publishing Co., Inc.
[3] Sears, P., and others: Effective reinforcement for achievement behaviors in disadvantaged children: The first year, Technical report 30, Stanford University, 1972, Stanford Center for Research and Development in Teaching, School of Education.

HOW I SEE MYSELF, ELEMENTARY FORM

1. Nothing gets me too mad	1	2	3	4	5	I get mad easily and explode
2. I don't stay with things and finish them	1	2	3	4	5	I stay with something till I finish
3. I'm very good at drawing	1	2	3	4	5	I'm not much good in drawing
4. I don't like to work on committees, projects	1	2	3	4	5	I like to work with others
5. I wish I were smaller (taller)	1	2	3	4	5	I'm just the right height
6. I worry a lot	1	2	3	4	5	I don't worry much
7. I wish I could do something with my hair	1	2	3	4	5	My hair is nice-looking
8. Teachers like me	1	2	3	4	5	Teachers don't like me
9. I've lots of energy	1	2	3	4	5	I haven't much energy
10. I don't play games very well	1	2	3	4	5	I play games very well
11. I'm just the right weight	1	2	3	4	5	I wish I were heavier, lighter
12. The girls don't like me, leave me out	1	2	3	4	5	The girls like me a lot, choose me
13. I'm very good at speaking before a group	1	2	3	4	5	I'm not much good at speaking before a group
14. My face is pretty (good looking)	1	2	3	4	5	I wish I were prettier (good looking)
15. I'm very good in music	1	2	3	4	5	I'm not much good in music
16. I get along well with teachers	1	2	3	4	5	I don't get along with teachers
17. I don't like teachers	1	2	3	4	5	I like teachers very much
18. I don't feel at ease, comfortable inside	1	2	3	4	5	I feel very at ease, comfortable inside
19. I don't like to try new things	1	2	3	4	5	I like to try new things
20. I have trouble controlling my feelings	1	2	3	4	5	I can handle my feelings
21. I do well in school work	1	2	3	4	5	I don't do well in school
22. I want the boys to like me	1	2	3	4	5	I don't want the boys to like me
23. I don't like the way I look	1	2	3	4	5	I like the way I look
24. I don't want the girls to like me	1	2	3	4	5	I want the girls to like me
25. I'm very healthy	1	2	3	4	5	I get sick a lot
26. I don't dance well	1	2	3	4	5	I'm a very good dancer
27. I write well	1	2	3	4	5	I don't write well
28. I like to work alone	1	2	3	4	5	I don't like to work alone
29. I use my time well	1	2	3	4	5	I don't know how to plan my time
30. I'm not much good at making things with my hands	1	2	3	4	5	I'm very good at making things with my hands
31. I wish I could do something about my skin	1	2	3	4	5	My skin is nice-looking
32. School isn't interesting to me	1	2	3	4	5	School is very interesting
33. I don't do arithmetic well	1	2	3	4	5	I'm real good in arithmetic
34. I'm not as smart as the others	1	2	3	4	5	I'm smarter than most of the others
35. The boys like me a lot, choose me	1	2	3	4	5	The boys don't like me, leave me out
36. My clothes are not as I'd like	1	2	3	4	5	My clothes are nice
37. I like school	1	2	3	4	5	I don't like school
38. I wish I were built like the others	1	2	3	4	5	I'm happy with the way I am
39. I don't read well	1	2	3	4	5	I read very well
40. I don't learn new things easily	1	2	3	4	5	I learn new things easily

Fig. 1. From Gordon, I.: Studying the child in school, New York, 1966, John Wiley & Sons, Inc.

SELF CONCEPT SCALE

	Excellent	Very good	Better than most	OK	Not so good
1. Being good at sports	_____	_____	_____	_____	_____
2. Learning things rapidly	_____	_____	_____	_____	_____
3. Making friends easily with my own sex	_____	_____	_____	_____	_____
4. Having new, original ideas	_____	_____	_____	_____	_____
5. Getting my school work done on time and not getting behind	_____	_____	_____	_____	_____
6. Being able to read well	_____	_____	_____	_____	_____
7. Being a good size and build for my age	_____	_____	_____	_____	_____
8. Remembering what I've learned	_____	_____	_____	_____	_____
9. Being willing for others to have their way sometimes	_____	_____	_____	_____	_____
10. Solving problems in ways others haven't tried	_____	_____	_____	_____	_____
11. Being confident, not shy nor timid	_____	_____	_____	_____	_____
12. Knowing how to do math	_____	_____	_____	_____	_____
13. Being good at things that require physical skill	_____	_____	_____	_____	_____
14. Being a good student	_____	_____	_____	_____	_____
15. Being a leader—one to get things started with my own sex	_____	_____	_____	_____	_____
16. Thinking up answers to problems—answers no one else has thought of	_____	_____	_____	_____	_____
17. Being able to concentrate	_____	_____	_____	_____	_____
18. Being interested in science; learning about things that scientists do	_____	_____	_____	_____	_____
19. Being attractive, good looking	_____	_____	_____	_____	_____
20. Having brains for college	_____	_____	_____	_____	_____
21. Making other people feel at ease	_____	_____	_____	_____	_____
22. Learning about new things even when other people aren't interested—studying about things on my own	_____	_____	_____	_____	_____
23. Getting a lot of fun out of life	_____	_____	_____	_____	_____
24. Writing creative stories and poems	_____	_____	_____	_____	_____
25. Being a good athlete	_____	_____	_____	_____	_____

Fig. 2. From Sears, P., and others: Effective reinforcement for achievement behaviors in disadvantaged children: The first year, Technical Report 30, Stanford University, 1972, Stanford Center for Research and Development in Teaching, School of Education.

SELF CONCEPT SCALE—cont'd

	Excellent	Very good	Better than most	OK	Not so good
26. Being able to apply what I've learned					
27. Having plenty of friends of my own sex					
28. Seeing new ways of thinking about things and putting ideas together					
29. Spending most of my time on my work, not goofing off					
30. Having good handwriting even when I'm hurried					
31. Being not too skinny, not too fat					
32. Having brains					
33. Being sensitive to what others are feeling					
34. Being able to see things in my mind easily when I want to					
35. Being able to change things when they don't suit me					
36. Being able to spell correctly					
37. Enjoying games and sports					
38. Being smart					
39. Being active in social affairs with my own sex					
40. Being interested in new things; excited about all there is to learn					
41. Well organized; having materials ready when needed					
42. Learning about people around the world and being interested in them					
43. Having nice features (nose, eyes, etc.)					
44. Knowing what to do for the right answer to a problem					
45. Being easy to get along with					
46. Letting my imagination go when I want to					
47. Enjoying myself in school					
48. Doing well in art work, painting or drawing					

Fig. 2, cont'd. For legend see opposite page.

SELF CONCEPT SCORE SHEET

Child's name _____ Teacher _____ School _____

Scorer _____ Date _____

STANFORD CENTER FOR RESEARCH AND DEVELOPMENT IN TEACHING

Items	Physical ability	Attractive appearance	Convergent mental	Social relations same sex	Social virtues	Divergent mental	Work habits	Happy qualities	School subjects	Total
1 to 6	1		2	3		4	5		6	
7 to 12		7	8		9	10		11	12	
13 to 18	13		14	15		16	17		18	
19 to 24		19	20		21	22		23	24	
25 to 30	25		26	27		28	29		30	
31 to 36		31	32		33	34		35	36	
37 to 42	37		38	39		40	41		42	
43 to 48		43	44		45	46		47	48	
Total										
No. items	4	4	8	4	4	8	4	4	8	48
Average										

Excellent = 5 Better than most = 3 Not so good = 1
Very good = 4 OK = 2

WHAT ARE GOOD AND POOR SELF IMAGES?

When we say a person has a good or a strong or a positive self image, we mean that the person is relatively satisfied, as opposed to relatively dissatisfied, with the self perceptions that are important to him at that time and place in life. As mentioned previously, when we categorize perception-evaluations in certain ways, we can determine that those categories remain fairly constant from one person to another. Each category includes discrete perception-evaluations that cause one to feel, in a relative way, adequate or inadequate, accepted or unaccepted, appreciated or unappreciated, and so forth.

Several important writers have given attention to what constitutes a positive impression of oneself. Combs, for example, sees a positive self image resulting from seeing oneself as generally liked, wanted, acceptable, and able, possessing dignity and integrity.[4] Such a positive self image does not mean that the person never feels doubt, inadequacy, or anxiety. On the whole, however, such people see themselves as more adequate, more able than not, most of the time. Kelley describes fully functioning persons (that is, persons with positive self images) as thinking well of themselves, thinking well of others, and recognizing their interrelationship with others.[5] Those persons hold good human values and are secure enough to accept mistakes and profit from them.

Rogers sees such a person as one who is in the process of forming answers to such fundamental questions as "What is my purpose in life? What am I striving for? What do I want to be?" The person, in this process, shows a sensitive openness to experience and a relative nonuse of defense mechanisms.[6]

Maslow writes of man's "inner nature" and notes that psychological health requires that this inner nature receive acceptance, love, and respect from others, as well as from oneself. The inner nature includes a force toward health, growth, clarification of identity, and self-actualization.[7]

Teachers would find little to disagree with in these professional opinions. Their main concern lies not so much in whether students have accurate self perceptions as in whether students feel relatively good about themselves. And of course they would like to know how students do perceive themselves.

If we put together the ideas of authorities such as those referred to here, we can form a useful picture of some of the important things a person with a good self image might think.

I am unique, though similar to others.
My appearance and personality satisfy me.

People care about me.
People support my ideas, opinions, and activities.

I recognize my need for others.
I belong.

I have a sense of purpose in life.
I have ability to do.

I am successful.
My efforts are recognized.

These statements, although they reflect self perceptions that a person with a good self image might have, are not to be considered in the sense of either-or—either I have ability or I don't have ability. No one has absolute confidence in his ability; no one feels perfectly sure about his sense of purpose. The perceptions should be thought of as "more so than not"—I am more able than not able; I have more sense of purpose than of purposelessness; I am more successful than not successful.

Moreover, the statements represent categories of perception-evaluations. For example, if "my appearance and personality satisfy me," that is because the great number of individual perceptions about body build, eyes, hair, strength, happiness, outgoingness, dependability, and so on, when put in the balance, lean more toward the positive than toward the negative in my mind. The categories are entirely artificial, arranged to summarize self perceptions in a convenient way. Their number could be expanded greatly or further reduced. As shown here, however, they correspond fairly well with the way various authorities have expressed their views.

Since teachers are concerned with their students' having good self images, as related to the categories presented, a short scale

---

[4] Combs, A.: A perceptual view of the adequate personality. In: Perceiving, behaving, becoming, Washington, 1962, Association for Supervision and Curriculum Development Yearbook.

[5] Kelley, E.: *Ibid.*, Chapter 2.

[6] Rogers, C.: *Ibid.*, Chapter 3.

[7] Maslow, A.: *Ibid.*, Chapter 4.

1. How I feel about the way I look

   Size ___ ___ ___
   bad   ok   good

   Face ___ ___ ___
   bad   ok   good

   Hair ___ ___ ___
   bad   ok   good

2. How I feel about the way I behave

   In class ___ ___ ___
   bad   ok   good

   On the
   playground ___ ___ ___
   bad   ok   good

   At home ___ ___ ___
   bad   ok   good

3. How I feel about the way people treat me

   Teachers ___ ___ ___
   bad   ok   good

   Others
   my age ___ ___ ___
   bad   ok   good

4. How I feel about the way I play

   Indoor
   games ___ ___ ___
   bad   ok   good

   Outdoor
   games ___ ___ ___
   bad   ok   good

5. How I feel about my work in school

   Math ___ ___ ___
   bad   ok   good

   Reading ___ ___ ___
   bad   ok   good

   Science ___ ___ ___
   bad   ok   good

   Art ___ ___ ___
   bad   ok   good

   Music ___ ___ ___
   bad   ok   good

6. (Optional)

   What I think is best about me _____

   What I think is worst about me _____

Fig. 3. How I feel about myself.

such as the one shown in Fig. 3 might be useful to them. The scale should be modified in its content and wording in accord with the age of the students with whom it is used.

A caution: If you intend to use this scale or any other scale with students in school, be sure to show it first to the building principal. Occasionally, parents object to their children responding to such questions, so the principal should approve in advance your using the scale.

WHAT IS THE RELATION OF SELF IMAGE TO SCHOOL ACHIEVEMENT?

Most teachers agree: Students who think well of themselves also happen to do better in school. Unlike many of education's truisms, this one has basis in fact. In this section we will take a brief look at some of the findings of investigators who have searched for a relationship between self image and school achievement.

Studies

Gowan, in 1960, searched for factors that might be related to the academic achievement of high school and college students.

Included among factors found were student self confidence, self acceptance, and overall positive feeling about the self.[8]

Shaw, Edson, and Bell divided bright high

---

[8] Gowan, J.: Factors of achievement in high school and college, Journal of Counseling Psychology 7:91-95, 1960.

school students into groups of high achievers and underachievers, then asked them to report on themselves using an adjective checklist. For the male students, though not for the females, they found significantly different ratings, in which high achievers more often chose adjectives such as intelligent, clear thinking, reliable, and enthusiastic.[9]

In a following study, Shaw and Alves found that male high school students who are underachievers have significantly more negative self images than achievers and are less accepting of themselves. Similar results were not found for female underachievers, however, who gave no clear indication of inferior self images.[10]

Thompson found similar evidence in a study of 500 English secondary school students. Three groups were compared—one composed of students judged well-adjusted, a second of students judged maladjusted, and a third of students who had made appearances in court. The second and third groups, when asked how they thought others perceived them, rated themselves significantly lower than did the well-adjusted group.[11]

Brookover, Patterson, and Thomas obtained self reports on a large number of seventh grade students. They found a significant positive correlation between students' perceptions of their own ability and their grade point averages.[12]

In a 1966 report comparing elementary grade students who were judged effective readers or ineffective readers, Brunkan and Sheni found notable differences in the views these two groups held of themselves. The effective readers had positive feelings about themselves, whereas the ineffective readers did not.[13]

This condition was shown again in a 1974 study by Black. Children who were reading below grade level were found to have significantly lower self images than children reading at or above grade level. The older the children, the lower their self images.[14]

Williams and Cole's study of sixth grade students, reported in 1968, showed significant positive relationships between measures of students' self images and their achievement in reading and mathematics.[15]

The same relationship was found between self image and science achievement. Alvord and Glass studied over 3000 students in the fourth, seventh, and twelfth grades. They found significant relationships between the two variables at each level.[16]

Caplin studied 180 intermediate elementary grade students, ninety white and ninety black, matched on socioeconomic levels. Among his findings were the following: (1) Overall, student scores on the self image scale used correlated significantly with scores on the Iowa Test of Basic Skills. The correlation was .52, significant for both black students and white students. (2) There were no

[9] Shaw, M., Edson, K., and Bell, H.: The self-concept of bright underachieving high school students as revealed by an adjective check-list, Personnel and Guidance Journal 39:193-196, 1960.

[10] Shaw, M., and Alves, G.: The self-concept of bright academic underachievers: Continued, Personnel and Guidance Journal 42:401-403, 1963.

[11] Thompson, B.: Self concepts among secondary school pupils, Educational Research 17:41-47, November 1974.

[12] Brookover, W., Patterson, A., and Thomas, S.: Self concept of ability and school achievement, Sociology of Education 37:271-278, 1964.

[13] Brunkan, R., and Sheni, F.: Personality characteristics of ineffective, effective, and efficient readers, Personnel and Guidance Journal 44:837-844, 1966.

[14] Black, F.: Self concept as related to achievement and age in learning-disabled children, Child Development 45:1137-1140, 1974.

[15] Williams, R., and Cole, S.: Self concept and school adjustment, Personnel and Guidance Journal 46:478-481, 1968.

[16] Alvord, D., and Glass, L.: Relationships between academic achievement and self concept, Science Education 58:175-179, April 1974.

significant differences in self image scores for boys and girls. (3) Black students' self image scores were significantly lower than white students' scores.[17]

Soares and Soares reported contrasting findings in 1969. They investigated the self perceptions of disadvantaged elementary students and compared them with advantaged students. They found that, overall, disadvantaged students had even more positive self perceptions than did the advantaged students.[18]

Zirkel and Moses reported similar findings. They studied 120 fifth and sixth grade white, black, and Puerto Rican students in Connecticut. No differences were found between black and white students' scores on the Coopersmith Self Esteem Inventory. Puerto Rican students, however, did make scores that showed significantly lower self images.[19]

Jones and Grieneeks found that for one group of university sophomores, measures of self image were better predictors of grade point average than were scores on the Scholastic Aptitude Test (SAT). These investigators tested 877 students and obtained separate correlations for males, females, and total group. The correlations between self image of ability and scores on the SAT ranged from .34 to .42. Correlations between self image of ability and grade point average ranged from .43 to .49. On the other hand, correlations between the SAT (that is designed to predict scholastic achievement) and grade point average ranged from .22 to .36.[20]

In a study of 150 university student teachers, Garvey compared grades made in student teaching with scores made on the Tennessee Self Concept Scale. She found significant relationships between good student teaching performance and high scores on self image, especially with regard to identity (what I am) and absence of confusion and uncertainty.[21]

At the other end of the educational ladder, Williams attempted to determine whether there was a relationship between self image and reading achievement for first grade children. She was unable to find such relationships, when comparing children's scores on the Coopersmith Self Esteem Inventory with various measures of reading achievement. Neither did she find relationships between self image and ethnic and socioeconomic backgrounds.[22] This study raised the following questions: (1) Do significant differences exist in self image among young children? or (2) Is there no relationship between self image and reading achievement at this age? or (3) Is the Coopersmith Self Esteem Inventory unable to show reliable differences among young children's self images?

Unlike Williams, Cicirelli and associates were successful in finding self image differences among primary age children. They devised a scale called Children's Self-Concept Index, consisting of a number of items with two possible answers. Children selected the answer—one of a pair of drawings—that

[17] Caplin, M.: The relationship between self concept and academic achievement, Journal of Experimental Education **37**:13-16, Spring 1969.
[18] Soares, A., and Soares, L.: Self-perceptions of culturally-disadvantaged children, American Educational Research Journal **6**(1):1969.
[19] Zirkel, P., and Moses, E.: Self concept and ethnic group membership among public school students, American Educational Research Journal **8**:253-265, March 1971.

[20] Jones, J., and Grieneeks, L.: Measures of self-perception as predictors of scholastic achievement, Journal of Educational Research **63**:201-203, January 1970.
[21] Garvey, R.: Self concept and success in student teaching, Journal of Teacher Education **21**:357-361, Fall 1970.
[22] Williams, J.: The relationship of self concept and reading achievement in first grade children, Journal of Educational Research **66**:378-380, April 1973.

they judged most like themselves. The instrument yielded adequate coefficients of reliability and validity. When they used it with several hundred children of various ethnic groups, they found significant positive correlations between these scores and scores made on various standardized reading tests.[23]

Conclusions

One hesitates to draw firm conclusions from the findings of studies such as those reported here, because the results do not seem to be sufficiently consistent. Tentatively, these generalizations seem to emerge:

1. A significant relationship exists between self image and academic achievement.

2. This relationship does not seem to become significantly strong until students reach the third or fourth grade in school.

3. It is debatable whether differences in self image exist between black and white students. The evidence seems contradictory. Some studies show differences favoring whites; others show no differences; and still others show differences favoring blacks.

4. Questions exist concerning whether males and females have different levels of self images. Some studies, at least, have revealed no differences.

5. Socioeconomic background does not seem to be related to self image.

6. Students with poor self images are seldom high achievers. On the other hand, it is not uncommon for students with good self images to be low achievers.

Cause and effect

It should be clearly recognized that correlational studies such as those cited previously do not show cause and effect. Thus, we cannot conclude that self image directly affects academic achievement. Nor can we conclude the reverse—that academic achievement directly affects self image. To show that good self image causes higher achievement, one would first have to find the means of raising individuals' self images during a period while they were not attending school. Then, assuming the self images remained high, one could determine whether academic achievement increased.

Self image has, in fact, been improved in the school setting. Landry, Schilson, and Pardew worked with 4-year-old preschool children. They reported significant increases in self image following a Self Concept Enhancement Program.[24]

Other studies have shown improvements in self image, but questions remain about causal relationships. Calsyn and Kenny, for example, did a longitudinal study of 556 adolescent students. They concluded that improved achievement was more likely to raise self image than vice versa.[25] For the most part, we can be fairly sure that poor self image tends to accompany low achievement, whereas good self image tends to accompany higher achievement. Since we don't know which causes which, or whether in fact either causes the other, we must seek ways to attempt to increase both achievement and self image among the students.

WHAT IS THE RELATION OF SELF IMAGE TO MENTAL HEALTH?

Mental health, mental illness: There's so much disagreement about what these terms

---

[23] Cicirelli, V., and others: Measures of self-concept, attitudes, and achievement motivation of primary grade children, Journal of School Psychology 9:383-392, Winter 1971.

[24] Landry, R., Schilson, E., and Pardew, E.: Self concept enhancement in a preschool program, Journal of Experimental Education 42(4):39-43, Summer 1974.

[25] Calsyn, R., and Kenny, D.: Self concept of ability and perceived evaluation of others: Cause or effect of learning achievement? Journal of Educational Psychology 69:136-145, April 1977.

mean it seems foolhardy even to bring them up. Some people say health and illness should refer only to the physical—to muscles, bones, nerves, blood vessels, and what have you. You can't talk about "mental" health or illness, they say. You can talk about physical illnesses of the brain, such as injuries or chemical imbalances or germ-related diseases, that cause people to act in unexpected, inappropriate, or undesirable ways. But "mental" health and illness don't make sense.

Other people say you're showing your biases when you talk about mental health and illness. What you are doing, they say, is making value judgments about other people's behavior. Who says your way is any better than theirs? If they want to keep to themselves, why isn't that just as good as socializing? If they get depressed, why shouldn't they? There are plenty of good reasons for intelligent people to get depressed these days. Besides, who ever proved that happy means the same as healthy? Happiness is sometimes a sign of ignorance, a lack of empathy, or an absence of concern.

Still others point to creative geniuses who would have been considered mentally ill in many respects. Rousseau, who so greatly influenced our concept and treatment of children, failed to care for his own. All six of them took their turns in the orphanage. Hemingway constantly sought ways to show his manliness. He ended it all in suicide. Van Gogh was hardly your archetype of the well-adjusted man. Beethoven, Chopin, and an impressive list of composers, musicians, writers, and artists led rather unusual lives, to put it mildly. The point is this: People who really produce, who really contribute, often show bizarre traits that we comfortable, well-adjusted, nonproducers call crazy.

Despite these objections, we will give attention to mental health and illness anyway. The behaviors these terms generally refer to seem to have to do with concepts of the self. To see why this is so, we will note behavior traits of the mentally healthy and contrast them with behavior traits of the mentally ill. This comparison points out relationships between self image and mental health.

There are different ways of approaching the matter of mental health. Three of them (take your pick) are (1) identifying the traits of "healthy," "fully functioning" persons, (2) identifying the traits of persons who are inhibited in some way from doing all they are capable of doing, and (3) identifying the conditions that bring on ill health.

Let's consider each of these approaches briefly.

Healthy traits

Mental health seems to boil down to this: It is an overall state of the emotions, as those emotions influence ability to perform normal functions. We usually assume one's mental health is good unless we see evidence to the contrary. We don't often say "There goes a healthy person," or "That's a healthy person because . . ." But that's probably what we should do. Emphasizing the positive reminds us of the positive, whereas emphasizing the negative . . . well, you know where that leads.

How, then, do we recognize mentally healthy persons? Kelley summarized his ideas about mentally healthy people (he calls them "fully functioning") in these ways:

1. They think well of themselves.
2. They think well of others.
3. They recognize their interdependence with others.
4. They see themselves in a process of becoming.
5. They see the value of mistakes.
6. They develop and hold values related to the welfare of people.
7. They live in keeping with their values.[26]

[26] Kelley, E.: The fully functioning self. In Perceiving, behaving, becoming, *op. cit.*, pp. 9-20.

Rogers takes a similar approach. He writes that persons moving toward full functioning show these traits:

1. An openness to experience, without defensiveness
2. A recognition that they are in a constant process of fluid change
3. A trust in their own experience and acceptance of their feelings[27]

Combs points out that the self images people possess determine whether they are maladjusted or well adjusted. In writing of well adjusted people, he mentions such traits as:

1. They know who they are.
2. They feel they are liked and wanted.
3. They feel they are accepted and successful.
4. They feel a oneness with others.
5. They are maximally open to experience.[28]

Other writers have developed longer lists of healthy traits. Anderson, for example, includes the following among attributes of mental health:

1. High level of self esteem
2. Obtaining gratification through approved avenues
3. Security
4. Confidence
5. Courage
6. Stability
7. Orderliness
8. Adaptability
9. Self discipline
10. Self reliance
11. Interest in others[29]

These descriptions by Kelley, Rogers, Combs, and Anderson are clear and to the

point. Everyone's concern lies with how to foster these traits in persons. Several well-accepted procedures are in use today. We will examine some of those procedures in Chapter 5. But now let's look at some of the "unhealthy" traits that have been identified.

Unhealthy traits

Unhealthy traits include behaviors and attitudes that inhibit adequate functioning. That simply means that people with one or more of these traits cannot do all they are capable of doing, that they function with much discomfort, or that their potential development is unnecessarily stifled.

For Kelley, Rogers, and Combs, psychologically unhealthy traits would include:

1. Poor self image
2. Poor attitudes toward others
3. Feelings of rejection
4. Feelings of failure
5. Closed mind toward new experience
6. Static view of the self
7. Fear of failure
8. Distrust of own feelings

For Anderson, the traits would presumably include:

1. Low self esteem
2. Insecurity
3. Fearfulness
4. Instability
5. Slovenliness
6. Rigidity
7. Self indulgence
8. Lack of interest in others

Maslow has pointed out some of the illnesses people suffer when they lack an adequate value framework. When they are uncertain about what is worth striving for and what is not, they may begin suffering from anomie, cynicism, apathy, and hopelessness. Maslow pointed out that these psychological illnesses, when allowed to progress, often

[27] Rogers, C.: Toward becoming a fully functioning person. In Perceiving, behaving, becoming, *op. cit.*, pp. 21-33.
[28] Combs, A.: A perceptual view of the adequate personality. In Perceiving, behaving, becoming, *op. cit.*, pp. 50-64.
[29] Anderson, C.: School health practice, St. Louis, 1972, The C. V. Mosby Co.

manifest themselves in physical illnesses of one sort or another.[30]

Causes

What brings on these unhealthy traits, anyway? Some of the more serious seem to result from home influences. Rousell and Edwards did a follow-up investigation on young adults whose home conditions had first been studied fifteen years previously. They identified psychopathological behaviors in some of these people and found relationships between the behaviors and the kind of home atmosphere in which they had been raised. In summary, they found many significant correlations, ranging up to .50 and above, of which the following are most interesting:[31]

Behavior of mother	Effect in young adulthood
Permissive (neglectful)	Neuroses and psychoses among females
Warm punitive	Neurotic disturbances among females
Aloof (disinterested)	Psychopathological disorders among males
Warm overindulgent	Strong anxiety and psychotic disturbances among males
Cold punitive (rejecting)	Phobic and psychotic disturbances among males

Among the specific disorders identified were hypochondriasis (imaginary illness), depression, hysteria (violent emotional outbreaks), paranoia, schizophrenia, mania (excessive excitement), and various phobias (abnormal fears).

Less severe instances of mental ill health may come as a result of the following kinds of experiences:

1. *Failure to establish self identity and clarify roles.* Who am I? What am I capable of? What is expected of me? What is important to me? What are my purposes in life? Of what value am I?
2. *Prolonged, repeated frustration and failure.* Others expect too much. No one is ever satisfied. I am unable to please. I am continually below par. Others are always better than me. I can do nothing right. I am powerless.
3. *Sustained rejection by "important others."* Parents/teachers/peers don't like me. They prefer brother, sister, other students to me. They never smile or talk kindly to me. They won't listen to me. They don't recognize my problems. They always criticize, use sarcasm, put me down. They never seek me out, never include me.
4. *Loss of psychological support, from sudden changes in environment and/or persons.* Everything familiar is gone. I'm alone, cut off. Everything's strange. These are not my ways. These are not my people. I do not know the ways, the rules. This unknown terrifies me.

Cures

Teachers are not doctors. They are not psychotherapists. They cannot be expected to perform cures on all the mental illnesses their students have. They can't do much to change students' home environments. They can't change parents' personalities.

Hopeless? Not exactly. There are things teachers can do to help students function better. Granted an impressive array of "can'ts" stands between them and their students. But there are also several "can do's":[32]

1. Learn to recognize symptoms of high anxiety, such as nervousness, frequent swallowing, perspiration on palms and face, rapid heartbeat, and extreme misbehavior. Then change situations that cause anxiety by lowering the threat of failure or by changing to alternative, success activities.

---

[30] Maslow, A.: Some basic propositions of a growth and self-actualizing psychology. In Perceiving, behaving, becoming, *op. cit.*, pp. 34-49.

[31] Rousell, C., and Edwards, C.: Some developmental antecedents of psychopathology, Journal of Personality 39:362-377, September 1971.

---

[32] See Chapter 5 for elaboration of activities and techniques.

2. Practice activities and techniques that enhance the self. Examples of activities include value clarification, Gestalt games, and morality instruction. Examples of techniques include nonpunitive teaching, student-centered teaching, and positive reinforcement.

3. Provide low threat activities that ensure frequent success for every student. A variety of such activities are described in later parts of this book. Generally, they involve breaking the curriculum down into small, easily mastered parts, combined with systematic positive feedback to students.

4. Provide a warm, supportive classroom climate. This can be accomplished through use of accepting techniques, valuing the student, and nonpunitive approaches.

We have some evidence that approaches similar to those described here can have positive effects on students' mental health. Griggs and Bonney, for instance, in a one-semester program for fourth and fifth grade students, emphasized causes of behavior. They used books such as *Why People Act as They Do* and found that, as a result, the children became more accepting of others. The children also made significant positive changes in performance on a mental health analysis scale.[33]

In other studies, Van Koughnett and Smith worked with black elementary school students from segregated, low economic areas. They succeeded in helping the students develop much more positive feelings about their own worth and ability to succeed in school.[34] Baron, Bass, and Vietze developed a praise-reinforcement procedure that significantly improved young black women's self image.[35]

Studies such as these provide increasing assurance that we can affect students' self image and thus their mental health. In Chapter 5, we will examine rationale and strategies for enhancing the self.

---

[33] Griggs, J., and Bonney, M.: Relationship between "causal" orientation and acceptance of others, "self-ideal self" congruency and mental health changes for fourth and fifth grade children, Journal of Educational Research **63**:471-477, July 1970.

[34] Van Koughnett, B., and Smith, M.: Enhancing the self concept in school, Educational Leadership **27**:253-255, December 1969.

[35] Baron, R., Bass, A., and Vietze, P.: Type and frequency of praise as determinants of favorability of self-image: An experiment in a field setting, Journal of Personality **39**:493-511, December 1971.

5

Enhancing the self

So here we are. Beautiful and homely. Brave and fearful. Eager and reluctant. Loved and rejected. Whizzes and duds. Sought and avoided. Confident and timid. Powerful and powerless. Some of us only a mother could love. We are the fortunate ones, even so. Mothers' rejections have scarred some of us forever.

How have we come to be this way? Are our traits immutable parts of the universe, preordained and foisted on us? Are we precast as pawns, knights, or queens in some cosmic game? Is beauty really truth, and truth beauty, and that's all we ever need to know?

No. If I think myself ugly, it's because I have learned it. Learned it from others. If I think myself worthless, it's because people and circumstances have taught me so. If I think myself capable, it's because my modest accomplishments have been recognized. We are what we have learned ourselves to be.

What we have learned ourselves to be directs our behavior. When we see ourselves as failures, we tend to fail. When we see ourselves as rejected, we tend to reject. When we see ourselves as achievers, we tend to achieve. When we see ourselves as loved, we tend to love. We don't always do so, you understand. But much of the time we do; we behave in ways consistent with what we believe about ourselves.

This congruence of self perception and behavior tell us much. It tells us why people act as they do. It helps us understand them, tolerate them, accept them. It helps us predict what people will do. Our predictions won't always be right, but they will be better than chance. It tells us how people will react to each other and how they will behave in groups. It tells us what kind of activities they will choose. It tells us how they will approach learning situations and how well they will see those situations through. It tells us about people's self discipline, stubbornness, flexibility, resiliency, motivation, stability, and what have you.

For these reasons alone, knowledge of people's self images is eminently desirable. Yet there is another fact about self image that demands attention. That is the fact that self image is learned; it is not innate. And since it is learned, it is in a constant process of change, because throughout our lives we continually learn things about ourselves that cause changes in self image. Self image is not static. It is fluid and malleable.

Imagine what this fact suggests: People

who have poor self images can learn better ones. If we feel incapable, we can learn to feel capable. If we feel rejected, we can learn to feel accepted. If we feel ugly, we can learn to feel beautiful. And if it is true that we act in accord with what we believe about ourselves, then we can improve the quality of our functioning through learning to think better of ourselves.

Therapists

Psychologists agree that self image is learned. They agree that it changes throughout life. Sometimes these changes occur rapidly, in great leaps. Sometimes they occur slowly, in tiny steps. But the self image is never static, just as the self is never static. Both are continually changing.

Therapists work hard at changing self images. Poor self images can be crippling. They can depress performance and inhibit satisfaction to a distressing degree. The purpose of therapy is to reduce these crippling depressions and inhibitions. The therapeutic process, in its essence, is no great mystery. If a person functions poorly because he sees himself a chronic failure, then he needs to experience success often enough to think of himself as successful. If he relates to others poorly because he sees himself as rejected, then he needs to experience situations in which he is accepted by others. If his daily functioning is depressed because he sees no sense or purpose to life, then he needs help in finding and clarifying life goals whose pursuit brings a sense of fulfillment.

Therapy is easier pronounced than produced. Still, the concept on which it rests is simple enough. You provide new learnings to remake old learnings. What results are new behaviors to push out old behaviors.

Teachers

Teachers are occasional therapists. Their influence often helps students think better of themselves, as more capable, more successful, more accepted. But their efforts are seldom systematic. They are hit and miss, because they have never been put into a coherent framework of concepts and procedures. Since their efforts are not systematic, they miss the mark some of the time. In the worst cases, teachers' efforts can do more harm than good, especially when they reject students who already feel rejected, overly restrict students who already feel hemmed in, or write off as failures students who are crying for the tiniest mark of success.

Moreover, teachers have never been strongly encouraged to think about students' self images. They realize students have good and bad feelings about themselves and that those feelings do influence school behavior. They want students to think better of themselves and better of school. But teachers rarely have had instruction in specific approaches to enhancing the self. They have not been strongly encouraged in that direction by professional and public opinion, which still tunes in almost solely on academic achievement, not realizing how closely achievement is related to self image. Sure, psychologists and some professors and a few other people here and there keep harping about the importance of the self and its influence on behavior. The newspapers, though, get excited mostly about boys' hair styles, new buildings, and poor reading scores. Parents clamor for return to the basics—that is, reading, phonics, English grammar, and respect for adults. They want all kids shaped up, made to toe the mark, taught a little respect—all kids except their own, of course.

Despite the chilling effects of these realities, teachers in ever growing numbers are beginning to pay as much attention to Mary and John's self images as to their knowledge of punctuation. The tempo of this change in focus will inevitably increase, for three basic reasons:

1. Teachers, despite what sensationalists might bandy about, really do care how students feel about themselves. They want them to feel happy, secure, able, successful, and concerned about others.
2. Enough attention has been given to self image during recent years so that useful, workable approaches for enhancing the self have been clarified. Now teachers can find out what to do and when and how to do it.
3. Teachers are extremely distressed by hostility and conflict in the classroom. Improvement of student self image is a way to improve interpersonal relations. Teachers will seek to enhance students' self image because it serves their own interests as well.

Given these incentives, what can teachers do to enhance students' self images? Rather than speak in generalities, let's examine some organized approaches that hold promise of success. We will look at seven such approaches. They are communication, classroom meetings, facilitation, values development, creativity, behavior modification, and mastery/competence/success.

COMMUNICATION

Maybe you think of school as basics and frills, basics being the history, math, English, and sciences, and frills the art, music, games, plays, and so on. We often talk about school that way. Much of the time, though, we'd do better to think of school as "talk," or more accurately as communication between people. Psychiatrists and clinical psychologists increasingly recognize that communication— you may see them use the words "interaction" and "transaction"—play a powerful role in the feelings people have toward themselves and others.

Ned Flanders has shown that talk goes on most of the time in school. His work in interaction analysis turned up a "⅔ rule," an observation that in a typical classroom, teacher and students are talking two thirds of the time, and the teacher is talking two thirds of

that time. He has also shown that the kind of talk used by teachers influences students' academic progress and attitude toward school.[1]

We know self image is shaped in part by what "significant others" say and do. Teachers certainly hold significant positions in students' lives. The things they say and do have effect. For these reasons, we need to examine kinds of talk that go on between teachers and students. We need to improve the quality of that talk as much as we can.

Teachers use three different types of talk with students. These types are:

1. *Informing talk.* In this type, teachers give factual information, explain procedures, and give directions and assignments.
2. *Eliciting talk.* Eliciting talk usually asks questions or commands; it calls for student responses, which can be either verbal or behavioral.
3. *Reacting talk.* This is talk that teachers make in reaction to student talk and behavior. It consists of two subtypes:
   a. *Acceptance*, which is approval and encouragement: Yes, right, very good, you're on the right track, atta girl. (Teachers also use many nonverbal accepting reactions, such as smiles, nods, pats, and other gestures.)
   b. *Rejection*, which is disapproval and squelching: No, stop that, you missed the point, pay attention. (Teachers also use many nonverbal rejecting reactions, such as frowns, stares, shakes of the head, and so on.)

The important thing in all teacher talk is the *meaning* it conveys to the student. The words used may not carry evident meanings. For example, a teacher may say "Come on, dagburn it, let's get with it." Those words carry different meanings, according to tone of voice and personality of the teacher. They

---

[1] Flanders, N.: Using interaction analysis in the inservice training of teachers, Journal of Experimental Education **30:**313, 1962.

can be serious and cutting, or they can be good-humored and encouraging.

Flanders has developed a scheme for analyzing verbal exchanges between teacher and students.[2] One of the things his scheme can do is show whether a teacher tends to be "indirect" or "direct," in general. Indirect teachers accept, praise, encourage, and help clarify feelings and meanings. Direct teachers tend to control, reject, lecture, and moralize. When you compare the effects of these two styles on learners, you find in general that students of indirect teachers learn more and like school better.[3]

Thomas Gordon has worked on interpersonal communication from a different perspective.[4] He noted that when adults talk with students about matters of morals, values, behavior styles, and other such topics, what they say often causes frustration, anger, hostility, and counterattack, or they may cause students to lie, hide their feelings, feel guilty, or just stop talking. When these reactions occur, the communication process has obviously bogged down.

To prevent this occurrence, Gordon urges parents and teachers to learn to identify and avoid styles of talk that cripple communication. He has identified twelve such styles, which he calls the "typical twelve":

1. Ordering, directing, commanding
2. Warning, admonishing, threatening
3. Exhorting, moralizing, preaching
4. Advising, giving solutions or suggestions
5. Lecturing, teaching, giving logical arguments
6. Judging, criticizing, disagreeing, blaming
7. Praising, agreeing

8. Name calling, ridiculing, shaming
9. Interpreting, diagnosing, analyzing
10. Reassuring, sympathizing, consoling, supporting
11. Probing, questioning, interrogating
12. Withdrawing, distracting, humoring, diverting[5]

When talking with students, you should do your best to avoid the typical twelve. Instead of using them you should:

1. Listen actively, maintaining eye contact and showing you are following what the student is saying
2. Reflect back, by paraphrasing or summarizing, the strong feelings students express
3. Use "I-messages," in which you tell the student how the situation makes you feel. At the same time avoid "you-messages," in which you place blame on the student
4. Together with the student, search for constructive, cooperative solutions to the problem, without blame or antagonism

From yet another perspective, Eric Berne has considered the ego states that people use when they communicate. He has labeled his approach "transactional analysis," which he has described in several scholarly works and in the popular books *Games People Play* and *What do You Say After You Say Hello?*

Basically, Berne believes that a person has three different ego states he can use in communicating[6]:

Parent: In this state one thinks, acts, and talks as his parents did to him when he was a child. He admonishes, corrects, controls, and reacts in stereotyped ways.
Adult: In this state, one appraises situations objectively and dispassionately, functioning like a computer taking into account various possibilities and probabilities learned from past experience.

[2]Amidon, E., and Flanders, N.: The role of the teacher in the classroom, Minneapolis, 1963, Paul S. Amidon and Associates, Inc.
[3]Flanders, N.: Teacher influence, pupil attitudes, and achievement, Washington, D.C., 1965, United States Government Printing Office.
[4]Gordon, T.: Parent effectiveness training, New York, 1970, Peter H. Wyden/Publisher.
[5]*Ibid.*, pp. 48-49
[6]Berne, E.: What do you say after you say hello? New York, 1972, Grove Press, Inc.

Child: In this state one thinks, feels, and acts as he did when a young child, somewhere between the age of two and five. This state remains strong and alive in all of us, regardless of our age.

These three ego states comprise everyone's personality, Berne believes. An individual can move from one to the other and often does so when communicating.

Thus, when two persons communicate, six ego states come into play—three for each person:

Person 1	Person 2
Parent	Parent
Adult	Adult
Child	Child

It is important to know which states are being used by two people during communication. So long as the states are complementary, communication proceeds well and effectively. But when transactions are "crossed," problems occur.

This concept of transactional analysis was used by Thomas Harris in his book *I'm OK– You're OK.*[7] Harris writes of four kinds of interaction postures among people, having to do with feelings about oneself and others, that affect communication. These four postures are:

I'm Not OK—You're OK
I'm Not OK—You're Not OK
I'm OK—You're Not OK
I'm OK—You're OK

Harris believes that full communication is most likely to occur in the fourth instance, in which individuals are accepting of both themselves and others. He thinks people can learn to be more accepting—and thus enhance communication—by attending to the following:

[7] Harris, T.: I'm OK—You're OK, New York, 1967, Harper and Row, Publishers.

1. Recognize that you have three sets of data—those of Parent, Adult, and Child—that must be processed during communication. Parent is closed to new data and reacts in stereotyped ways, taking the "how dare you" and "tsk tsk" attitudes. Adult looks for the comparative, the probable, the factual—who, what, when, where, why, how. Child shows emotions, pleasures, fantasies, with tendencies to tears, whining, giggling, in hopes of signs of love and direction.
2. Assess your own reactions during communication to see whether they are Parent, Adult, or Child.
3. Learn to use your Adult; let it be in charge because it permits change. Parent and Child resist change, seeking to maintain the status quo.

Harris goes on to give suggestions about how to stay with your Adult during communication[8]:

1. Know your own Child behaviors—your fears, vulnerability, delights, and means of expressing them.
2. Know your own Parent behaviors—your admonitions, injunctions, fixed positions, and ways of expressing them.
3. Be sensitive to your Not OK feelings, which all of us have.
4. In conflict situations, count to ten to delay automatic Child reactions and allow Adult reactions time to occur. Think before you speak. Restraint allows Adult to compute appropriate responses.
5. Be sensitive to the Child in others. When in doubt, stroke. We fear the Parent in others, but we love the Child in them.
6. Remember that you need a strong Adult, but you need your Parent and Child, too. You simply need to curtail the destructive qualities in Parent and Child.
7. Clarify your system of values. They tell you what's right and wrong, worthy and worthless—information the Adult must have to function.

[8] *Ibid.*

CLASSROOM MEETINGS

Coleman, in his 1960 report that compared educational opportunities of white and black students, made a relatively unnoticed but highly important finding: There is a *pupil* factor that has more influence on learning than all the *school* factors combined. That pupil factor is this: A strong relationship exists between school achievement and the extent to which a pupil believes he has control over his own destiny.

William Glasser, author of the acclaimed *Reality Therapy* and *Schools Without Failure* cites the Coleman finding to support his conviction that "classroom meetings" should be a part of the regular school curriculum.[9] Glasser advocates frequent use of three kinds of classroom meetings:

1. The Social-Problem–Solving Meeting
2. The Open-Ended Meeting
3. The Educational-Diagnostic Meeting

All three of these kinds of meetings are intended to accomplish two specific ends: The solution of student problems and the fostering of students' convictions that they do, in fact, have significant control over matters of importance in their school lives.

Let's briefly consider each of these three types of classroom meetings.

The social-problem–solving meeting

The primary purpose of this type of meeting is to solve educational problems of individuals, groups, class, and school. It helps students avoid the all too common reactions to difficult problems—evasion, lying, giving up, and dependence on others. This kind of classroom meeting exposes problems for open, honest discussion. The teacher takes the lead but always remains warm, open, accepting, and nonjudgmental. Here are

guidelines Glasser suggests for conducting the meetings:

1. *Problems eligible for discussion include those of the school, the class, or any individual member of the class.* Problems can be brought up by any student, and can have to do with himself, other students, teachers, parents, administrators, and so on. Teachers also bring up problems they see. Problems usually have to do with behavior. Often, though, they may have to do with feelings of loneliness, fear, anxiety, or rejection. The problems, whatever they may be, are placed out for open, frank discussion by the total group.

2. *The purpose of the discussions is to find solutions to problems.* Students quickly learn that the purpose of the meeting is to solve problems in constructive ways. It is never to find fault, punish, or place blame. Instead, the purpose is to help people with problems find more suitable ways to behave. The tone is always positive.

3. *Meetings should be conducted with teacher and students seated in a tight circle. Their length should be appropriate to the age of the students.* Glasser believes that the circle seating enhances the value of the meetings. He believes too that the meetings should not be too long. Between ten and thirty minutes is about right for primary grade children; thirty to forty-five minutes is appropriate for older students. More important is that the meetings be held on a regular basis.

Open-ended meetings

Glasser considers open-ended meetings indispensable. The more of them you have, he says, the more relevant your teaching will be.

In this type of meeting, students are encouraged to bring up any ideas they react to strongly—ideas that interest, puzzle, perplex, frustrate, anger, delight, motivate, or whatever. The ideas may be related to the

---

[9] Glasser, W.: Schools without failure, New York, 1969, Harper and Row, Publishers.

school curriculum, but they don't have to be. The main purpose is to explore, consider, talk about; it is not necessarily to find factual information or correct answers.

Ideally, discussions should turn back in a natural, unforced way to curricular topics. Most students never suspect that many of their most pressing concerns relate to sociology, anthropology, biology, physics, communication, mathematics, music, and art. Teachers can help relate concerns to curriculum. They shouldn't force it, though. If you have to choose between school curriculum and pursuit of interesting ideas, stay with the ideas.

Educational-diagnostic meetings

These meetings have to do with teaching-learning activities in the class. The purpose is to help the teacher get feedback concerning students' reactions. This feedback can indicate first of all what the students find interesting, challenging, clear, useful, fun, boring, and frustrating. These reactions can focus on several things. They can be concerned with activities and materials. They can focus on teachers' instructional methods and evaluation procedures.

Second, the information provided from this feedback should be used to advantage. If a procedure is unclear, the teacher undertakes to make it clear. If a topic is dull, the teacher explores, with the class, ways to instill excitement into it. If students dread written tests, other means of evaluation can be used, such as analysis of work completed, observation during work activities, and student self appraisal.

This kind of meeting can be unnerving for teachers. Most of us identify closely with what we do. We see our teaching activities as extensions of our selves. When they are criticized, we believe that our selves are being criticized. Therefore, it should be made clear in this kind of meeting, as in others, that blame and harsh criticism have no place. Emphasis, as always, is placed on constructive, positive alternatives. Teachers' self images are fragile, too.

FACILITATION

What should students learn? How should they learn it?

Those two questions have produced enough printed material in the last fifty years to reach all the way to Mars. Arguments about them have generated enough hot air to refuel the sun. No end is in sight. Those questions are basic in education and have been since Cro-Magnon or some such person decided you had to teach kids stuff or else their characters would be stunted.

Some of the writing has been bad, some of it good. Some bad writing has been pleasantly readable, some good writing terribly ponderous. Once in a while somebody manages a mix of stimulating ideas and clear, readable prose. Carl Rogers has done that.

Rogers writes of significant learning and of the teaching act. He thinks learning is significant if it has personal meaning for the learner. Usually, the learner takes the initiative in that kind of learning. Nothing is forced on him, nothing spoon fed. The learner opens his eyes and says "Hey, I want to know more about that. How do I do it?" Rogers calls that kind of learning "self-initiated."

He sees teaching as a rather important aid to such learning. Only he doesn't call it teaching. He looked at dictionary definitions of teaching and rejected all of them as irrelevant or damaging to significant learning. He uses the term "facilitation of learning." By facilitation he means the help teachers give learners in clarifying what they want to learn, in arranging necessary activities, in finding the personal meaning of those learnings, and in maintaining a psychological climate that nurtures, rather than represses, the process of learning.

Significant learning, Rogers says, has these qualities:

It is self initiated.
It involves learners' feelings as well as their intellect.
It makes behavior and attitude differences in the learner.
It is evaluated by the learner.
Its essence is meaning.[10]

We can all think of instances in our work, hobbies, and play in which learning of this type occurs. But how can it be made to occur in school, day after day, month after month?

The answer, for Rogers, lies in remaking the teacher's role so that it becomes, truly, one of facilitating learning. Rogers is so convinced of this idea that he writes "Here then is a goal to which I can give myself whole-heartedly. I see *the facilitation of learning* as the *aim* of education . . ."[11]

And this process of facilitating—Is it another grand sounding idea without a shred of practicality to it? No, says Rogers, not at all. Most teachers can make the change if they really want to. Here are some of the things they must attend to:

Realness. They must be genuine people, without front or facade. They must meet learners on a person-to-person basis, not a teacher-to-student basis. There must be no pretense, no falsity.

Acceptance. They must care for the learner in a nonpossessive way, accepting his feelings, his opinions, his totality as a person. They must respect the student by showing they recognize as worthwhile his preferences, hopes, and aspirations.

Understanding. They must respond to students in ways that show they know how students feel about things. This kind of understanding is not evaluative. They don't say "I understand what's wrong with you." They don't judge. They try to see things through the student's eyes. Their comments reflect his feelings—his anger, frustration, pleasure, excitement. They show they know how he feels and why he feels that way.

Trust. They must believe students behave intelligently most of the time. They must show this belief through allowing students a significant voice in expressing their desires, in organizing their own learning activities, and in selecting from among optional activities. They must listen to students. They must allow them to decide how they want to work; they must allow them to establish rules of behavior. Then they help arrange details to facilitate decisions students have made.

The four qualities mentioned—realness, acceptance, understanding, and trust—all help, as Rogers says, reduce the threat to the self. When threat to the self is high, one does not learn well. When threat to the self is low, one's horizons remain open; learning can proceed.

These traits are necessary for teachers who wish to facilitate learning. There is still more to facilitating, however. Rogers lists several fairly specific things teachers do to facilitate learning.[12] Among them are:

1. *Setting the initial mood for the class.* In talking with students, the teacher shows genuine interest in them. This allows the traits previously described—realness, acceptance, understanding, and trust—to be communicated in subtle ways.

2. *Eliciting and clarifying the purposes of individuals and the group.* There is no need to manufacture a purpose for the entire group. Different interests normally exist. Students should be helped to pursue purposes important to them. This means that several different activities will often be occurring simultaneously in the classroom.

---

[10] Rogers, C.: Freedom to learn, Columbus, 1966, Charles E. Merrill Publishing Co.
[11] *Ibid.*, p. 105.

[12] *Ibid.*, pp. 164-166

3. *Organizing activities and making resources available.* The teacher's role is not one of making students learn what they don't want to know. Rather, it's helping them learn what they do want to know. This means teachers should strive to obtain quickly all the material resources needed in activities a student selects.

4. *Making oneself available as a resource to the group.* The teacher wishes to be used by the group, as a counselor, advisor, or person already experienced in the activity. He or she does not force himself on students, but does work alongside them, naturally and easily. At times, when conditions indicate, the teacher remains apart, allowing students to try, make mistakes, and succeed on their own.

5. *Sharing one's own feelings and thoughts with the group.* The teacher, participating as a group member, shares feelings of satisfaction, elation, frustration, anger, and disappointment. He or she always makes clear that these emotions are personal and does not make judgmental statements about students, so that blame is fixed on them.

As you read these ideas about facilitation, which have come mostly from the writings of Rogers, several questions probably have arisen in your mind:

Don't I know more than the kids about what they should be learning?
These ideas are fine for older students, but how could they possibly work at the primary level?
Won't the students go completely wild if I don't enforce standards of conduct?
Most parents want the "basics" stressed in their children's schooling. What will they say about teaching like Rogers advocates?
How do I get my administrators to go along with a scheme such as this?
If I try this, how do I work into it?

Enough teachers have begun using the facilitation approach to give us a few answers to such questions.

First, the personal traits of realness, ac-

ceptance, understanding, and trust should be cultivated, regardless of the teaching style you use. The trust you show carries over into a conviction that, given a variety of alternatives, students will seek and select those that make sense for them.

You can get parents behind you if you take pains to communicate with them. Invite them to open house at school. Send notes to them. Call them on the phone. Explain what you are trying to do. Involve them with the class. Get them to help with class projects and other activities.

Administrators will usually support you if they think your program is educationally sound. Discuss your ideas with your principal. Explain in detail what you want to achieve and how you intend to go about it. Be sure the principal doesn't get caught off guard when a parent calls.

Primary grade teachers have been moving in this direction by making more activity options available to students. Students select from the options. Teachers talk individually with students and with the total group to tune in to their preferences. Many teachers now start the day with an extended open or free choice period. Students select from a very rich environment the various learning games and activities they prefer.

As teachers, whether primary, upper grade, or secondary, begin using open activity periods, they usually find, to their surprise, that the level of disruptive behavior goes down instead of up. Students actively engaged in doing things that interest them show less inclination to bother others.

As for your moving away from a traditional role and into a facilitating role, a good first step is to set up a variety of alternative activities or learning centers in your classroom. Allow students a free choice period. During that period, make a point of talking individually with students about their interests, desires, and feelings. Find out what they like most and least about school. Show a genuine personal interest in them. Show through your actions that you want to help. When you do that, you are well on your way.

VALUES DEVELOPMENT

What do you think of, specifically, when you think of your self? Your face, your hair, your body? The window behind your eyes? Clothing? Occupation? Demeanor? Talents? Wittiness? Your importance and power? If someone said stop and think about yourself for thirty seconds, most of us would quickly touch on physical appearance, relations with others, and special abilities. These traits hold key positions in our self image. We hardly think of ourselves without thinking of them.

But there is another factor that is every bit as important in our makeups as appearance, relationships, and talents. That factor is our values. Lumped together, these are called our system of values, which is the totality of what we consider good and bad, right and wrong, important and unimportant, just and unjust, desirable and undesirable.

Our system of values directs our activities. It points us one way or another. It guides us like a rudder—convenient in the calm, essential in the storm.

Oddly enough, most of us cannot accurately specify our values. On minor issues, such as styles of dress or grooming, it hardly matters. Anything goes. Well, almost. But on the larger issues, many of us swing to and fro like leaves in the wind. We waver in matters in which individual rights clash with the common good, human justice bumps against personal interest, or law and order tangles with personal liberty. We have difficulty not only in acting consistently, but even in explaining what and why we believe as we do.

Values development and values clarification can improve this condition. They are significant ways of enhancing the self. They help us know where we stand, because they require us to think things through. They give us direction. They give us foundations on which to base our actions. They help us acquire an increased sense of self-ness. I am the I that thinks thus, believes thus. This is where I stand, and this is what I stand for. This is what's important to me.

Teachers have long recognized the importance of values and value development. They had little to go on, however, so far as techniques to bring about student awareness of values. That has changed in recent years. Several writers, most notably Louis Raths and Sidney B. Simon, have developed strategies for helping students clarify values they hold, that is, for knowing consciously what it is they believe subconsciously. These writers stress valuing and values clarification as processes for bringing values to the conscious level.

Raths, for example, points out that traditional attempts at value development such as providing good examples and having frank discussions have been ineffective.[13] He argues that teachers should help students build their own value systems, by using a strategy consisting of two parts: (1) establishing a climate of psychological safety, and (2) using a clarification procedure. Here's what he means.

Psychological safety. A "safe" climate is required before clarifying procedures can be used. Students must feel safe in expressing their deeply felt beliefs. This climate can be maintained by showing concern for the ideas of every student. You show concern by listening to ideas, responding to them, and remembering them. To facilitate sharing of ideas, you organize activities that encourage students to express their beliefs, attitudes, and feelings about important issues.

Clarifying procedures. This part consists of various nonjudgmental responses teachers

---

[13] Raths, L.: Clarifying values. In Fliming, R., editor: Curriculum for today's boys and girls, Columbus, 1963, Charles E. Merrill Publishing Co.

make after students express opinions. Often the responses are questions, for example:

(Summarize student expression and ask) Is that what you mean?
Can you give me an example?
How long have you felt that way?
Where do you think your idea comes from?
Should everyone think that?
Have you thought of any other possibilities?

Sometimes the follow-ups are accepting comments, such as:

I see what you mean.
I think I understand better now.
I imagine it was difficult for you to decide.

Through clarifying procedures, teachers try to encourage students to do three things:

Choose: freely, from alternatives, after careful consideration
Prize: the choice, that is, be pleased with it and willing to affirm it publicly
Act: repeatedly on the basis of the choice[14]

Simon reports several interesting strategies he and his associates are using to help students learn the process of values clarification.[15] One strategy is called "Things I love to do." Students list, as quickly as they can, twenty things they really love to do. Then they code the listed items to show which ones involve risk, which ones their parents might have loved, which ones will probably not be on the list five years from now, and so on.

Another of Simon's strategies is called the "Personal coat of arms." The teacher has students take a sheet of paper and draw a large triangular shield, like those used by knights of old. Then they divide the shield into six sections, by drawing a dotted line from top to

bottom and two lines from side to side, so it looks something like the one shown above. The following things are put into each section:

Section 1: Draw two pictures. One represents something you are good at. The other represents something you *want* to be good at.
Section 2: Make a picture that shows something that you feel so strongly about you would never give up.
Section 3: Make a picture that shows one thing that is very important in the lives of every member of your family.
Section 4: Draw a picture that shows what you would be or do, if you could be or do absolutely anything you wanted.
Section 5: Show something you wish every person in the world would believe.
Section 6: Write four words you wish people would say about you behind your back.

A recent book by Simon, Howe, and Kirschenbaum describes seventy-nine activities such as these for helping students clarify their values.[16]

Yet another strategy for exploring values has been developed by Clegg and Hills.[17] Included in their strategy is the suggestion that

---

[14] Raths, L., Harmin, M., and Simon, S.: Values and teaching, Columbus, 1966, Charles E. Merrill Publishing Co.
[15] Simon, S.: Values-clarification vs. indoctrination, Social Education **35**:902-905, 1971.

[16] Simon, S., Howe, L., and Kirschenbaum, H.: Values clarification, New York, 1972, Hart Publishing Co., Inc.
[17] Clegg, A., and Hills, J.: A strategy for exploring values and valuing in the social studies, The College of Education Record **34**:67-78, 1968.

teachers and students select an important issue and follow these steps:

Break the issue down into parts on which students can focus easily.
Consider the parts one at a time.
Develop a number of alternative possibilities for dealing with each part of the issue.
Explore the consequences of each alternative.
Each person identifies the alternative that seems most desirable under the circumstances.
Each person expresses the reason for the choice.

These strategies selected from the works of Raths and associates, Simon and associates, and Clegg and Hills are but samples that illustrate the new emphasis on values that has emerged in recent years. All aim at the same objective—the strengthening of the self through identification of values—so that students can come to say "Here's where I stand. Let me tell you why."

CREATIVITY

Have you ever thought of this? Were it not for creativity, human beings would still live, if they lived at all, as they did two million years ago. No spaghetti, no double knits, no Bill of Rights, no Eiffel Tower, no Mona Lisa, no moon shots, no Cabernet Sauvignon, no calendar, no autobahn, no Peanuts. In fact, we'd have almost nothing we associate with humanness. There are times, it is true, when it seems we'd be better off without them. But we get over that idea at once when the car or TV or watch goes on the blink.

All in all, of the behaviors that divide humans from the ape, no single factor stands out more clearly than the ability to invent. If in the education of the young we want to stress essentially human traits, we can do no better than stress and nurture that inventive ability, that creativity.

Creativity is a characteristic we all possess. Some of us don't seem to have our fair share; others have more than they know what to do with. But we all have the trait. What's more, we can improve what we have. We

can *learn* to be more creative. Don't let people tell you you've got it or you don't. You *do* have it. You *can* learn to make more of what you have. And it surely seems we can teach it to kids in school.

Several thinker-researchers have looked into the nature of the creative process. They have described it, and they have figured out how to foster it. We will look at four of them who have made especially outstanding contributions.

Guilford has been one of the great contributors to our knowledge of the creative process. He conducted studies into the structure of the intellect and identified one intellectual factor he called "divergent production."[18] Divergent production refers to a human tendency to produce, think of, and dream up multiple correct solutions to a problem. Instead of seeking a single answer to a question such as "What thing can I use to fasten these two boards together?" (answer: nail), divergent production asks "What are all the different possible things I can use to fasten these boards together?" (answers: nail, glue, string, giant clothespin, vice, bolt, adhesive tape, and many others). We all have this ability called divergent production. Some of us can use it better than others, but there is reason to believe we can all improve it through practice.

Guilford also stressed fluency and flexibility as essential elements of creativity. Fluency refers to the ability to generate quantities of ideas and words. A sample task might be: Name all the things you can pin together with a safety pin. Flexibility refers to the ability to make new relationships—to see new uses, arrangements, and possibilities. A sample task might be: One use of a safety pin is to fasten things together. Name all the other, different uses you can think of for a safety pin.

[18]Guilford, J.: Three faces of intellect, American Psychologist **14**:469-479, 1959.

Another great contributor to the field of creativity was Osborn, who invented the technique called brainstorming.[19] This technique (who hasn't heard of it?) has been put to widespread use in business and industry, not to mention education. Brainstorming is used when groups attempt to solve problems. It brings a great outpouring of ideas, all of which are initially accepted. None is judged or evaluated until later. Wild ideas are as acceptable as any other. They sometimes lead to the best solutions. Piggybacking on ideas and alterations of ideas already expressed are encouraged. Evaluation begins only after new ideas cease. Even then, ideas are judged not in terms of good-bad or right-wrong, but in terms of practicality, cost, difficulty, and other pragmatic values.

Osborn also developed a checklist that has proved useful in inventing new products. This checklist helps one look at objects or compositions, part by part, with an eye to modifying the object. Virtually all new products result from modifications, sometimes quite small, of already existing products.

Gordon is another of the notable contributors to making sense of creativity.[20] He has developed a training approach for improving creativity, which he calls "synectics."

Synectics procedures include the following three approaches:

1. *Personal analogy.* The individual is taught to identify and involve himself with the elements of a situation or problem. Example: Suppose you are a can opener. Tell how you move, how it feels to cut through the metal, how the can reacts to you, what you dislike most, and so on.

2. *Direct analogy.* The individual is taught to seek (invent) relationships between two things not usually considered related. Example: Describe all the ways you can think of in which an automobile is like a democracy.

3. *Compressed conflict.* The individual is taught to think of an item characterized by opposite words. For example, "An example of a repulsive attraction is _____."

Finally, we must make mention of our most prolific writer in school-related creativity, E. Paul Torrance. Torrance has composed tests of creativity and has written several books and articles on the subject. Many of his most valuable ideas are included in a recent article entitled "Creativity and Infinity."[21] The article deals specifically with using creativity approaches to help students feel more comfortable with the idea of infinity. The approaches Torrance suggests are widely applicable to many areas of the daily school curriculum.

Previously, I pulled together what I considered the ten best ideas of authorities in creativity.[22] Here you see a brief listing of a few of them:

1. *Ideas and associations.* Creative people seem to produce quantities of ideas (fluency) and make numerous associations among them. We can improve students' ability to do those two things by giving them direct practice in tasks such as:

Name all the things you can think of that are yellow and grow on a tree.
Name all the things that would happen if automobiles were no longer allowed in the United States.
Hawk: list nonbird objects that are similar or analogous to the hawk in shape, function, behavior, abilities, and origin.
Take two objects or ideas at random, for example, elephant and car. Make all the relationships you can between them.

[19]Osborn, A.: Applied imagination, New York, 1963, Charles Scribner's Sons.
[20]Gordon, W.: Synectics, New York, 1961, Harper and Row, Publishers.
[21]Torrance, E.: Creativity and infinity, Journal of Research and Development in Education 4:35-41, 1971.
[22]Charles, C.: Educational psychology: The instructional endeavor, St. Louis, 1972, The C. V. Mosby Co.

2. *Flexibility.* Creative people tend to be flexible in the way they look at things. That is, they see many different possibilities that usually don't come to mind at first. We can help our students become more flexible by giving them exercises such as:

Think of all the unusual uses you can for a shovel.
Think of ten different ways to get a cat down from a tree.

3. *Elaboration.* Creative people tend to be very good at elaborating ideas. If you give them a bare outline of an idea, they can fill in all the details. We can help students develop that ability by letting them do exercises such as:

Suppose we decide to get a pet for the classroom. What will we need to do to get ready for it?
Suppose our class decides to take a trip (to the park, the zoo, the next city, Hawaii). What plans do we need to make so everything will turn out the way we want?

4. *Manipulation.* The vast majority of new ideas and products come as a result of someone making a small change in an existing product. We can help students become adept at this technique by providing them exercises such as:

List all the characteristics of (an object in the classroom such as a shirt, book, table, window, and so on). Now change one of those characteristics so the object is better, more durable, or has a new use.
Use a checklist such as the following to invent a new object based on an existing object:
1. Can you change its shape, color, sound, odor, movement?
2. Can you make it bigger, stronger, taller, more durable?
3. Can you make it smaller, lighter, shorter, softer?
4. Can you rearrange its parts?
5. Can it be combined or blended with something else?

If you are interested in seeing other ideas for fostering creativity, similar to those presented here, you might like to look at my book, *Creative Writing Skills,* either book I or book II.[23]

BEHAVIOR MODIFICATION

Why do we behave as we do? Why do I, as I struggle with getting words on this page, experience an almost uncontrollable urge to get up and get a cup of coffee, although I just finished one ten minutes ago? Why do you read books for class assignments that you would not read otherwise? Why do you watch stupid television, take part in silly conversations, and eat candy you don't want or need?

Many psychologists believe a great part of human behavior can be traced to the consequences that follow it. You read a certain type of book and it brings you pleasure. You eat candy and the sweet wonderful taste has you grabbing for more. You don't read your textbook, so the teacher calls you down in front of the class, an experience so distasteful that you will read the boring text rather than have it happen again. After a while some of these acts become habit. They may stay with us for a time even though they don't bring us a reward of any kind.

The fundamental principles that underlie such ideas have been brought to a high level of understanding by one of the most famous and respected psychologists of all time. His name is B. F. Skinner, and his writings, such as "Teaching Machines," *Walden Two,* and *Beyond Freedom and Dignity,* continue to fan the flames of controversy.

Behavior modification is a practical application of the principles of reinforcement that Skinner has so ably described. Principles of reinforcement form part of a kind of learning called operant conditioning. If you want to

---

[23] Charles, C., and Church, M.: Creative writing skills, Minneapolis, 1968, T. S. Denison & Co., Inc.

teach an organism through operant conditioning, you wait for the organism to perform a desired act. Then you immediately provide a reinforcer. A reinforcer is anything that makes the organism more likely to repeat that act.

Suppose, for example, you want to teach a pigeon to roll a golf ball. You put a hungry pigeon and a golf ball together in a small enclosed area. (Skinner is not overjoyed with the fact that such enclosures are commonly called Skinner Boxes.) Now you wait until the pigeon moves toward the golf ball. As soon as it does, you supply a reinforcer, which in this case is a pellet of food. You wait until the pigeon moves toward the ball again. And again you supply the food. First thing you know the pigeon is touching the golf ball, then pecking and pushing it. All the while you reinforce each desirable movement (operant) the pigeon performs.

In common parlance, reinforcers are called rewards. When working with students, we watch for them to do a desired act, then we reinforce or reward them. Food is one of the best reinforcers for pigeons. It is very good for humans, too. But there are also other things that work well for humans. Those things include affection, praise, points, stars, plastic discs, privileges, and play money. Any activity can serve as a reinforcer, if students prefer it to the learning task. For instance, many boys like to play outdoors more than they like to practice the piano. They can have their piano practicing reinforced by being allowed to go outdoors to play immediately after practicing.

So far as teaching is concerned, we can markedly improve students' performance in learning tasks by using principles of reinforcement. This improved performance is noted in amount learned as well as in percent of on-task behavior. Kids just don't horse around and bother others nearly so much when the teacher is reinforcing the more desirable behavior.

Reinforcement procedures produce results. Massive evidence from studies involving varieties of learners and varieties of topics substantiates its effectiveness.

But why, you may ask, is behavior modification included in a discussion of techniques for enhancing the self? Certainly many people consider it *de*humanizing, as we noted in Chapter 3. It's okay for training dogs, pigeons, and rats, they say. But not for human beings. Kids need education, not training. They should be left free to choose, not coerced or manipulated, however scientific-sounding the technique might be.

Behavior modification is discussed here precisely because it does have value in enhancing the self. Whether it is an artificial technique is debatable. Skinner argues that all human behavior is shaped by random reinforcement and punishment. In his opinion we do what we do because of forces that reward or punish our behavior. Regardless of whether he is right, behavior modification, which entails the judicious systematic application of reinforcement, is very powerful in helping students feel successful, able, and productive. It helps them function in more cooperative and less hostile ways. It produces results with slow learners thought impossible only a few years ago. In short, it can effectively enhance the self—that is, make people feel better about themselves, able to interact better with others, able to produce higher quality work, able to keep at learning tasks longer than ever before.

True, behavior modification can be misused. It can make students more conforming, more submissive, less able to make decisions. But properly applied, it can produce the opposite results, as has been amply demonstrated.

How do teachers use behavior modification when they use it well?

First, they see that students have available to them learning activities that are relevant, interesting, and important.

Second, they carefully work out, in collaboration with students, rules of conduct to be followed when engaging in the learning activities. They talk with students a great deal, to be sure everyone agrees on what goes and what doesn't.

Third, they reinforce behavior, through praise, recognition, or whatever, of those students who engage in the activities, who follow rules, who try, who don't bother other learners.

Fourth, they ignore the behavior of students who violate the rules, as long as those violations do not seriously hinder the work of others. When violations occur, the teacher makes a point of praising students who are working in desirable ways.

Behavior modification, then, when used properly, can and does serve, to help students feel accepted, important, recognized, successful, able, and productive. It helps them acquire knowledge and skills. It helps them relate better to other students. Its methods are proved effective. All in all, it is a tool to be used to advantage in personalized instruction, not an evil device to be shunned.

MASTERY/COMPETENCE/SUCCESS

Ever notice how some kids take everything in stride? You throw problems in their path, they don't bat an eye. You have a bad day and grouch at them, they just plug along undaunted. You put them in stress situations, they astound you with their cool.

They have some special things going for them. One thing is high tolerance for frustration. Another is courage. Another is good sense. One quality, though, seems to stand out above the rest. That quality is self confidence.

You don't find this self confidence in overabundance. But you do find it distributed here and there among little kids, adolescents, and adults. People who have it always seem to outdo themselves when the going gets tough. They show it in sports, in discussions, in arguments, in presentations, in class assignments. They have that little something extra the rest of us wish we had.

This self confidence—this belief in one's own ability—comes from two main sources. One of these sources is feedback from others, who let us know in ways subtle and not so subtle what they think of our performances. Another source lies more within us. We see what we do and we judge it. It has to meet our own personal standards.

We all have continual opportunities for feedback about our acts. School furnishes a multitude of such opportunities. What goes on in school can really bolster self confidence. By the same token it can absolutely quash it. These things can happen because school furnishes so many conditions that bring on sweet success and devastating failure. Sometimes it seems the whole idea of school balances around success and failure.

Our society has always been success oriented. You are successful if you are able to do worthwhile things. You are a failure if you cannot. You probably know from experience how crushing failure can be. We remember instances in which we didn't do well enough to please ourselves or others. We got the F on the test. We got cut off the basketball squad. We got obliterated in an argument. How hard it is to pick ourselves off the floor and come back for more.

Yet, in subtle ways that's what happens to lots of people in school. It probably hasn't happened to you very much, or you wouldn't be far enough along the educational trail to be reading this book. But for numbers of students in school, failure is a way of life.

Robert Glasser, mentioned as the advocate of classroom meetings, has strongly urged that schools become success oriented instead of failure oriented. He says that when most students get a grade lower than B, it really means failure in their minds. They have fallen to the lower echelons of goodness. Glasser says we ought to do away with grades in schools.[24] They do too much harm to too many students. Instead of grades, he says, we should have credit. When you reach a certain level of competence in your math or history or English, you get credit. Until then, you don't get anything. For students who want to do more than is expected, you can add honors. But you don't rank students A through F.

For Benjamin Bloom, "mastery learning" is the key to success feelings.[25] He points out that teachers usually expect the following from their students:

About one third will fail or barely get by.

About one third will learn a fair amount, but not enough to be considered good students.

About one third will adequately learn what is taught.

In most cases, students meet the teacher's expectations. That means two thirds of them systematically get their motivation reduced, their aspirations lowered, and their self concepts bruised and battered.

This situation needn't occur, Bloom contends. At least 90% of all students could reach "mastery level" in material being taught, though not if they all receive identical instruction. Teaching strategies especially designed for mastery must be used. Such strategies include:

Variable rate provisions. "Slower" students can master material, but since they learn more slowly, they must have more time. Given this extra time, their final level of learning can be equal to that of the faster learners.

Instructional differences. Some students learn at a highly abstract level, working mostly on their own. Others can reach mastery only if they have concrete illustrations, ex-

planations, repetitions, and large amounts of reinforcement.

Tutorial help. With one-to-one help, many borderline students can reach mastery level. Cross-age tutoring, where "olders" help "youngers," has proved tremendously helpful in this regard. Such a program used in the Ontario-Montclair School District (California) produced outstanding learning gains for fifth and sixth grade students tutored three times per week, forty minutes each, by eighth grade students. The "olders" also showed unexpected academic gains, as well as gains in self concept, acceptability, and discipline.[26]

Okay, then, how do you make your school mastery/competence/success oriented? Or more importantly, how do you make your own teaching that way?

One thing you can do is what Glasser and Bloom suggest. You can stop giving grades. When a student's work reaches an acceptable level, give him credit and let him move on to something else. Don't give him anything until the work reaches a satisfactory level—not a C, not a D, not an F, not a frowning face.

A second thing you can do is break your curricular tasks down into steps that even the slowest learners can manage. That way they can see achievement. They can see progress. They can see they are successful because they are getting somewhere.

A third thing you can do is use a comprehensive set of performance objectives. (Now calm down, Humanists. You can let students have a lot of say about which objectives they want to attain, how they want to go about it, and how they want to pace themselves). Such a list of objectives first of all emphasizes performances. You show you are capable when you perform successfully. Secondly, learners know in advance what at least one significant

[24] Glasser, R., *op. cit.*

[25] Bloom, B.: Mastery learning. In Block, J., editor: Mastery learning: theory and practice, New York, 1971, Holt, Rinehart and Winston, pp. 47-63.

[26] Cross-age teaching. Ontario-Montclair School District, P.O. Box 313, Ontario, California 91761.

person (you) sees as evidence of success. Thirdly, when learners show their ability to perform tasks, they build, block by block, that stout feeling of competence we want them to have.

A fourth thing you can do is find ways to provide special teaching and tutoring, as Bloom has suggested in the mastery learning strategies.

A fifth thing you can do is allow students to play a strong role in evaluating their own work. They always make judgments about it anyway. But when you let them make official judgments, you are telling them that they are competent not only to *do*, but to *judge* as well.

You may have noticed that this section has the words mastery, competence, and success in its title. All three were included for a good reason. People can be made to feel successful in school even when they develop no competence. Programs that produce this unfounded feeling of success have been derogatorily called feel-good programs—anything at all is okay as long as the learners feel good about it. Feelings of success *are* important. Evidence of growing competence is just as important. In the long run, it's absolutely essential. Incompetents can't be fooled into feeling successful forever. Worse, students who do not gain competence, which means the knowledge and skills to solve problems,

are getting cheated in school, regardless of how successful they might feel. What we want to do is help students increase their real competence, through mastery learning, and get them to feel successful at the same time.

You may have a growing feeling that this competence/success stuff is overrated. Maybe you think it's not nearly important enough to make all this fuss over. Not likely. You can hardly overemphasize competence and success. Not if you are concerned about how students think of themselves. Not if you want them to become independent enough to launch into new learnings without fear and trembling. Not if you want them to build their self confidence enough to withstand the shock of failure—failure that is bound to come in some measure as they become adventurous enough to try the unknown.[27]

---

[27] For an outstanding example of a success oriented program, see the article, Succeeding with success environment by Anne C. Sapp in American Education 9:4-10, November 1973. This article describes Project Success Environment, a program in the Atlanta Public Schools that emphasizes three things: (1) Each student receives work at his own level of ability. (2) The work is structured to maximize success. (3) Teachers use positive reinforcement that combines verbal praise with tangible reward. The Project classes, compared with control classes, are more work oriented and less disruptive, and the students' gains in reading and math have been twice as great.

6

Styles of learning

RESEARCH

Teachers notice many things about the way students approach learning. They notice some dive headlong into every activity, whereas others go more slowly. Some look for adventure, others for security. Some like to work in groups, others like to work alone. Some like to read, others like to work with their hands. Some seem unusually dependent, almost unable to start activities by themselves. Others seem independent and eager to go on their own. Some like noise and movement; others like quiet and order.

You can probably add several observations of your own. These personal differences vis à vis learning exemplify a construct called "learning style." When we refer to learning style, we are alluding to personal ways of approaching learning situations. Related terms include "cognitive style," which refers mainly to what goes on in the mind, and "sensory modalities," which refers to the senses (hearing, seeing, touching) that individuals prefer to use when learning.

Learning style has been talked about for forty years and more, yet we still know little about it. Several investigators have tried to shed light on the idea. Their findings, although not overly clear and consistent, are beginning to provide hints about how to work more effectively with different kinds of students.

You may have seen some of the technical terms used to label learning styles. Bruner, for example, concluded in his research on concept formation that students could be grouped as conservative focusers or gambling focusers, depending on their approach to a given task.[1] Gamblers take chances. They leap ahead. Conservatives prefer to get everything into perspective and alter only one detail at a time.

Gardner has used terms from classical Gestalt psychology, describing tendencies toward "leveling" and "sharpening."[2] A learner who sharpens puts emphasis on significant parts of what is being learned, so that those parts stand out as larger or more important than might be warranted. They tend to remember details in the new learning better than they do the total context. Levelers, on the other hand, tend to make features of new learnings blend together, become compati-

---

[1]Bruner, J., Goodnow, J., and Austin, G.: A study of thinking, New York, 1956, John Wiley & Sons, Inc.
[2]Gardner, R., and others: Cognitive control: A study of individual consistencies in cognitive behavior, Psychological Issues 1(4):22-30, 1959.

ble, and merge into unity to a degree greater than what might be justified. They tend to remember the total situation better than its details.

Guilford, in his studies of the structure of the intellect, has identified "convergent production" and "divergent production" as separate facets of intellectual functioning.[3] Convergent production refers to the production of ideas along a single plane and to the finding of single, correct solutions to problems. Divergent production refers to the production of ideas along varying planes and to finding several different appropriate solutions to problems. People are capable of both these kinds of intellectual activity, but some (the intuitive dreamers?) seem inclined toward divergent production, whereas others (the logical realists?) seem more inclined toward convergent production.

Kagan, in studying the ways learners form concepts, concludes that some learners seem to be more "impulsive" in their approach, whereas others seem to be more "reflective."[4] Impulsive learners move quickly to conclusions, often settling on the first response that occurs to them. Reflective learners, if not slower-gaited, at least spend more time carefully considering various possibilities.

In addition to the impulsive and reflective styles, Kagan noted styles he called "analytic" and "thematic." The analytic-style learner notes and sorts out all the details of material being learned, attempting to identify them and see how they fit together. The thematic-style learner acquires a global cognition of material being learned, concerning himself not so much with the various parts and their relationships as with overall impression, meaning, and impact.

Witkin, in his studies into cognitive functioning as related to personality characteristics, identified two styles of learning that seem to have special importance for teachers—"field-dependent" and "field-independent."[5] The field-dependent person requires strong support from others around him. He tends to be fearful and anxious. He has difficulty taking the initiative and working on his own and tends to be submissive to others, especially those in positions of authority. The field-independent person functions in quite a different way. He can take initiative and organize. He often assumes a dominant role. He shows confidence and self assurance.

One of the largest investigations into styles has been coordinated over a period of years by Runner.[6] Using a specially designed questionnaire, the Runner Studies of Attitude Patterns (RSAP), Runner has succeeded in finding the means to categorize people with regard to "styles of life" and "styles of action." Four of each have been identified, and they combine to form sixteen basic personality styles. The styles of life and the styles of action are presented below:

Styles of life	Characterization: more inclined than most to seek:
Adventure oriented	New experiences
Comfort oriented	Reassurance of routine
Affiliation oriented	Personal acceptance
Recognition oriented	Public admiration

Styles of action	Characterization
Reactive	"Compelled" to act/over-react
Responsive	Inclined to experiment
Restrained	Deliberate, logical behavior
Mechanical	Acts with little feeling or thought

[3] Guilford, J.: Three faces of intellect, American Psychologist 14:469-479, 1959.
[4] Kagan, J.: Impulsive and reflective children. In Krumbolz, J., editor: Learning and the educational process, Chicago, 1964, Rand McNally & Co.
[5] Witkin, H., and others: Psychological differentiation, New York, 1962, John Wiley & Sons, Inc.
[6] Runner, K.: A theory of persons, San Diego, 1973, The Runner Associates, and Philadelphia, 1973, Research for Better Schools, Inc.

In another extensive study, Witkin and associates followed 1548 college students from entry into college through graduate and professional study. They found (1) that students tended to shift into areas of study compatible with their own cognitive style, and (2) that students achieve slightly better in areas of study compatible with their cognitive style.[7]

Runner reports several studies that have been carried out by other investigators. Two of these investigations that have special importance for teachers were done by Torrance. In one study Torrance identified college students as "freedom-oriented" or "control-oriented." He had them perform tasks on a test of originality. Then he gave them two different types of feedback—"evaluative feedback" and "creative feedback." Upon repeating the test of originality, the freedom-oriented groups made great gains after creative feedback, but only small gains after evaluative feedback. Conversely, the control-oriented groups made greater gains when given evaluative feedback than when given creative feedback.[8]

In a later study, Torrance trained 50 freedom-oriented and 50 control-oriented college students in techniques of creative problem solving. He then assigned the students a "fuzzy" problem to solve. Eighty-four percent of the control-oriented students expressed a need for more structure in the problem. Only 26% of the freedom-oriented students expressed that need.

In a similar study, Wiederanders and Harvey explored the relationship between student learning styles and types of feedback from their teachers. They found that students who were oriented to authority and personal relationships responded better to *personal* feedback. Students who were abstract task-oriented responded better to *impersonal* feedback.[9]

Other studies have investigated the relationship between learning style and achievement. Coop and Brown divided college students into two style groups—"analytic" and "non-analytic." They provided both groups two kinds of instruction identified as "teacher structured" and "independent problem solving." They found that the teacher structured method produced superior achievement gains for both groups.[10]

Different results were obtained by Grieve and Davis. They identified ninth grade geography students as "analytic" and "global" and then provided both groups two types of instruction—"discovery" and "expository." Instruction had to do with the geography of Japan and with the use of geographic materials in new situations. They found that:

Extreme *global* students did significantly better in the discovery method than in the expository method.
Extreme *analytic* students did significantly better than global students in ability to use geographic materials in new situations.[11]

Messer investigated primary grade children who had failed a grade and were repeating it. When rated on a "reflection-impulsivity" scale, repeaters were found to be signifi-

---

[7] Witkin, H. A., and others: Role of the field-dependent and field-independent cognitive styles in academic evolution: A longitudinal study, Journal of Educational Psychology **69**(3):197-211, June 1977.

[8] Torrance, E. P.: Freedom control orientation and need for structure in group creativity, Sciences d'Art—Scientific Aesthetics 8(1):1971. Reported in Runner, K., *op cit.*

[9] Wiederanders, M. R., and Harvey, O. J.: Effects of conceptual system and quality of feedback on voluntary task persistence, Journal of Educational Psychology 69(4):442-451, August 1977.

[10] Coop, R., and Brown, L.: Effects of cognitive style and teaching method on categories of achievement, Journal of Educational Psychology 61:400-405, October 1970.

[11] Grieve, T., and Davis, J.: The relationship of cognitive style and method of instruction to performance in ninth grade geography, Journal of Educational Research **65:** 137-141, November 1971.

cantly more impulsive than other children, though the same in verbal intelligence.[12]

Messer's findings seem to be explained by the findings of Odum, McIntyre, and Neale. They too placed kindergarten children into "impulsive" and "reflective" categories and found the following:

Impulsive students made twice as many errors as did reflective students.

Reflective students took more time to do their work but tended to get the correct answer sooner. They were also better able to apply their knowledge to new situations.[13]

The type of task seems to play a role. Rollins and Genser identified third and fourth grade children as "impulsive" or "reflective" and compared their performance on problem-solving tasks. They found that reflective children were faster in problem solving when the task had *few* dimensions. Impulsive children were faster when the task had *many* dimensions.[14]

SYNTHESIS

You can see that the investigators cited here use different labels to describe learning styles. Let's lift those labels from their contexts and see what they look like in isolation:

Gamblers	Conservatives
Leveling	Sharpening
Analytic	Thematic
Convergent	Divergent
Impulsive	Reflective
Field dependent	Field independent

[12] Messer, S.: Reflection-impulsivity: Stability and school failure, Journal of Educational Psychology **61**:487-490, December 1970.

[13] Odom, R., McIntyre, C., and Neale, C.: The influence of cognitive style on perceptual learning, Child Development **42**:883-891, September 1971.

[14] Rollins, H. A., and Genser, L.: Role of cognitive style in a cognitive task: A case favoring the impulsive approach to problem solving, Journal of Educational Psychology **69**(3):281-287, June 1977.

Adventure oriented	Reactive
Comfort oriented	Responsive
Affiliation oriented	Restrained
Recognition oriented	Mechanical

Now let's try to pull together all these notions of learning style and put them into patterns teachers can recognize in their own classes of students.

Most of the researchers identified learning styles by placing behaviors into either-or categories—either gamblers or conservatives, either impulsive or reflective, and so on. Teachers can probably see, among their students, three rather distinct styles of approaching learning stiuations, rather than just two.

One of these styles is free-wheeling, impulsive, novelty-seeking, adventurous, and somewhat frenetic. Learners with this style try to sample ideas and materials quickly. They react to them hurriedly and intuitively, ready to move on to something else. They seem almost compulsive on their verbal and motor responding. They are likely to form overall emotional reactions to the situation and to parts of the situation, without recognizing details or the ways the parts fit together. They don't seem overly concerned with doing things the "right" way or with giving the right answer. These students might tend to score higher on tests of creativity than on tests of intelligence or achievement. Teachers might think of them as *Adventurers;* that is the term we will use here.

A second style is more reflective and analytic. Learners with this style are usually willing to work at tasks provided, but they may not seem too anxious to begin nor anxious to finish and move on to something else. They take a more restrained approach to the situation. They may become intrigued with details, how parts work, how they fit together. They may be willing to work on a topic for a long while, trying to be sure to understand it or get it right. These students often seek feedback from the teacher or from other authorities to be sure they are on the right track. They may or may not score high on tests of creativity, but they will probably do well on intelligence and achievement tests. Teachers might think of these students as *Ponderers,* the term we will use here.

A third style is more mechanical, plodding, and hesitant. Learners with this style are quite dependent on others. They do not take the initiative; they depend on the teacher to tell them what to do and to get them started. They do not work well by themselves, preferring to be in groups with other students. They require external motivation, which may be provided in the form of social and tangible reinforcement. They tend to lose interest quickly and become discouraged easily. They require urging and evidence of progress. These students tend to rank below average in both creativity and achievement. Teachers might call them *Drifters.* We will use that name here.

Comfort conditions

Associated with learning styles are certain conditions that afford learners special comfort or satisfaction. Of course it is true that we continually learn things simply for the pleasure or the necessity of learning them. We pay attention to events in the news; we delve deeply into matters in our work and play. We absorb information as we travel, watch TV, talk with friends, and just go through the routines of normal living.

Yet, it is also true that when engaging in new tasks and learning experiences each of us seeks one or more attendant conditions— conditions that make us feel more comfortable and satisfied in the situation.

One of these comfort conditions is *structure.* Structure is like a good road map. It lets us know what to expect, where we are going, and how to get there. We do not have to be anxious about the unexpected, nor fear conditions with which we cannot cope.

A second condition is *latitude.* Although many learners seek structure, many others feel hemmed in, restricted, and stifled when asked to fit their activities into a preset pattern. In truth, structure can suppress much creativity. Too, many of us feel much more comfortable if we are allowed to do things our way, at our own pace.

A third condition is *affiliation.* Many of us willingly undertake tasks as part of a group, that we will not undertake alone. Group belonging can provide a sense of camaraderie, an esprit de corps, and above all psychological support that motivates and comforts. For these reasons we often seek to associate ourselves with others when approaching new learning situations.

A fourth condition is *recognition.* Many of us avidly seek recognition from others for the work we do. In fact, we often do work we would not do otherwise simply to gain recognition. Recognition is important because it serves to enhance the self. Others see our work as good and praiseworthy. We consider our work an extension of ourselves and thus eagerly acknowledge the praise as directed to ourselves instead of to what we have done.

Virtually all of us seek one or more of these four comfort conditions when engaging in learning situations—at least when engaging in repeated learning situations like those available in school. Some of the comfort conditions always seem linked to the Adventurer, the Ponderer, or the Drifter. For example, the Adventurer seeks latitude, whereas the Drifter seeks structure.

But learning styles and comfort conditions don't match up consistently. The adventurer, while seeking latitude, may also seek affiliation, recognition, or both; but he will not likely seek structure. The Drifter, while seeking structure, may also seek affiliation and recognition but probably not latitude. The Ponderer, meanwhile, may seek either structure or latitude, together with affiliation or recognition.

Now let's see in summary form what kinds of combinations of cognitive style and comfort conditions teachers can expect among their students:

	Comfort conditions	
Style	**Likely**	**Possible**
Adventurer	Latitude	Affiliation
		Recognition
Ponderer	Structure	Latitude
		Affiliation
		Recognition
Drifter	Affiliation	Recognition
	Structure	

In addition to comfort conditions, another factor that has an important relationship to learning style is what we commonly call feedback.

Feedback

Feedback refers to the responses made to learners, especially those responses that help them to work, keep on the track, and to improve. It includes such things as:

Rejecting responses: For example, verbal: "no, wrong, stop that"; nonverbal: frowns, shaking head, snapping fingers

Accepting responses: For example, verbal: "good, right, go on"; nonverbal: smiles, nodding, touching

Other reinforcing responses: For example, awarding of privileges, giving points and tangibles, allowing preferred activities

Corrections: For example, pointing out right answers, indicating where errors exist, how mistakes should be corrected

Evaluations: For example, indicating whether student work and behavior are good, poor, on the right track

Teachers provide much of this feedback. Other feedback can be provided through self checking devices and through student self evaluation. Still other feedback comes in the form of comments from other students.

Different learning styles call for different kinds of feedback. The Adventurers do not go out of their way to seek teacher approval. Neither do they require heavy doses of positive reinforcement, as might be provided in programs of behavior modification. Overall, they operate more on the basis of inner feelings than on others' reactions, though teacher and peer responses do have some effect.

What kind of feedback, then, suits Adventurers best? Generally, what helps them most are comments such as: "All right, have you thought about . . .? What do you think might happen if . . .? Why don't you look at . . .?" In other words, they thrive on comments that suggest new possibilities, that expand their horizons. Kind words from teachers help, too, but they aren't necessary to keep the Adventurers going.

The Ponderers need a different type of feedback. They tend to be preoccupied with whether they are doing things right or wrong. What teachers think about their work makes a difference. They seek out evaluative judgments, hoping for positive ones, of course. But when they are on the wrong track, they want to know it and make things right. They respond well to positive reinforcement and to programs of behavior modification.

The Drifters can only be kept working at tasks through constant guidance and feedback. As we have noted, they require both structure and physical nearness of the teacher. Their comportment ("good" and "bad" behavior) varies from spontaneous, habitual annoying of others to willing compliance to withdrawn quietness. They are seldom able to start themselves on school learning tasks. Once started, they cannot sustain their activities for long. To progress, they must experience almost constant success, enhanced through systematic positive reinforcement. Both their task activities and their comportment respond dramatically to behavior modification. Since they are so easily distracted, boisterous behavior by others is almost sure to disengage them from learning activities.

Having taken note of feedback judged effective with different students, let's add it as

| | Comfort conditions | | |
Style	Likely	Possible	Feedback
Adventurer	Latitude	Affiliation Recognition	Expansion of possibilities, suggestion of alternatives, occasional positive comments
Ponderer	Structure	Latitude Affiliation Recognition	Suggestions, evaluation, corrections, positive reinforcement
Drifter	Structure Affiliation Recognition	Recognition	Guidance, urging, positive reinforcement

a third facet to the "styles" and "comfort conditions" presented previously (see chart).

TEACHING STRATEGIES

Examination of the styles/comfort conditions/feedback summary just presented indicates that rather distinct teaching strategies are needed for the different categories of students identified. Such general strategies, appropriate to the three categories of students, will be mentioned briefly. In following chapters the strategies will be examined in detail.

First, though, let it be understood that all students in the class participate in group activities part of the time. Discussions, dramatizations, group games, and some art and music activities require a group format. We can think of these group activities as one layer of the curriculum.

A second layer of the curriculum consists of the instructional activities used for students of different learning styles. The strategies of this second layer are considered here.

Too, it must be understood that the activities and materials within different strategies vary according to the ages of students. So also do the degrees of structure and the ways of providing different kinds of feedback.

For Adventurers

Adventurers seem to thrive on novelty and diversity. They react impulsively, rapidly, as if there were not enough time to examine everything. Just as quickly they leave an activity or topic to try another. They require latitude. They resist being forced into established ways of doing things. They are not overly concerned with right answers or right ways. They are concerned with interesting possibilities.

Individualized "open experience" strategies and creative project approaches seem well suited to Adventurers. These approaches give them great exploratory latitude, opportunity to follow interesting leads, and alternative activities. Possibilities in various curricular areas can be made virtually limitless. Many people think the open experience approach is just a "leave 'em alone and let 'em go" style of teaching. They are greatly mistaken. The open experience approach requires that teachers make much special preparation. So does the creative project approach. Since students help select their own topics and activities, teachers must provide an exceptionally rich environment in each subject area. Reading, for example, requires a great number and variety of books, magazines, newspapers, reference books, and reading games. Science requires quantities of reading materials, charts, models, diagrams, and objects such as wires, cells, microscopes, prisms, lenses, measuring devices, aquaria, terraria; the list seems to go on forever. And so it is for every curricular area in which optional work activities are provided.

Furthermore, teachers must keep track of what students do and how they react to the experiences they select. Students should plan their activities and reach agreement with the teacher concerning their suitability. Regular conferences must be held. Records of those conferences, of activities undertaken, and of student reactions to the activities must be kept. Samples of student work should be kept with the records.

For Ponderers

Ponderers approach learning activities in a reflective, analytic, touch-all-the-bases manner. They do not leap in pell mell. They take hold of the task and begin to work away at it. They show concern for the right way, the correct answer. They work well on their own and produce good quality work.

A structured individualized strategy seems best suited to the Ponderers' learning style. Programs such as diagnostic-prescriptive teaching, modularized instruction, and behavior-referenced learning centers exemplify this strategy. Objectives, procedures, and necessary materials are all specified in these approaches. Self checking devices provide quick feedback concerning correctness of work completed. Teachers suggest corrective measures where needed and supply additional reinforcement.

The behavior-referenced approaches such as those mentioned here come in considerable variety. Many such programs are commercially available, often coming in kit or packaged form. The commercial materials are expertly prepared and sequenced; however, they are costly, and often they are not well suited to a particular group of children.

Teachers can prepare their own sets of behavior-referenced materials, especially suited to their students. The preparation of these materials is not difficult. However, it is time-consuming, because it requires the listing of specific objectives, the preparation of work activities designed for each objective, and the preparation of checking and record-keeping devices. The load can be reduced and the procedure made more enjoyable when three or four teachers work through it together.

For Drifters

Drifters have difficulty beginning work and keeping at it, at least in most school learning activities. They take little initiative, and the slightest distraction causes them to disengage from the activity. Teachers must continually encourage, urge, and supply positive reinforcement.

For these reasons, individualized work does not seem appropriate for Drifters. They need the stimulation of the teacher's presence, together with the psychological support of other classmates. Small group instruction, directed by the teacher, seems more desirable. The work provided should be carefully structured so that directions are very clear and work sessions short and varied. The structure should provide frequent, continual evidence of success. Students should have their progress pointed out. Their learnings should have immediate, evident application to lifelike problem situations. They need to apply and practice very quickly what they learn.

Coupled with this success approach, teachers should apply systematic programs of behavior modification consisting of three parts:

1. Setting up clear objectives and rules of conduct
2. Ignoring minor failures and breaking of conduct rules
3. Rewarding success and desired behavior

The reward aspect may take the form of personal praise, the awarding of privileges, or the awarding of tangible reinforcers such as tokens and candy.

Topics and approaches

Earlier we noted that many areas of the curriculum do not lend themselves well to individualized instruction. Some activities are best done in large groups, regardless of differences in students' learning styles.

Examples of some of the curricular subjects, topics, and activities best approached through large group instruction include:

Elementary: Art, music, physical education, health, creative writing, drama, social studies, sharing, discussions, class projects

Secondary: Drama, group music, team sports, class discussions, class projects, typing, home economics, foreign language

Other subjects and topics lend themselves quite well to approaches in which content, objectives, activities, or time schedules are made different for different students. These program differences are provided to coincide with students' abilities, interests, working tempo, and styles of learning.

Examples of some of the subjects and topics that lend themselves well to individualized approaches include:

Elementary[15]: Reading, mathematics, spelling, grammar, handwriting, science

Secondary: Virtually all subjects within the areas of natural science, mathematics, social sciences, and English. Class discussions in these areas, of course, require group participation.

From these examples you can see that personalized instruction, since it is always directed at what is best for each student, sometimes takes the form of individualized work. At other times it takes the form of small group instruction and at still other times the form of large group instruction.

To conclude this discussion of learning styles and teaching strategies, let's take note once more of the following points:

1. Large group instruction often best serves the interests of individual students. This is evident when group interaction is desired, as in group discussions, projects, team games, and other such activities. Student differences in learning style do not call for different teaching approaches in large group activities.

2. At other times small group instruction best serves the needs of certain students. This is the case when interaction is not particularly desired, yet the students, because of their learning styles, cannot function well without structure and the physical presence of the teacher. We referred to these students as Drifters.

3. Individualized instruction, at certain times, best suits the needs of many students. This is true when students have learning styles characterized by initiative and some perseverance. Some of these students (Adventurers) seek diversity, novelty, and the opportunity to explore. Other students (Ponderers) prefer structure, sense of direction and accomplishment, and teacher feedback.

The continual intent of personalized instruction is to provide learning activities, comfort conditions, and teacher feedback that best provide for each individual member of each class.

---

[15] Kindergarten and first grade are special cases. Some work can be individualized at these levels, but most is best done in large and small groups directed by the teacher.

III

STEPS TO INDIVIDUALIZATION

*providing suggestions on how
to begin individualizing portions
of the instructional program,
followed by descriptions of tried and
true approaches to individualization,
through*

7
Proceeding calmly

8
Recipes and rationales

7

Proceeding calmly

The word "shibboleth," which in Hebrew means freshet, found a remarkable use in an ancient war between the Gileadites and the Ephraimites. Both groups spoke the same language, but the Ephraimites could not pronounce shibboleth in the same way the Gileadites did. So the Gileadites used the word as a test; friend could be separated from foe by having questionable persons pronounce it.

Today, shibboleth has different meanings in English. One of those meanings is "a pet word or phrase of a particular group." Education has its share of shibboleths—some say more than its share—few of which are more prominent than "individualization." Almost all teachers say individualization is important. Who would deny that a person learns better when being taught something worthwhile, suited to special needs, at a level neither too difficult nor too easy, with pacing neither too fast nor too slow, using materials and activities suited to a particular learning style or preference.

Yet, few teachers individualize very much, because it takes know-how, careful planning, and some effort to get things going. They could begin more easily if they would reflect on the importance of smallness.

THE IMPORTANCE OF SMALLNESS

Ramon Ross, the noted author and story-teller, has a saying that makes a great deal of sense. What the world needs, he says, is lots of really good *small* ideas. We already have plenty of big ideas. The trouble is, those big ideas, such as solving world hunger or stopping inflation or ensuring a lasting peace, are awfully hard to deal with. They are so big and cumbersome you can't get hold of them. What we don't have is good small ideas, things we can really get our teeth into, that would finally make the big ideas work.

When discussing matters of education and teacher training, Ross will listen, face without expression, while the fine sounding big ideas are bandied about. If at last someone mentions a small, practical first step, his eyes will light. "Now there's a *real* small idea!" he will say. If you asked Ross he wouldn't think much of the big idea of individualizing instruction. He would be enamored, however, of any small ideas that would help people make a start. You have to take that first step, he would say, before you can take the second.

Let us then be mindful of Professor Ross. Let us seek the small ideas that give us toeholds on individualizing. In short, let us remember the importance of smallness and proceed calmly.

PERSONAL DIFFERENCES

We have already noted the variety of educationally important differences that exist among students. We saw that differences in *intellectual development* allow some students to learn more rapidly and abstractly than others.

We saw that differences in *language ability* allow some students to learn verbal material and verbally presented material much more easily than others.

We saw that differences in *background of experiences* enables some students, more easily than others, to relate to and profit from content being taught.

We saw that differences in *preferred styles of learning* enable some students, more than others, to engage profitably in the instructional activities and materials being used.

We saw that differences in *personality* cause students to react differently to teachers' personalities and teaching styles.

We saw that *self image* is mixed inextricably into the educational process and is related to school achievement.

These differences all point to the need for individualizing instruction, and this is where the big idea bugaboo rears its ugly head. How can any teacher hope to make up individual teaching plans for each and every student that would take all these important factors into account? The answer is that teachers can't. They can't do it all. Not completely. But they can do a great deal fairly easily. They can think small, as Ramon Ross says. They can light a candle instead of cursing the darkness, as Eleanor Roosevelt said. They can take the first steps first.

PUT ON THEIR COATS

If you were to individualize instruction completely, you would have to plan individ-

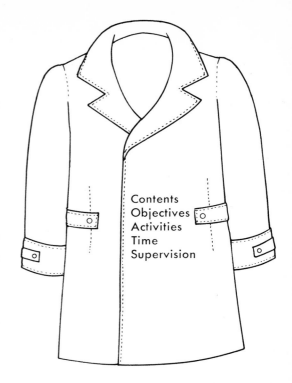

ual programs for each of your students. Each of those programs would have to have its own special *content*, *objectives*, and *activities*. The different content and activities would call for different instructional materials. Each plan would have its own pace, rhythm, and allotment of *time*. You would *supervise* learning differently for each plan.

As we said, there is no feasible way teachers can make such individual plans. Even if there were, it would be impossible to manage instruction when every student was doing something different, with different materials, at different rates of speed.

This tells us a simple basic fact: It is impossible, within the present school setting, to individualize instruction completely. Therefore, when we speak of individualizing as a practical matter, we are speaking of partial individualization.

The question then becomes, how much, to

what extent can I individualize my teaching? Given my particular students, the school's curriculum requirements, our physical facilities, the materials at hand, and the schedule requirements, what can I do to begin matching instruction to my individual students? The answer lies in the students' COATS.

Remember that acronym "COATS," and you will always have a handle on individualizing instruction. Now there's a *real* small idea. It works like this: To take the first step toward individualizing instruction, make some small adjustments, in accordance with individual students' needs, in *either*

Content—the subject matter being studied

Objectives—the outcomes expected from the study of the subject matter

Activities—the procedures and materials students use while learning

Time—the amounts of time students are allowed for work or completion of assignments

or

Supervision—the amount and type of control you exercise over students at work and the way you talk with them

If you make variations in even one of these aspects, you are individualizing instruction. The more variations you make, the more you are individualizing. Remember, though, it is not feasible to vary all the elements for all the students all the time. You reach a point of diminishing returns. It is impossible to say where the optimally effective point lies between no individualization and complete individualization. Too many uncontrolled factors, such as age of students, type of facilities, teacher helpers, teacher personality, and school demands come into play. However, we can hypothesize that the optimal point lies somewhere near the intersection of *feasibility* and *student match*.

This hypothesis is illustrated in the following diagram. The solid line denotes *feasibility*—the ease with which the teacher can arrange, present, and control instruction. The broken line denotes *student match*—the extent to which instruction matches the needs of individual students regarding content, objectives, activities, time, and supervision.

Even with no individualization, we see a degree of match between students and COATS. That's because content, objectives, activities, time, and supervision are selected for an imaginary student who is "average" in all human variables that affect learning.

Instructional feasibility is at its highest with no individualization. That's because methods, materials, schedules, and the like are all prearranged for the imaginary average

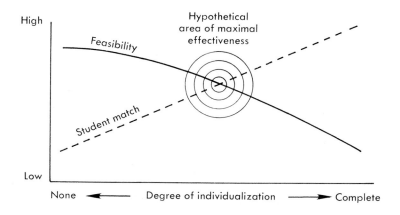

High

Hypothetical area of maximal effectiveness

Feasibility

Student match

Low

None ◄——— Degree of individualization ———► Complete

student. Feasibility remains high as small variations in COATS are made, then declines as the variations become greater and thus more awkward to manage.

FIRST STEPS

Herbert Kohl, in his fine little book *The Open Classroom*, says "start with 10 minutes a day." He was talking about an open experience approach to teaching (which incidentally is one major way of individualizing instruction). We can as easily apply his idea to any approach to individualizing instruction and the advice remains sound.

Ten minutes a day is a way of starting small. It is that toehold, that first step. It gets you going. As the students get used to it and you get the kinks worked out, you can increase to 20 minutes a day and so on. In reading, for example, you might allow students to read whatever they wished for 10 minutes each day. In English, they could write about whatever they wished. In biology, they could work on individual projects.

Instead of starting with a certain amount of time each day, you might want to think in terms of a few students. Perhaps you have six students who are advanced in general science and capable of working on their own. You give them individual assignments they complete on their own, while you teach the rest of the students in your customary way.

Yet another way of taking the first step in individualizing focuses on production. Many areas of the curriculum stress two levels: one level is basic knowledge and skills, which all students need to acquire. You can teach that level to the total class. The other level is a productive level—students are expected to do creative, productive work using the basic knowledge and skills from the first level. You can individualize this second level by allowing students to choose, from among several options, what they wish to work on. Or you can assign them individual work, based on special needs and abilities you have seen.

The point is this: by beginning small, you set a firm foundation for further individualization. You can decide which of COATS you want to vary for your students. You can work out your procedures, acquire your materials, and take care of all the details without undue difficulties. Meanwhile, the students adjust to the new approach. They have to learn new routines and new expectations. Starting small eases the transition. Once you have things organized and students have adjusted, it's very easy to individualize further.

ADJUSTING THE COATS

Contents, objectives, activities, time, and supervision—these are the elements that we manipulate when individualizing instruction. In Chapter 8 you will see an introduction to specific approaches that have been developed for varying the elements, for adjusting the COATS. Before reading those recipes and rationales, you might want to know a bit more about the elements referred to as COATS.

Contents refers to the subject matter with which students are working. In traditional, nonindividualized instruction, the subject matter—contents—is exactly the same for all students. If the course is Modern American Poets, all students study the same material at the same time. If the course is Eighth Grade Reading, all students work together at the same skills using the same materials.

Some individualized programs vary the contents for different students. They can provide this variation in three different ways: (1) options within a topic, (2) optional topics within a subject, and (3) options among subjects.

The first, options within a topic, allows students to select from different sources of information provided or suggested by the teacher. Suppose for example that the topic is "control of the Panama Canal." Sources of information from which students could select might include newspaper articles from Panama, the United States, and the USSR. They might include essays in *Time*, transcripts from "Meet the Press," speeches given in Congress, and in the United Nations General Assembly, and television broadcasts or videotapes of interviews with the President of Panama. They might include historical accounts of political events surrounding the construction of the Panama Canal. Each of these sources provides different information, different interpretations, and different viewpoints on who should control the Canal and how it should be done. The teacher may assign options or students may select them.

A second way of varying contents is to provide optional topics within a subject. Suppose the subject is American History, focusing on the westward movement. Students might choose or be assigned to delve into different aspects of this movement, such as Manifest Destiny, the major routes westward, modes of transportation, what lured the settlers on, the wagon trip from Missouri to California, Indians along the way, or the Hispanic tradition in the Southwest.

A third way of varying content is to allow students to work at different subjects during a given period. This approach is feasible only in elementary schools and secondary schools that have "cores" or individual study programs. Students are encouraged and assisted in subject matter work they select because of special interest, special aptitude, or special need. This approach is most commonly seen in open experience education, alternative school programs, free-choice periods, and programs for the mentally gifted.

Objectives are the intended outcomes of teaching. They are specifications, made in advance, of what students will be able to do as a result of the instruction they receive.

Normally, objectives are held constant for all students. Some teachers individualize instruction by setting forth different objectives for different students. This can be done even when the content is the same for everyone.

One way to make variations in objectives is to set higher or lower standards of accomplishment for individual students. Suppose the contents under study are addition facts in arithmetic. All students are provided the same contents (as well as the same activities, time, and supervision), but some may be expected to complete 30 problems correctly in 15 minutes, while others may be expected to complete 25, 20, or 15.

Another way to vary objectives is to begin with a master list of objectives within a given subject, but not expect all students to reach all the objectives. Suppose, for example, the topic is Environmental Studies. Given the same contents and materials, students accomplish as many of the objectives as they can within the time allowed. They may be encouraged to work toward the objectives in fixed order, or they may be allowed to skip around to sample aspects related to health, conservation, aesthetics, and so forth.

Another very common way of varying objectives can be seen in the teaching method called diagnostic-prescriptive teaching (DPT). Students are "diagnosed" to determine which objectives they need to work toward and are then given individual instructional "prescriptions" that lead to the attainment of specified objectives.

Activities refers to the procedures, materials, and interactions provided to facilitate student learning. They are what students *do* while studying the contents under consideration. Familiar kinds of activities include reading, writing, listening, discussing, observing, drawing, working problems, and so forth.

Teachers often individualize instruction by providing a variety of activities, even though the contents and objectives may be held constant for everyone. One example of this is modularized instruction, a method explained in detail in Chapter 10. In this approach, the contents and objectives are kept the same for all students. Optional activities are provided, all of which lead to attainment of the objectives. The options ideally offer different avenues to learning. Some stress reading, others stress viewing media, still others stress interviewing and discussing. Students are allowed to select the activity option that best suits their interests, abilities, and preferred styles of learning.

Another example of varied activities is open experience. The subject might be art and the objective might be to produce a product that illustrates the use of form, line, and composition. Individual students decide whether they will work singly or in pairs; they select the materials they need to complete the product, and they arrange a means of displaying it to best advantage.

Time refers to the number and schedule of minutes, days, or weeks for which students work at given topics. Ordinarily time is held constant for all students. They all do algebra during a 50-minute period. They all have two weeks to get their book report ready. At the end of the specified time, some will have done very well, some will have done moderately well, and some will have done poorly.

Some teachers are now individualizing instruction by providing variable amounts of time. They recognize that some students work slowly and methodically. Those students need more time to complete their work than do students who are naturally faster.

Recent research in mastery learning has provided additional evidence for the desirability of varying time limits. Investigators have found that almost all students, given sufficient help and time, can reach high levels of achievement—levels called "mastery." It take some students much longer than others, but they ultimately learn the material as fully as the faster students. Many people believe it better to learn less material but learn it well than to cover more material but learn it poorly.

With this in mind you may want all your

students to reach high levels of achievement before moving ahead to their next learnings. Some will progress much faster than others. The slower ones will be learning the material well. They will simply cover less of it.

Supervision refers to the guidance, conrol, and communication used by the teacher. Students react differently to urging, praise, exhortation, structure, support, and correcion. Some need to be spoken to gently. Others respond better to firm words. Some need direct supervision. Others work just as well when the teacher is out of the room. Some want to be told exactly what to do. Others like the latitude to do things their own way.

Teachers must be very tactful in their supervision of students. They must be fair and consistent. Yet, they increase their effectiveness by interacting differently with different students.

This fine line requires that the same basic expectations be held for all students—expectations that they abide by class rules, do work at a level commensurate with their ability, and respect the rights and feelings of others. Within those expectations, teachers may need to relate to individual students differently. If the students seem to think the teacher is unfair or is showing favoritism, frank discussions should be held to explain why different students receive somewhat different attention and treatment.

ALL SUBJECTS WERE NOT CREATED EQUAL

There are three final points to remember as you take the first steps in individualizing instruction: (1) it is much harder to individualize instruction in some subjects than others; (2) it is difficult to individualize instruction for primary grade children; and (3) some subjects should not be approached at all through individualized instruction.

When it comes to subjects, individualized instruction is

Easier and more desirable in	More difficult, or questionable, in
Knowledge and skill acquisition in "basic" subjects such as reading, English, mathematics, natural sciences, and social sciences	Group music
	Team games and sports
	Interaction exercises
	Group discussions
	Debates
Individual music, art, sports	Voice choir
	Drama
Special interest projects	

Although individualization enhances some parts of the curriculum more than others, any part can be individualized to the extent that:

It can include "free" exploratory experiences, and

It can be structured into directions and responses that individuals can follow on their own.

When it comes to students, individualized instruction is

Easier with	More difficult with
More advanced students	Primary grade children
Students who read well	Students who read poorly
Students who are good at following directions	Students who do not follow directions well
Students who have had prior individualized experience	Students who have had no individualized experience

But even under difficult conditions it can be done, especially if you have help from aides, parent volunteers, or cross-age tutors.

In conclusion, think of individualization in small terms. Look for *real* little ideas as places to start.

8

Recipes and rationales

We begin this chapter with an overview of strategies useful in individualizing instruction. You will learn which aspects of instruction are changed when adapted to individual students and what characteristics of teachers and students prompt those changes. You will learn about experience-referenced and behavior-referenced approaches—how they differ and what they try to accomplish. You will find brief descriptions of strategies within each of these approaches. You will see some hints on how to begin individualizing. Finally, you will find a summary of management details you must handle in any strategy you decide to use.

The Planning Guide on the next page will help you get an overall view of how to individualize instruction.

TYPES OF INDIVIDUALIZATION
Behavior-referenced

Behavior-referenced strategies emphasize the attainment of specific behavioral objectives. Those objectives are established before instruction is presented. They specify in observable terms exactly what you want students to be able to do as a result of instruction. They include three essential parts:

1. The desired behaviors are specified: for example, "Give a worksheet showing 10 acute and 10 obtuse angles, the student will be able to identify which are obtuse and which are acute, within one minute. 100% accuracy."[1]
2. Appropriate instruction is provided to enable students to perform the specified behaviors.
3. Criterion measures, such as tests, specified acts, or work products, are analyzed to see whether the student has reached the objectives.[2]

Experience-referenced

Experience-referenced strategies place emphasis on providing quality learning experiences for students. Quality means the experiences are relevant, multi-optional, intriguing to students involved, and rich with materials. Specific behavioral objectives are not used, because they are believed impossible to define, unpredictable, or irrelevant. Instead of stating objectives, one describes the experience. Examples are: "The student will be given the opportunity to hold and pet a baby rabbit," "The student will be given the opportunity to ride with an on-duty highway patrolman."

---

[1] This is an example of a behavioral objective. Instructions for preparing or obtaining behavioral objectives are presented in Chapter 9.
[2] Criterion measures are described in detail in Chapter 9.

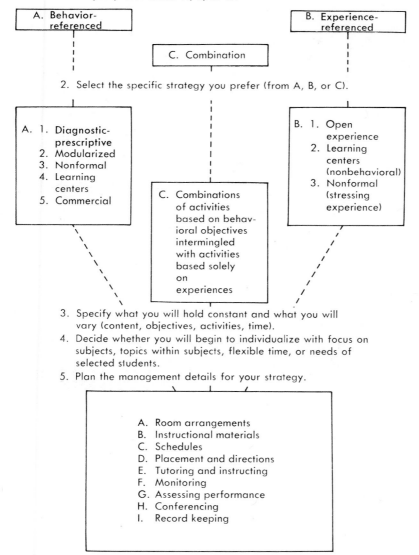

1. Select the general type of individualized instruction you prefer (either A, B, or C).

A. Behavior-referenced

B. Experience-referenced

C. Combination

2. Select the specific strategy you prefer (from A, B, or C).

A. 1. Diagnostic-prescriptive
   2. Modularized
   3. Nonformal
   4. Learning centers
   5. Commercial

C. Combinations of activities based on behavioral objectives intermingled with activities based solely on experiences

B. 1. Open experience
   2. Learning centers (nonbehavioral)
   3. Nonformal (stressing experience)

3. Specify what you will hold constant and what you will vary (content, objectives, activities, time).
4. Decide whether you will begin to individualize with focus on subjects, topics within subjects, flexible time, or needs of selected students.
5. Plan the management details for your strategy.

A. Room arrangements
B. Instructional materials
C. Schedules
D. Placement and directions
E. Tutoring and instructing
F. Monitoring
G. Assessing performance
H. Conferencing
I. Record keeping

Teachers and/or students decide what sorts of experiences are desirable for each student. Teachers strive to maximize the quality of the experience, which can be modified continually on the basis of feedback from students.

Combinations

Combination strategies place emphasis on both quality experiences and specific objectives. The combination approach is often used in creative or aesthetic topics. In art, for example, you may decide that a student "needs" a particular experience. Skills inherent in the experience may be defined behaviorally. Aesthetic intents may not be definable; thus, attention is also focused on the quality of the experience.

STRATEGY SELECTION: BEHAVIOR-REFERENCED
Diagnostic-Prescriptive Teaching (DPT)[3]

Beginning with an extensive list of behavioral objectives, teachers test students to determine—"diagnose"—areas of weakness. On the basis of this diagnosis, teachers assign activities intended to correct the weaknesses identified. These assignments are called "prescriptions." DPT requires:

1. Sets of *behavioral objectives* that cover the curricular area or topic
2. *Diagnostic tests*
3. *Prescriptive activities*
4. *Criterion tests* to determine whether objectives have been reached

Modularized instruction[4]

Teachers prepare instructional modules that guide learners to the attainment of objectives in a given topic. A module usually consists of the following parts:

1. Directions for using the module
2. A pretest. If students pass, they are given credit without going through the module.
3. Introduction to the topic
4. Goals of the module
5. Short-range specific behavioral objectives
6. Enabling activities, related to each specific behavioral objective. Two or three alternate activities, each using different types of materials, are made available for each objective. Students select the activity they prefer.
7. A posttest
8. Remedial work, if performance on the posttest is not acceptable

Nonformal basic programs, with objectives[5]

Nonformal basic programs take many forms. They are structured by teachers, often in cooperation with students, and they use behavioral objectives. Usually, they involve a single subject area. Reading is probably the most common subject in elementary schools, whereas individual projects are most common in secondary schools. Though these programs use behavioral objectives taken from teachers' manuals, curriculum guides, or other sources, students may be given leeway in their choice of activities and materials and in their use of time to teach the objectives. Teachers and students hold conferences periodically for the purpose of keeping track, making suggestions, correcting problems or errors, and deciding on future work.

Specific learning centers[6]

A learning center is a place in the classroom that contains activities and materials for

---

[3] Diagnostic-prescriptive teaching is described in Chapter 9.
[4] Modularized instruction is described in detail in Chapter 10.

[5] Nonformal basic programs are discussed in detail in Chapter 11.
[6] Learning centers are described in detail in Chapter 12.

a given topic. It includes directions for using the center, assignment or task cards, perhaps pre- and posttests, and record keeping devices. "Specific" means the center uses behavioral objectives. These learning centers are similar to interest centers, but the emphasis is on instructional rather than leisure or supplemental activities. They are often used in conjunction with group instruction. Basic instruction is given in groups, then drill, application, expansion, and enrichment are carried out in the centers. In some cases all activities, including basic instruction, are included in the center.

Commercial programs[7]

Commercial programs, such as those from SRA, Scholastic, IPI, IGE, PLAN, and others, have been available for many years. They divide a subject area into small parts with different levels of difficulty, provide interesting instructional activities and materials, include self checking devices and record forms that show student progress through objectives and experiences. They tend to be well prepared, high in quality, and expensive. They are very good if you can afford them.

STRATEGY SELECTION: EXPERIENCE-REFERENCED
Open experience[8]

Students identify or select topics they want to pursue. They make the selection on the basis of their own interests, not those of the teacher. They may decide, in group discussions, to pursue one large topic together (such as making and using a greenhouse) and to work at it in teams. However, persons are free to work individually at whatever they choose.

Teachers may leave the choice of topics entirely up to the students, or they may require that students choose topics in one particular area, or in two or three areas, such as math, art, reading, or creative writing. Once topics are selected, teacher and students confer on procedures, materials, and so on. The teacher may give hints but does not direct or even make strong suggestions that imply student compliance.

This approach does not use behavioral objectives unless the student requests them. Neither does it use exams unless requested. Both teacher and students play parts in evaluation. Students evaluate themselves—their progress, interest, and satisfaction. They also give evaluative feedback to the teacher concerning the relevance and richness of the experiences. Teachers evaluate the experiences, activities, and materials in terms of student interest and participation. They also consider the importance of the topic as students see it, the quality and quantity of materials available, and student feeling of satisfaction from the experience. In addition, they look for completed work projects, if any, and they solicit student feedback regarding all aspects of the experience. They do not criticize student work unless asked to do so.

Exploratory learning centers[9]

This approach entails setting up one or more learning centers in the classroom. Students participate by bringing in materials and helping arrange activities. As described in the section on learning centers, topic, task cards, and other materials are present in the center. However, in the exploratory center, specific behavioral objectives are not used. The emphasis, again, is on the quality of the experience, rather than on specific outcomes. Assignments will be stated in terms of learn-

---

[7]Commercial programs are discussed briefly in Chapter 14.

[8]Open experience is described in detail in Chapter 13.

[9]Learning centers are described in detail in Chapter 12.

er activities, for example, "Listen to 'In The Hall of The Mountain King' and note any feelings you have about the music, as well as any images you see while listening."

The experiences are judged on the basis of student involvement, with willingness and enjoyment, on any work produced, and on feedback students provide.

Nonformal basic programs, without objectives[10]

Given normal curricular topics and materials related to them, students arrange their own schedules of activities. They may choose to work in textbooks, workbooks, reference materials, audiovisual materials, games, or magazines. They may choose to draw, construct, dramatize, or whatever. They are expected to devote a minimum amount of time to each specific topic. Since behavioral objectives are not used, student accountability is shown in work produced, in records kept, and in conferences with the teacher. Students may work individually, in pairs, or in small groups.

STRATEGY SELECTION: COMBINATIONS

As shown in the Planning Guide, combination strategies include emphasis on both specific behavioral objectives and quality experiences. The kinds and numbers of combinations are virtually limitless. No attempt will be made to list them here. They usually occur within a topic that combines skill and knowledge development with exploratory, creative, or aesthetic activities. Skills and knowledge objectives are stated behaviorally. Exploratory, creative, and aesthetic activities may be stated in terms of the experiences themselves.

Art is an example we used previously.

---

[10]Nonformal basic programs are described in detail in Chapter 11.

Skills and knowledge, behaviorally defined, are developed in certain activities. Those activities, in turn, may be incorporated into a creative production experience, such as drawing or macramé.

Literature is another example. Students acquire knowledge, behaviorally defined, of, let us say, symbolism or figures of speech. This knowledge is acquired within a larger experience context that provides exploration into the work of an author such as Fitzgerald—an experience that presumably has desirable though unpredictable effects on readers.

In general, subjects such as art, music, literature, creative writing, and drama lend themselves nicely to strategies that emphasize both experiences and specific objectives.

CONSTANTS AND VARIABLES

In reality, individualized instruction is a grand ideal we strive for. Completely individualized programs fall beyond our reach. Like carrots before our nose, they dance ahead of us as we gallop after them.

Why? Because to completely individualize a program you have to provide exactly the right *content, objectives, activities, time allotments,* and *supervision* for each student. Individuals would have subject content suited to their own peculiar needs and interests. They might have their own special set of objectives to guide their learning. Activities would be matched exactly to their interests and learning style. And they would have available whatever time might be necessary to complete, to everyone's satisfaction, the activities undertaken, whether they work fast or slow, continually or occasionally, intensively or superficially.

In this light, you see, a completely individualized program is a virtual impossibility. No teacher can manage activities when students are all on different time schedules. Therefore, many individualized plans hold time constant. That is, a specific amount of time is alloted to individual work each day. Since no teacher can develop a complete, different set of behavioral objectives for each student, many plans hold the same objectives for all students while varying the activities or time schedules. And so it is with content and activities, which cannot be specially selected for each student without undue effort by the teacher.

For these reasons, we must realize that it is unrealistic to think of setting up "completely" individualized programs for every class. Individualization, in some ways, is a state of mind in which you make continual efforts to fit instruction to differences among students. This instructional fit (and you may think that's exactly what it is) increases to the extent we can make content, objectives, activities, time, and supervision variable—at least, as variable as school policy and our own physical and mental resources will allow.

You should make a basic decision as you individualize instruction: You should decide whether, which, and to what extent you will vary content, objectives, activities, time, and supervision for your students. This decision should be made consciously, not accidentally, and students should understand what is being done and why.

BEGINNING THE PROGRAM

Don't think you have to have a 100% full-blown individualized program ready before you can begin. Chapter 7 stressed that you should start small. Learn your way as you go. Let students learn their way, too. You can expand as you and the students get in the swing of things. Here are some ways to begin:

With certain topics. Many teachers concentrate first on a single topic or subject. Once they get organization and management of that topic smoothed out, they add another topic, and so gradually increase the scope of individualized work. Beginning topics often

include language, mathematics, and individual projects.

With certain times. Another way of beginning is to set aside part of each day or period for individual work. You allow students to choose their activities. Most teachers expect students to do something "worthwhile" and to be accountable for it, through conferences, work produced, records kept, and other means.

With certain students. Almost every class has students who can work on their own, responsibly and productively. Some students will be far ahead of others, some far behind. These students often do not profit from group instruction aimed at the middle. Many teachers individualize instruction for such students while providing grouped instruction for the remainder of the class.

MANAGEMENT DETAILS

Your good ideas don't automatically work just because they seem good. They will fizzle before your eyes if you don't attend to details. This last section touches on several details—the grease, pivots, and cogs—that run the machinery of individualized instruction.

Room arrangement

If you have your own elementary or secondary classroom, you can facilitate individual work with special attention to:

Location of work areas. You need to arrange a quiet area (for study, reading, writing, and similar activities), an audiovisual area, a drama and discussion area, a production center, and a game area. Noisy areas should be placed near each other and away from quiet areas.

Placement of low-level room dividers between noisy and quiet areas. Bookcases, files, and tables serve this purpose well, and they provide additional work and storage space. Mobile easels and bulletin boards serve too, and they give extra display space.

Location of the teacher's station so that all areas of the room are visible from it and so students can move to and away from it without disturbing others.

If you have to change classrooms during the day, incorporate as many of these suggestions as possible.

Materials: collection, storage, and retrieval

Collection. Individualized work requires quantities of materials, and it takes time and effort to collect them. A list of desirable materials would be virtually endless and cannot be included here, but enterprising teachers and students can accumulate an astonishing amount and variety in a short time. Teachers will be responsible for most printed materials such as books, charts, task cards, worksheets, and tests, but students can help greatly with almost everything else.

Storage. Where you find individualized instruction you will find file cabinets, bookcases, tables, shelves, cupboards, cans, carboxes—almost anything that can hold instructional materials. You can make shelves from boards and concrete blocks. Cardboard boxes and wooden crates decorate and stack easily. Cupboard space can be increased by bringing discarded cabinets and chests of drawers into the classroom and having students paint them. Casters can be added to make them mobile.

Retrieval. Essential materials should be labeled or coded so they can be easily secured and accurately returned to storage. Colors, numbers, and graphic symbols can be used for coding. There should be a clearly identified place for everything, and when not in use everything should be in its place. Student cooperation is essential to keep the classroom from becoming an utter mess.

Schedules

Scheduling of student work periods is commonly done in the following ways:

Established time periods. All students work at their individual projects or whatever at a given time. They should know immediately what they are to do. When they are working on individual projects, they seldom need directions from the teacher. When they are working within a given topic, as in DPT in math, very explicit directions are required. Young children can receive directions orally; the children then act out the directions several times to be sure they have them well in mind. Older students can refer to a list of directions posted in the room.

Self scheduling. During a designated period, students select from available options. They may write their names on a master list or place name tags in a pocket chart to show their selections. This provides a record of who is working where, and it shows which activities still have work space available.

Rotation. Students move among established activities, as from one learning center to another, according to a schedule made by the teacher. The rotation often occurs on a day-to-day basis, so that by the end of the week students will have gone through several different activities. Rotation scheduling can be simplified by assigning colors to groups or individuals, then using a tagboard wheel to show which colors go to which activities.

Negotiated schedules. Teacher and student confer together to decide on activities for the week. This allows students greater self direction. It also helps in attending to special needs, such as those associated with emotional or behavioral problems, that require activities other than what are usually allowed.

Placement and directions

In behavior-referenced plans, students are placed in activities according to predetermined need. This need may be identified through diagnostic testing, pretesting, teacher observation, or student identification of own needs. Specific work assignments are also made on the basis of identified need. Assignments can be made in various ways, using such devices as:

Prescriptions, related directly to needs identified in diagnostic testing. Prescriptions are often related to diagnostic test items by code.

Task cards, which give assignments and directions; they are commonly used in learning centers.

Oral directions, given during group or individual conferences

Written directions, given after assessment on a pretest or after analysis of completed work

Progressive steps, as in task sequence in levels of commerical materials like those of SRA

In experience-referenced plans, placement and assignments can be made in four main ways:

Self selection of content and activities by students

Negotiation between student and teacher, resulting in an agreement such as a "contract"

Optional choice by students, from among options available, as might be the case with learning center activities

Direct assignments made by the teacher

Tutoring and instructing

Some individualized programs can be set up so students instruct themselves from materials provided. Most plans, however, require some individual tutoring or group instruction, especially when skill development is involved. Teachers must demonstrate the skill, pinpoint errors, and give remedial instruction as necessary. This function requires a scheduled time and place, when instruction is given to students who need it.

Monitoring

Watching over student work is necessary in all but the most "open" plans, to ensure that:

Students are working purposefully.

Help is given when students encounter difficulties that hinder progress.

Student errors in process or product are noted.

Students requiring special tutoring are identified. Teachers can monitor while moving about the room. Or if they station themselves at a central position, they can monitor while doing other work such as conferencing, checking, recording, and planning.

Assessing performance

Most teachers want to keep close account of the quantity and quality of work students do. They do this through several means, such as:

Observing student behavior during activities.

Observing student work in progress and noting errors or difficulties. Errors can be corrected individually when noted, or students can be called for small group tutoring at a specified time.

Analyzing products of student work, such as completed worksheets, art projects, and others. Errors or difficulties can be noted for later correction.

Testing, both diagnostic and criterion.

Self checking or self appraisal by students.

Conferencing

Teachers must talk with students on a regular basis. Some teachers like to concentrate the conferences into one or two days; others prefer to have a conference time every day.

Conferences can be scheduled during free choice times, free reading, project work, or at any time when individualized work is in progress. A pocket chart with name tags can be used for students to request conferences if needed at unscheduled times. Conferences should be used for discussing successes and pleasures, errors, difficulties, plans for remedial work, plans for further activities, and so forth. Brief records of each conference should be kept.

Record keeping

It's no fun, but record keeping is an essential part of any individualized program. Teachers cannot possibly keep in mind all the accomplishments, strengths, errors, difficulties, and suggestions of every one of the students in the program. Yet such details are necessary for keeping track of student progress, for recommending future work, and for conferencing with parents and other teachers.

Master checksheets are useful for recording activities students have selected, begun, and completed, and for keeping track of behavioral objectives attempted, reached, or not reached. Scores made on diagnostic tests, prescriptions based on them, scores made on criterion tests, and remedial work required should all be recorded, in the briefest form possible. Student performance over a period of time should be charted (students can do this) to show progress. Individual folders containing many samples of finished work should be kept. Records of conferences should also be kept; index cares are useful for this purpose.

How complete should records be? As a rule of thumb, you are keeping adequate records if you can tell from them, within a couple of minutes, what individual students' strengths and weaknesses are, what they have attempted to do, what their successes and failures have been, what they elect during free choice time, and what has been suggested for future work.

•   •   •

At this point we conclude our rapid overview of individualized instruction. You can see that very different types of programs can be established, according to one's philosophy and preferences in working with learners. Yet these different programs have elements in common. By attending to those elements, as outlined in this chapter, you can draw up plans that suit both you and your students. More important, you can manage necessary details, which are the key to any program's success.

Now we will move on to detailed examinations of strategies that have proved themselves workable in individualized instruction.

IV

MODELS FOR INDIVIDUALIZING

in which six models, well established in individualized instruction, are presented, complete with rationales, details, and examples, through

9

Diagnostic-prescriptive teaching

When you complete this chapter, you will be able to prepare, organize, and use diagnostic-prescriptive teaching (DPT). The chapter is set up in diagnostic-prescriptive format, and you can work through it as if you were a student in a DPT program.

Proceed in this way:

1. Take the diagnostic test, which follows.
2. Check your test answers. An answer key is provided on p. 112.
3. Notice that each item on the test is coded. The codes refer to other material you will find in the chapter and elsewhere in this book. For each item you miss, find and read the material coded to it. Those materials are your prescriptions. You may find it helpful to discuss them with other students.
4. When you have completed your prescriptions, retake the diagnostic test. It will now serve as your criterion test. You may set your own passing score, which you will no doubt want to be quite high.
5. Based on the results of the criterion test, give yourself credit or repeat prescriptions as necessary.

Diagnostic test

True or False

_____ A1   1. "Diagnosing" in diagnostic-prescriptive teaching refers to the process of

determining each student's levels of verbal and performance intelligence.

_____ A1   2. "Diagnosing" in DPT refers to the process of identifying specific learning disabilities.

_____ A1   3. "Diagnosing" in DPT refers to the process of deciding which students should receive remedial instruction.

_____ A1   4. "Diagnosing" in DPT refers to the process of deciding which students should go into special education classes for part of each day.

_____ A1   5. "Prescribing" in DPT refers to the process of composing objectives for each student.

_____ A1   6. "Prescribing" in DPT refers to the process of making assignments based on students' needs.

_____ A1   7. "Prescribing" in DPT refers to the process of communicating with students' parents about their instructional needs.

_____ A1   8. "Prescribing" in DPT refers to the process of informing students about what they need to do to come up to grade level.

Multiple choice. Write letter of correct answer in blank at the left.

_____ A2   9. Which of the following is not part of the teacher's basic role in DPT?
   a. Assessing student performance
   b. Conferring with the school psychologist
   c. Suggesting activities and materials

Answer   Code

d. Helping students who have difficulties with assignments

_____ A2   10. Which of the following is not one of of the teacher's main responsibilities in DPT?
a. Grouping students
b. Making assignments
c. Identifying performance levels
d. Giving instruction when indicated

_____ A3   11. Which of the following is part of the student's role in DPT?
a. Tutoring other students
b. Checking other students' work
c. Selecting instructional activities
d. Completing assigned tasks

_____ A3   12. Which of the following is part of the student's role in DPT?
a. Helping compose behavioral objectives
b. Performing pre-assessment activities
c. Bringing materials from home
d. Working in small groups

_____ B,L   13. Which of the following is not a desirable part of a behavioral objective?
a. Action verb
b. "The teacher will . . ."
c. "The student will . . ."
d. Criterion of acceptability

_____ B,L   14. Which of the following is not a desirable part of a behavioral objective?
a. Enjoy
b. Draw
c. Write
d. Kick

_____ B,L   15. Which of the following is not a desirable part of a behavioral objective?
a. Understand
b. Translate
c. Orally report
d. Do forty pushups

_____ B,L   16. The main purpose of behavioral objectives in DPT is
a. Providing instructional materials
b. Grouping students
c. Showing educational intents
d. Orienting parents

The following test items each have one notable error. The error can be:
a. Confusing wording
b. Trivial matter

c. Multiple correct answer
d. Strong hint as to correct answer

Place the letter of the error in the blank to the left of each item.

Answer   Code

_____ C   17. Sabu rode an _____ , a large animal of India.

_____ C   18. Holmes thought it not an unreasonable possibility that Watson would not have deemed the theft an impossibility.

_____ C   19. The President's chief advisor was ___ _____ .

_____ C   20. The name of George Washington's horse was _____ .

_____ C   21. The boy actor who rode elephants in the movies was _____ .

_____ C   22. The insects that pollinate avocado blossoms are
a. Hummingbirds   b. Winds
c. Bees   d. Spiders

Code

Write your answers on a separate sheet of paper.

A1,A2,D,L   23. Describe how you would diagnose students in (you choose the topic). Tell, in order, what you would look for and how you would look for it.

A1,A2,E,L   24. Describe how you would make student prescriptions, based on the diagnosis conducted in item 23.

_____ F   25. Diagram a classroom to show how it should be arranged for a DPT program like you described in items 23 and 24. Show locations of all essential parts.

_____ G   26. Describe *responsibilities* and *procedures* for storing, retrieving, and replacing tests and instructional materials.
Tests: storing, retrieving, replacing
Instructional materials: storing, retrieving, replacing

_____ H   27. Students sometimes require tutoring. Describe how you would provide for tutoring by the teacher, peers, and cross-age tutors.
Teacher:
Peers:
Cross-age tutors:

_____ I   28. Part of the teacher's role in DPT includes observing students, helping

Code

them, and keeping track of what they have done. Describe how you would perform each of these tasks.
Observing:
Helping:
Keeping track:

J 29. You will need to schedule regular conferences with students. Describe how you will take care of:
Scheduling:
Conferencing:

K,L 30. You will need to keep accurate records. Describe how you will record the following:
Work attempted:
Work completed:
Level of performance:
Student attitude:

PRESCRIPTIONS
A1 The nature of diagnostic-prescriptive teaching

All advocates of individualized instruction have the same great goal in mind. That goal is providing instruction that best suits the needs and abilities of each and every student. That much they agree on.

But that's where the agreement stops. Nowhere can you see differing philosophies of teaching more clearly than in the forms individualized instruction takes. Some programs are very open. They allow students great latitude in deciding what they will learn and when, where, and how they will learn it. Other programs are highly structured. They attempt to identify specific needs of students and then provide instruction to meet those needs.

Diagnostic-prescriptive teaching (DPT) exemplifies the second category. In essence, it is an approach to teaching that consists of four parts:

1. *Establishing objectives,* which in DPT are extensive groups of behavioral statements describing educational intents. Everything else in DPT relates back to this group of objectives.

2. *Diagnosis,* which is the process of ascertaining which objectives the student has already reached and which he has not.
3. *Prescription,* which is the process of describing activities to be undertaken that will lead to objectives as yet unreached.
4. *Criterion measurement,* which is the process of determining whether the student, after completing prescribed activities, has reached intended objectives.

Of these four parts, the first three—objectives, diagnosis, and prescription—give DPT its unique quality as a method of individualizing instruction.

In truth, the terms used in DPT hint at more than they entail. *Diagnosis,* for example, has a medical connotation that implies the search for a disorder or malfunction of some sort and a probing into the cause of that malfunction. Diagnosis in DPT doesn't do that at all. Instead, it simply identifies areas presumed ripe for instruction. That is, it tells which objectives the student has already reached and which he has not. Occasionally, it reveals consistent error patterns, as in mathematics for example, that cause repeated process mistakes. Usually, though, it merely assesses performance levels, which has caused some people to suggest that DPT should more properly be called "assess-assign teaching."

Diagnostic-prescriptive teaching is concerned with skill development and knowledge acquisition in normal instructional programs. It is not concerned with mental (IQ) measurement. It is not concerned with identification of learning disabilities, which are learning failures attributable to physiological or psychoneurotic causes. (Identifying such causes would fall into the realm of true diagnosis.) Nor is it concerned with deciding who should receive "remedial" instruction, except when error patterns are identified that must then be retaught and relearned correctly. To repeat, diagnosis in DPT is usually nothing more than a procedure of determining what a student can and cannot do in a particular topic or subject area.

Prescription, like diagnosis, has no medical overtones in DPT. Prescription is concerned with informing students about what they need to do to move toward a specified objective. It does not entail the formulation of new objectives, since the objectives have already been established in range and depth. It is not concerned with "grade level" or communicating to parents. It simply informs students about what they need to do next. In a way, prescription is just a fancy name for assignment.

A2 The teacher's role in DPT

The teacher's role in DPT is clear cut. Beginning with the bank of behavioral objectives, the teacher does these things:

1. Explains DPT, gives directions, and establishes rules of conduct
2. Diagnoses, usually through testing
3. Prescribes, based on diagnostic results
4. Monitors and tutors, while students work on prescriptions
5. Tests, to see whether students have reached new objectives as a result of completing their prescriptions
6. Keeps records, usually in the form of objectives reached

Let's look at some of these tasks in a bit more detail.

Determining objectives. DPT is a behavior-referenced type of instruction. That means it is used to help students acquire specific observable behaviors. These behaviors provide evidence that learning has occurred. Attention is focused on what learners become able to *do.* If they are to acquire knowledge, they must become able to perform acts (repeat, write, explain) that show they have acquired the knowledge. If they are to acquire skills, they must become able to perform acts

(draw, alphabetize, throw) that show acquisition of the skills.

If ready-made DPT programs are used, they will contain sets of behavioral objectives. If teachers are preparing their own plans, they must either locate and obtain sets of behavioral objectives or prepare objectives of their own. In another prescription you will see how behavioral objectives are prepared.

These sets of objectives are necessary in DPT because everything else relates to them. Diagnosis determines which of the objectives students can reach without instruction. Prescription is used to enable students to reach objectives not already attained. And criterion measurement, like diagnosis, determines which objectives the students have attained after completing prescribed activities.

Diagnosing. As described, diagnosis is based on behavioral objectives. It tells three things:

1. Which of the behaviors students can already exhibit
2. Which of the behaviors students cannot exhibit
3. What specific misconceptions might be causing students to make errors

Most DPT programs use short answer tests to diagnose deficiencies and difficulties. These tests are quick and easy for teachers to check, and students can easily check them using answer keys.

However, other procedures can also be used in diagnosis. Teachers can ask students to demonstrate skills and observe their successes and failures. They can ask them to do oral or written work, then review the work to determine strength and weaknesses. They can check children individually in conferences. They can give exams using long answers, if they wish, much like the diagnostic test at the beginning of this chapter. All these methods have their advantages, but none is as easy to use as the short answer test.

Prescribing. Usually, DPT programs are preplanned and organized so that activities and materials, related to each behavioral objective, are ready for immediate use. Teachers prescribe the activities indicated by the diagnostic test. They don't ordinarily sit with each student and plan out, starting from scratch, activities thought desirable. They could do so, of course, but that would require large amounts of class time, when the teacher can best be helping students who are at work on prescribed tasks.

Therefore, teachers prepare learning activities in advance, so that when they make a prescription, all they have to do is direct the student to the prepared activity. This activity will include directions that older students can read and follow on their own. Younger children must have directions explained orally.

Tutoring and instructing. Ideally, the materials in diagnostic-prescriptive programs provide basic instruction for students. Things don't always work out as intended, though. You can expect to spend a lot of time working directly with learners. Despite your best intentions, directions, instruction, activities, and materials, students will get confused. They may not understand directions. They may not be able to locate materials on their prescriptions. They may keep repeating errors. You have to watch for these difficulties and you have to correct them.

Criterion testing. Once students have completed their prescriptions, we check to see whether they have reached the objectives we have set. This step is often called criterion testing, but it should be called criterion "measurement" instead. There are many ways of measuring student performance. Testing is only one; sometimes it is a good way, but often other ways are better.

Rather than testing, for example, we might want to analyze work that students have completed. We might want to observe students at work, to note their progress, their attitudes, and their problems. We might want to

conference with them individually. Sometimes we might want to have group evaluations.

When we do use tests, though, the items should be very similar to those on the diagnostic test. We want the criterion test to measure the same things the diagnostic test measured—namely, whether students can perform acts specified in the objectives. Often, the criterion test can be exactly the same as the diagnostic test.

Recording. Diagnostic-prescriptive teaching requires that we keep very accurate records of diagnoses, prescriptions, and especially of criterion measures. These records can be kept in simplified form, and they do not require much time if done properly. What is needed is a folder for each student and a master checksheet such as the sample shown below. We want to record the following information for each student:

What	How
1. Diagnostic test results	Place tests in student folders.
2. Prescriptions assigned	Circle code on diagnostic tests.
3. Prescriptions completed	Cross out circled code numbers.
4. Criterion measures	Note on master Checksheet.
5. Problems and difficulties	"Problem" section in folder.
6. Suggestions for future	"Suggestions" section in folder.

The folder needed for each student is self-explanatory. The master checksheet can be prepared by writing students' names down the side and the code number for each objective across the top. The chart is then marked off into grids. Inside each appropriate square of the grid, you can mark the date that shows when the student achieved the objective. A sample checksheet is shown on pg. 98.

Some teachers prefer keeping a separate profile card for each student. This card can contain the same information as the master

MASTER CHECKSHEET SAMPLE

Students	Objectives												
	21	22	23	24	25	26	27	28	29	30	31	32	33
Amy													
Bill													
Carl													
Dotty													
Elton													
Frank													
Gisele													

checksheet, and it can be kept in the student's folder.

Looking at the folder, then, you can tell quickly what a student has been working on, what he has achieved, and what specific difficulties he has encountered. Samples of completed prescriptions can also be kept in the folder.

Redirecting. Once a student's performance has been measured and recorded, we must decide what to have him do next. In DPT, the student does one of two things. If criterion measurement reveals satisfactory performance, the student gets credit for objective attainment and moves on to further work. If criterion measurement shows that objectives have not been reached, the teacher makes new prescriptions. Prescriptions made previously may be repeated. It is better if an alternate set of prescriptions is available, so the student can do new activities with new materials related to the same objective. After completing these remedial activities, the student again asks for criterion measurement.

A3 The student's role in DPT

Students in DPT exercise little choice or self direction. They know they are to take diagnostic tests, that they must complete pre-

scriptions based on those tests, and that after completing the prescriptions they must demonstrate competency in one way or another.

Sometimes students forget the procedure, especially if it includes coded materials. To avoid this, you can post directions in a conspicuous place, and students can refer to them if necessary. The directions might look something like this:

1. Take diagnostic test.
2. Check test.
3. Get prescription.
4. Find material in file cabinet. Make sure the number and color of materials match those shown on your prescription.
5. Complete prescription.
6. Show completed work to teacher.
7. Take criterion test, if necessary.

B Behavioral objectives

Behavioral objectives—oh, those demonic devices. How many teachers have blasphemed at their name, overwhelmed and frustrated by them. For ten years after the appearance of Robert Mager's book *Preparing Instructional Objectives*, teachers fussed and fumed over the insistence that they write all objectives to show outcomes of instruction, stated in terms of observable student acts. Suddenly, they could no longer write:

"Do pp. 10 and 11" because that didn't name an outcome of instruction, nor
"Cover the concept of sound" because that named a teacher act instead of a student act, nor
"Fully understand multiplication by fractions" because 'fully understand' was not an observable act.

What, then, could they write (or say or think) when preparing objectives? When you get right down to it, it's quite simple; it just took a little getting used to—about ten years' worth, in fact. Here's what you do:

FIRST: you have to decide what you want students to *be able to do* **after** instruction is completed. Thus, you don't think of learning activities, materials, or lectures; you think first and foremost about what students are to become able to do. This means you have to think of verbs that describe observable student acts—action verbs such as tell, write, throw, name, list. You can't use verbs that don't describe observable student acts—verbs like know, understand, enjoy, or appreciate.

SECOND: you must have evidence—as objective and impartial as possible—as to whether students have, after instruction, become able to do what you decided they should. That means you have to see or hear them do the specified act, or you have to observe a product they have produced. To do that you usually need a direct object for your action verbs. For example:

Write	poem
(verb)	(object)
Name	states in the union
List	causes and effects

THIRD: as you become more sophisticated, you name conditions you consider necessary in students' performance. For example, you name

Givens: "Given pencil, paper, and crayons, the student . . ."
Limitations: "Without the use of books," "Within 15 minutes . . ."
Criteria: "80% correct," "accurate in the judgment of the instructor"

Thus, when you get the idea all put together in your head, you can write objectives that look like this:

"Given paper, compass, straightedge, and pencil, the student will be able to construct a square, within five minutes, with 100% accuracy."

Still, teachers balked at the idea of writing up lists of such objectives for all their instruction. Why? Time. It takes many and many an hour to make up lists of objectives, like the sample above, that adequately covers all your instructional intents.

You can beat the time problem, though, in two ways. One way is to locate ready-made objectives. You can find very complete lists of behavioral objectives, made by good objective writers, in school districts, curriculum libraries, and in books such as those from the Instructional Objective Exchange (IOX) at the University of California at Los Angeles. Using such lists, you simply select objectives suitable for your students, making small changes here and there as necessary.

Another way is to write your own objectives, but in the briefest form possible. You do well enough if you write only an action verb and its object, leaving out the givens, conditions, and so forth. Such verb-object objectives look like this:

Sing	Row, Row, Row Your Boat
Add	decimal fractions
Jump	rope
Write	cinquains
Associate	words with pictures

You can see objectives written this way in the materials contained in prescriptions *K* and *L*.

A final comment about behavioral objectives. They do make teaching and learning more precise and efficient. They are necessary in diagnostic-prescriptive teaching because they specify the behaviors you are trying to diagnose and develop. They needn't worry you, like they have so many teachers in the past, because you can either find ready-made objectives or you can quickly prepare your own, using the verb-object format.

To prove it, try your hand at writing five verb-object behavioral objectives. You choose the topic. Talk your efforts over with another student and ask your instructor if you are on the right track.

C   Test item construction

Test writing can be very complicated business, especially when it comes to writing items for standardized tests. There, everything is supposed to be valid, reliable, and discriminating.

When you make items for your own diagnostic and criterion tests in DPT, you need reliability and validity, too. An item is "reliable" if a student answers it the same way (correct or not) time after time. An item is "valid" if it measures what it is supposed to measure. For example, a mathematics item written in obscure language, might not be valid. It might be testing reading ability instead of mathematics ability.

To help make your test items more valid and reliable, you need to pay close attention to a few reminders such as the following:[1]

1. Be sure the test directions are very clear.
2. Do not include questions on trivial matters.
3. Use simple wording, language, and sentence structure.
4. Don't include more than one problem in one item.
5. Try to include items that have only one correct answer.

---

[1]Charles, C.: Educational psychology: The instructional endeavor, St. Louis, 1972, The C. V. Mosby Co., pp. 333-334.

6. Don't use trick statements or double negatives.
7. True-false items should be clearly either true or false, not yes and no, maybe, or sometimes.
8. Do not use words that give hints about correct answers, such as all, always, none, never, totally, exactly, completely, and so on: avoid a, an, singulars, and plurals before blanks, such as "Toby rode an ——————————, a large animal of India."
9. Be sure that one item doesn't give the answer for another item.

With these suggestions in mind, see if you can identify the error in each of the following items:

1. *(Fill in the blank).* The Wright brothers discovered many principles that are still used in the construction of an ——————— .
2. *(Fill in the blank).* The Wright brothers did their work in ——————— .
3. *(Write the answer in the space provided.)* What was the name of the Coast Guardsman who befriended the Wright brothers when they were conducting their important tests at Kittyhawk?

——————————————————————

4. *(Write your answer on the back of the page.)* Describe how the Wright brothers made and used their wind tunnel and what the most important things were that they found out from using it.
5. *(Circle the correct answer.)* What was the name of the place in North Carolina where the Wright brothers conducted their important tests?
   Raleigh
   Kittyhawk
   Big Moon
   Seabreeze
6. *(Circle one: true or false.)* The Wright brothers worked very well as a team, and they made millions of dollars from their discoveries.
7. *(Circle one: true or false.)* The Wright brothers, while neither was known as a mathematical expert, nonetheless were not unsuccessful in disproving existing tables of air lift over curved surfaces.

Answers:

1. Word "an" gives hint to answer.
2. Many correct answers possible, should have only one.
3. Trivial information.
4. Two problems in single item; should be only one.
5. Correct answer provided by item 3.
6. Partly true; partly false.
7. Wording too involved, not clear.

D Diagnostic tests

You can find commercial diagnostic tests of all sorts, for language, reading, mathematics, and what have you. Those kinds of tests can be incorporated into diagnostic-prescriptive programs; however, most teachers prefer making their own diagnostic tests. That way each test item can tie directly to one of the behavioral objectives.

In this section we will examine a few teacher-made materials developed for use in diagnostic-prescriptive teaching.

The first sample comes from a comprehensive mathematics program developed and used by the San Diego, California City Schools.[2] It shows both the diagnostic and the criterion test for one subtraction skill/concept. The behavioral objective to which it relates is

"The student will be able to solve subtraction examples using two 2-digit numerals, with renaming."

The code (3N3-01) refers to level (3), strand (N = number operations), topic (3 = subtraction), and subobjective (01 = "demonstrates basic subtraction facts, sums to 18"). Notice that the diagnostic and criterion tests are not identical. They do, however, involve the same concepts and processes.

The answer keys for the diagnostic and criterion tests are shown on pp. 102 and 103. Notice the middle column entitled "description of detractor." It shows common types of errors children make in subtraction, and it helps point out error pat-

---

[2] Correlated instructional guide for diagnostic prescriptive teaching. DPT—Elementary mathematics level 3, 1973, San Diego City Schools.

Diagnostic			Criterion		
1. 18 −13	A. B. C. D.	15 5 25 31	A. 27 −14		Answer _____
2. 35 −13	A. B. C. D.	22 12 48 28	B. 43 −22		Answer _____
3. 52 −37	A. B. C. D.	15 89 25 29	C. 62 −35		Answer _____
4. 76 −39	A. B. C. D.	115 47 37 43	D. 75 −49		Answer _____
Code no. 3N3-01			Code no. 3N3-01		

Diagnostic test			Description of detractor	Criterion test	
1. $\begin{array}{r} 18 \\ -13 \\ \hline \end{array}$	A ☐ 15 B ☒ 5 C ☐ 25 D ☐ 31		Subtracted ones and wrote down a ten Summed the tens subtracted the ones Summation	A. $\begin{array}{r} 27 \\ -14 \\ \hline \end{array}$	Answer: 13
2. $\begin{array}{r} 35 \\ -13 \\ \hline \end{array}$	A ☒ 22 B ☐ 12 C ☐ 48 D ☐ 28		 Error in tens subtraction See 1-D Sum of ones subtraction of tens	B. $\begin{array}{r} 43 \\ -22 \\ \hline \end{array}$	Answer: 21
3. $\begin{array}{r} 52 \\ -37 \\ \hline \end{array}$	A ☒ 15 B ☐ 89 C ☐ 25 D ☐ 25		 See 1-D Reversal of digits Lost track of regrouping did not charge tens digit	C. $\begin{array}{r} 62 \\ -35 \\ \hline \end{array}$	Answer: 27
4. $\begin{array}{r} 76 \\ -39 \\ \hline \end{array}$	A ☐ 115 B ☐ 47 C ☒ 37 D ☐ 43		See 1-D Lost track of regrouping did not charge tens digit See 3-C	D. $\begin{array}{r} 75 \\ -49 \\ \hline \end{array}$	Answer: 26
Code no. 3N3-01			The student will be able to solve examples using two 2-digit numerals, with renaming	Code no. 3N3-01	

Subobjectives (basic text references)				Manipulative materials/activities	Pupil supplementary texts	Teacher reference	Audiovisual
a. Basic subtraction facts sums to 18				Bean war (III M)	See basic reference sheet	Fun and Games with Mathematics, p. 79	FS Box "Arithmetic Practice Set 1" (addition and subtraction combination)
	2	3	4	Cars in garages (III M)		Developing Insights into Mathematics, Wirtz, Workjobs, pp. 151, 169, 210, 211	FS 511.2 "Subtraction Through 9"
				Tor This (Fun and Games With Mathematics)			
				Colorfax 6, 13, 17, 20, 23, 26, 52, 55, 58, 61, 64, 65, 67, 69, 72			FS Adding and subtraction (Part I numbers 1-10) (Part II 10 and more)
				Beans, Wirtz worksheets pp. 14, 15, 16, 17		Sourcebook in Mathematics, pp. Tc 47-64	
T. E.	40-53, 75 85, 80-87 147-148 161-165 170-173	56-58 63-65 76-79		Walk on number line		Games and Aids for Teaching Math, pp. 71-73	MPF 511.2 "Inverse operations"
				Number combination board—Workjobs			
				The number cans—Workjobs			
				The beans—Workjobs			
				Dice, beans, Lola May's worksheet IN3-01			
P. E.	19-32, 40 50, 55-62 116-117, 128-132, 137-140	36-38 43-45 56-59		Sum fun			
				Numo			
				Project Mathematics Activity Kit K-3, Cards N12, N15, N25, N26			
				Bead task cards, Level II, III, IV			
				I Win, Set 1, Deck 2 Set 1, Deck 4 Set 2, Deck 6			
				See Calculator			
				Beanstick War III M			
				Numberline Fun—Games and Aids for Teaching Math			
b. 2-digit minus 2-digit numerals, no renaming Example: 76 −33				Dienes blocks, Wirtz worksheets 95, 99, 100 (Teacher selects appropriate number to be subtracted) Beans, beansticks	MIP: Chap. 5, 17, 19, 22, 23 EPC: 306 Add. Wes. 59, 61 Elem. Math. Enrich. 49	Developing Insights into Mathematics, pp. 95, 99, 100 Operations with Whole No. 40-43	FS: "Subtraction" 511.2 "Subtract to Find"
	2	3	4				
T. E.		129-132-135	70				
P. E.		103 106-109	46				

Code No. 3N3-01

Key objective: The student will be able to solve subtraction examples using two 2-digit numerals, with renaming.

Code No. 3N3-01

terns that might require special attention.

For other samples of diagnostic test material, see p. 111 on prescription L in this chapter, and pp. 150-153 in Chapter 11.

E Prescriptions

Once you have completed diagnosis, through which you discovered what students could and could not do, you are ready to make instructional prescriptions. The beauty of DPT is that since all prescriptions relate to pre-established behavioral objectives, prescriptions can be made up in advance. You have them ready, and all you do is supply whichever ones a given student needs. This procedure can be carried out entirely by the students, past the primary grades, if you have the prescriptions coded so they can be located easily.

The sample prescription shown on p. 108 comes from the San Diego DPT Mathematics Program, and it relates directly to the diagnostic test from the same materials, previously shown.

For an example of prescriptions in a DPT reading phonics program, see p. 112 in this chapter.

F Classroom arrangement

The classroom does not require extensive preparation for diagnostic-prescriptive teaching. There are certain provisions you must make, but beyond those you can arrange things in ways as orthodox or avant garde as suits your fancy.

Basic classroom provisions you must make for DPT include:

1. *Accessible storage for diagnostic tests, prescriptions, and criterion tests.* You may want to include answer keys so students can check their own tests, or you may prefer to do that yourself. Metal file cabinets and cubby hole shelves serve well. The file cabinet can be locked, but only one student at a time can use it conveniently. Shelves allow several students at a time to obtain or return materials, but it is difficult to keep tests secure there, if that is a problem. You may want to keep diagnostic and criterion tests in

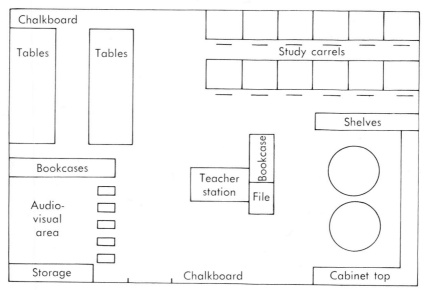

FIG. 4. Classroom arrangement.

a file that can be locked, but shelve the prescriptions along with instructional materials.

2. *Quiet work-study area.* One end of the classroom should be reserved for reading, study, and quiet work. Student tables, chair-desks, or individual study carrels can be kept in that part of the room.

3. *Activity centers.* The classroom should provide a few areas, away from the quiet study area, where activities can be done that require movement and moderate noise. Necessary instructional materials should be kept in the centers, so students in the quiet areas will not be disturbed or distracted.

4. *Accessible storage for instructional materials.* After receiving prescriptions, students should be able to get instructional materials easily and quickly. You don't want to get yourself tied up as materials dispenser. You need to code or label materials so students can recognize them, and you need to place them in locations where students can obtain and return them without your help.

One way of arranging a classroom to meet these four requirements is shown in Fig. 4.

If you are a teacher, try diagramming your classroom to show how you would arrange it for DPT. If you are not, sketch a hypothetical classroom the way you would want to arrange it.

G Materials: responsibilities and procedures

This prescription calls on you to get together with another student and talk over ideas for storing, retrieving, and replacing instructional materials. You can make any number of arrangements. Just decide who is responsible for each and what the working procedures should be. Try your best to think matters through and come up with a workable scheme. Use the plan you compose as the answer for item 26 on the diagnostic/criterion test.

Perhaps the outline shown below will help you.

H Tutoring

Suppose you have prepared your DPT program. You have designed it so the prescriptions will do the teaching—or rather, so students can teach themselves through the ac-

Task	Who is responsible	Procedures: 1, 2, 3
Test storage		
Test retrieval		
Test replacement		
Instructional material storage		
Instructional material retrieval		
Instructional material replacement		

tivities and materials described in the prescriptions. Everything looks as though it will work perfectly.

But it doesn't. A couple of students forget the procedures and get mixed up on what to do. One can't read a prescription. Another can't find needed materials. All these are minor problems that you correct quickly.

Then you notice three students having trouble with their prescribed activities. You notice they are hesitant or they are making errors as they work. They may have raised their hands or put out the red marker that means "help needed." You see them doing things wrong, learning wrong concepts. That's where you step in to tutor. Or that's where you have another student help those with difficulties.

Peer tutoring has been used since the beginning of education. More able students help less able. Those who can help those who can't. As it turns out, the tutoring is good for both students, which seems to bear out the observation that the best way to learn something is to teach it to someone else.

Cross-age tutoring, where older students help younger ones, has been around a long time, too. It played a big part in the one-room school house. It has been rediscovered recently, with high school students helping junior high students, junior high students helping fifth and sixth graders, fifth and sixth graders helping primary students. Research into the effects of cross-age tutoring has shown above average academic gains for both "olders" and "youngers."

And of course there's you, the trained professional. Peer and cross-age tutors teach by showing, demonstrating, and explaining. You teach that way when you tutor, too. But you can use an additional technique. You can question and use other strategies that help students clarify their own thinking, or that lead them into inquiry procedures.

Still, when you tutor, it's often to help students clarify one point so they can get on with their individual work. For that, you most often use expository teaching, a process in which you provide information to the student in the clearest manner possible. If you will turn to p. 159, you will find a brief description of expository teaching.

I Observing, helping, keeping track

Your teacher role in DPT doesn't allow you to test, prescribe, and then go have coffee the rest of the day. While you don't stay in a control position, directing all activities of all students all the time, you do have other duties—duties we might think of as higher level, more important. Those duties include observing, helping, and keeping track of what individual students are doing.

The *observing* duty is very important in DPT. For this, you behave much as Montessori urged teachers to behave many years ago. You step back and watch the students work, ever attentive and ever ready to render assistance, but never forcing it on the students. When still, you station yourself in a place where you can see the entire class. When moving, which is most of the time, you keep a sharp eye out for students who are struggling, making errors, or requesting help.

Occasionally, you may work alongside students, quietly and unpretentiously, either doing work similar to theirs or working at tasks of your own. You show that you are a working member of the class, but at the same time always ready to step in and help when needed.

The *helping* role cannot be stressed too strongly. Remember, though, that help must be rendered discreetly. You don't force it on students. You give it when they ask for it or when you see them making serious errors. In the previous section we examined the tutoring function in DPT. That's one way to give help. But there are other important ways, too.

For instance, you help when you encourage. Encouragement comes in many forms— mere physical presence, smiles, kind words, suggestions that show you care about students' work, pep talks. You help, too, when you support students, when you let them know they can make errors without fear of being put down and when you abide by their carefully considered decisions. You help when you redirect students who have taken a wrong direction, and of course you help when you suggest materials, show how, and explain.

Keeping track of what students are doing, where they have been, and where they are headed is as important in DPT as in any other individualized approach. It happens to be easier in DPT because everything revolves around behavioral objectives and related instructional activities. You always have an easy way to keep tabs on which objectives students have attained and which prescriptions they are working on at a particular time. In the section on record keeping we will examine a few forms that facilitate keeping track of students' progress.

J   Conferencing

One of the most important things you will do in your DPT program is conference with individual students. Set up a regular schedule, so you can talk privately with each student for at least a few minutes each week. During the conference you will want to give specific attention to several things, including:

1. *Reviewing* work the student has completed. Try to draw the student out freely, to talk of such things as progress, difficulties, and enjoyments encountered in the prescribed work.

2. *Appraising* knowledge and retention. As the student talks, see what he remembers from activities completed and see if he can express the personal meaning and significance the learnings have for him.

3. *Evaluating* progress, effort, and enjoyment. Find out what the student thinks about his own progress. See if he is satisfied with the effort he is making and with work procedures. See if he thinks he is getting anything worthwhile from the program.

4. *Talking* on an informal, friendly basis. Here is one of the bonuses you enjoy in DPT. You have time to talk with students, person to person. The talk needn't be about school matters. It can naturally turn to pleasures, problems, and what have you. This sort of conversation helps students see you as a real person. And it helps you see the students as real persons, too.

K   Record keeping

Keeping good records is quite a chore in most individualized programs. They aren't like regular teacher-directed classes, where students are all on the same page, doing the same worksheets, taking the same test. Instead, your students are doing different things, at different levels, and perhaps working toward different goals. Keeping records turns out to be just about the most time consuming part of individualized instruction.

But unlike other programs, DPT doesn't stagger you with record keeping chores. Actually, the whole matter is fairly easy. That's because you have to keep track, basically, of only one thing: which objectives each student has reached. You can do that by keeping individual folders that contain record forms. The forms show the behavioral objectives, which are the same for everyone in DPT. When a student reaches an objective, all you do is check it on the list, putting a date beside it to show when it was reached.

Many teachers also like to keep a master chart with objectives across the top and student names down the side. That technique shows at a glance which students are near the same level, and it helps in grouping them for short instructional sessions when necessary.

Let's look at some of the different kinds of record forms typically used in DPT. The following pages show three such forms:

1. An individual student profile card
2. A group/individual objective list, which can be stapled inside each student's record folder
3. A group master chart

For yet another form, see the phonics DPT samples presented on p. 110.

Text continued on p. 112.

STUDENT PROFILE CARD[3]

Name_____ INDIVIDUAL STUDENT PROFILE CARD MATH

Age _____ Grade_____ School _____ Date _____

Strand title	Numbers and operations					Geometry		Measurement								Graphing, statistics, and probability		Functions, coordinate graphing	
Strand code	N					G		M								P		F	
Topics	Sets and numeration	Addition	Subtraction	Multiplication	Division	Shapes and lines	Relationships	Money	Time	Linear measurement	Weight	Area	Volume and capacity	Angle measurement	Temperature	Collecting, organizing, and interpreting data	Probability	Patterns and ordered pairs	Plotting points
Topic number	1	2	3	4	5	1	2	1	2	3	4	5	6	7	8	1	2	1	2
Level 2	01 02 03 04	01 02	01 02	—	—	01	01	01 02 03	01 02	01	01 02	01	01 02	—	01	01 02	—	01 02	01
Level 3	01 02 03 04 05 06	01 02	(01)	01 02	01	01 02	01 02	01 02 03	01 02	01 02 03	01 02	01 02	01 02 03	—	01	01 02	—	01 02 03	01
Level 4	01 02 03 04 05	01 02 03 04	01 02 03	01 02 03	01 02 03	01 02 03	01 02 03	01 02 03 04 05 06	01	01 02	01 02 03	01	01 02	—	01	01	01	01	01

[3]From Correlated instructional guide for diagnostic prescriptive teaching. DPT—Elementary mathematics level 3. San Diego City Schools. This Profile Card has been modified from the original to include levels 2, 3, and 4. The tests and prescriptions previously shown were coded for level 3. The objective referred to by code 3N3-01 is circled on the card.

GROUP/INDIVIDUAL OBJECTIVE LIST

Directions: Circle and date code number to show attainment of objective.

Code	Objective
17-6-01	Identifies cause-effect relationships
02	Recognizes three kinds of logical fallacies
03	Locates logical fallacies in letters to editor
04	Correctly interprets information on graphs
05	Locates geographical boundaries on map
17-7-01	Defines propaganda
02	Names and describes three propaganda techniques
03	Locates three different propaganda techniques in magazine advertisements
04	Writes advertisement for imaginary product, using propaganda devices
05	Identifies and notes propaganda techniques in television commercials
17-8-01	Given premises, can draw logical conclusions
02	Defines and explains deduction and induction
03	Explains difference between fact and inference
04	Explains difference between denotation and connotation
05	Selects words having emotional impact

GROUP MASTER CHART

Students	Concepts/skills objectives												
	001	002	003	004	005	006	007	008	009	010	011	012	013

READING PROGRESS SHEET
(for letterbook 7-L1)

Skills and concepts   Student _____

	Objectives	Date reached	Comments
078	Identify sound /ℓ/, shape, and name of Lℓ		
079	Identify /ℓ/, initial position		
080	Write capital L		
081	Write lower case ℓ		
082.1	Identify /ℓ/, /d/, /s/, initial		
082.2	Write Lℓ, Dd, Ss correctly		
082.3	Associate /ℓ/, /d/, /s/, with corresponding letter		
083	Blend letters s,a,d; g,ℓ,a,d; to form words		
084	Add gl or s to ad to make word		
085.1	Discriminate between /ℓ/, /d/, /s/, /g/, in initial position		
085.2	Associate L, D, C, S, G with /ℓ/, /d/, /c/, /s/, /g/		
085.3	Write ℓ, d, c, s, g		
086.1	Identify /ℓ/ in initial and final positions		
086.2	Visually identify A, L, G		
086.3	Identify colors brown, yellow, green		
087.1	Identify /d/, /o/, /g/; write their corresponding letters; and blend them to make word dog		
087.2	Identify /ℓ/, /o/, /g/; write their corresponding letters; blend them to make word log		
088.1	Blend and read s,a,d; d,a,d; ℓ,o,g; d,o,g; d,o,ℓ,ℓ; g,a,s		
088.2	Associate words sad, log, doll, gas, dad, dog with corresponding pictures		
089	Discriminate between singular and plural		
090.1	Follow story with illustrations		
090.2	Explain meaning of a fable		
091.1	Read and write word "dolls"		
091.2	Read and write word "logs"		

DIAGNOSTIC/CRITERION TEST

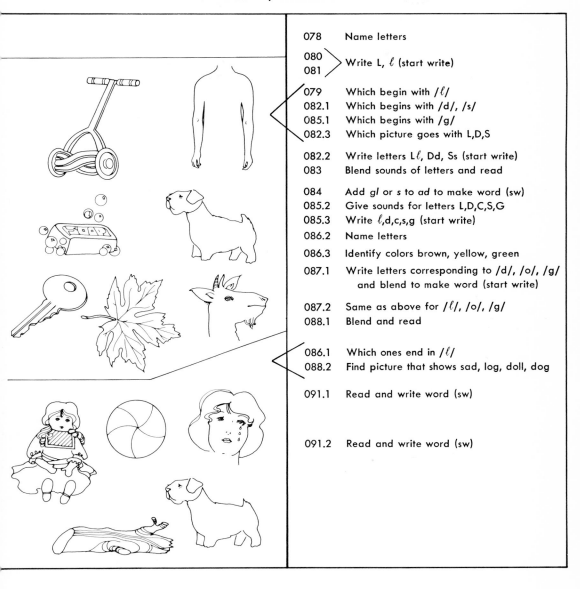

078	Name letters
080 081	Write L, ℓ (start write)
079	Which begin with /ℓ/
082.1	Which begins with /d/, /s/
085.1	Which begins with /g/
082.3	Which picture goes with L,D,S
082.2	Write letters Lℓ, Dd, Ss (start write)
083	Blend sounds of letters and read
084	Add *gl* or *s* to *ad* to make word (sw)
085.2	Give sounds for letters L,D,C,S,G
085.3	Write ℓ,d,c,s,g (start write)
086.2	Name letters
086.3	Identify colors brown, yellow, green
087.1	Write letters corresponding to /d/, /o/, /g/ and blend to make word (start write)
087.2	Same as above for /ℓ/, /o/, /g/
088.1	Blend and read
086.1	Which ones end in /ℓ/
088.2	Find picture that shows sad, log, doll, dog
091.1	Read and write word (sw)
091.2	Read and write word (sw)

PRESCRIPTIONS

Objectives		Prescriptions
078	Identify sound, shape, name of Lℓ	Cover, p. 1, pop-out, Test
079	Identify /ℓ/, initial position	p. 2, wsL-2a, wsL-2b, p. 8, Test
080	Write capital L	p. 3, cover, slate, Test
081	Write lower case ℓ	p. 4, cover, slate, Test
082.1	Identify /ℓ/, /d/, /s/ initial position	p. 5, wsL-5a, Test
082.2	Write Lℓ, Dd, Ss, correctly	p. 5, wsL-5a, Test
082.3	Associate /ℓ/, /d/, /s/ with corresponding letters	p. 5, wsL-5a, Test
083	Blend letters s,a,d; g,ℓ,a,d to make words	p. 6, 7 Test
084	Add gl or s to ad to make words	p. 7, wsL-7a, Test
085.1	Discriminate between /ℓ/, /d/, /k/, /s/, /g/ in initial position	p. 8, Tape 7 pt. I, Test
085.2	Associate L,D,C,S,G with /ℓ/, /d/, /c/, /s/, /g/	p. 8, Tape 7 pt. I, Test
085.3	Write ℓ, d, c, s, g	p. 8, Tape 7 pt. I, Test
086.1	Identify /ℓ/, initial, final position	p. 9, wsL-9a, Test
086.2	Visually identify A,L,G	p. 9, Test
086.3	Identify colors brown, yellow, green	p. 9, Test
087.1	Identify /d/, /o/, /g/, write their corresponding letters, and blend to make word:	p. 10, Tape 7 pt. II, Test
087.2	Same as above for /ℓ/, /o/, /g/	p. 10, Tape 7 pt. II, Test
088.1	Blend and read s,a,d; d,a,d; ℓ,o,g; d,o,g; d,o,ℓ,ℓ; g,a,s	p. 11, wsL-11a, Test
088.2	Associate words sad, log, doll, gas, dad, dog with corresponding pictures	p. 11, wsL-11a, Test
089	Discriminate between singular and plural	p. 12, Test
090.1	Follow story with illustrations	p. 13, 14, Tape 7 pt. III, comprehension questions, Test
090.2	Explain meaning of a fable	p. 13, 14, Tape 7 pt. III, Test
091.1	Read and write word "dolls"	p. 15, 16, Test
091.2	Read and write word "logs"	p. 15, 16, Test

L   Teacher-made DPT, kindergarten[4]

These materials are a small portion of a DPT program in kindergarten phonics. The program was built around the *Lippincott Kit 1: Beginning to Read, Write, and Listen.* These materials have to do with the letter L. They include objectives, diagnostic/criterion test, prescriptions, and a recording system.

Diagnostic test answer key

1. F		12. b	
2. F		13. b	
3. F		14. a	
4. F		15. a	
5. F		16. c	
6. T		17. d	
7. F		18. a	
8. F		19. c	
9. b		20. b	
10. a		21. d	
11. d		22. d	

[4] Based on materials prepared by Jan Seeley, Cajon Valley (Calif.) Schools.

23. Answer should contain mention of checking for attainment of objectives and perhaps notation of error patterns through testing, observing, analyzing products.

24. Check description against prescriptions A1, A2, E, L.

25. Diagram should show adequate location of and containers for tests, prescriptions, instructional materials, student work areas, teacher station.

26. Name storage containers and locations, who will retrieve and replace, how directions will be given.

27. *Teacher:* group, individually, questioning, expository teaching
Peer: specify who, buddy system, teaching style
Cross-age: source of tutors, routine

28. Answer should indicate style and purpose of observation, kind of help given and when, routines and reasons in keeping track of students' work.

29. Mention ways and times for scheduling; kinds of matters discussed in conferences, for example, problems, difficulties, progress, pleasures, comprehension, chit-chat.

30. Mention at least one way to keep track of specific objectives reached and when.

10

Modularized instruction

You probably know something about "unit teaching." That way of organizing instruction has been with us for a good many years. It came, at least in part, from John Dewey's insistence on activity curricula that would bring different disciplines together, in organized ways, for more lifelike learning.

Now launched into the space age, our terminology has been updating itself. Perhaps that's why we now have something called "modularized instruction," employing mysterious "modules" that one imagines flashing with red and green lights, computers humming, following the dictates of ground control.

You will be disappointed, or maybe relieved, to find that instructional modules are not marvels of auditory and optical wizardry. In fact, they bear a striking resemblance to their progenitor, unit teaching. They do, though, show advances in teaching precision and in providing more individual options for learners, especially in pacing and optional activities.

To take the mystery out of modularized instruction and to show the advantages it affords, this chapter is set up in module form. It will teach you how to prepare instructional modules of your own and how to use them in teaching.

DIRECTIONS

Although this module was prepared for individual learning, you don't have to work through it alone. If you prefer, as many students do, you can complete it in pairs or groups of three or four. In any case your instructor will be available to help as necessary—to suggest materials, to clarify procedures, to discuss progress, to help determine whether you have met objectives, and to suggest remedial work, if that should be necessary.

When you have finished this module, you will have familiarized yourself with the why's and how's of modularized instruction, and you will be able to make and use modules for teaching your own students.

MODULE ON MODULARIZED INSTRUCTION

I. *Prerequisites:* Read Chapter 8 on behavior-referenced instruction.
II. *Estimated time for completion:* 5 hours.
III. *Goal:* To provide information necessary for enabling teachers to plan and use modularized instruction in their teaching.
IV. *Preassessment:* Take the pretest. You must take this test individually. When you finish, get an answer key and check your work. If you think you have passed the test (about 80% or better), give the scored test to your instructor.

PRETEST: MODULARIZED INSTRUCTION

Name _____

Date _____

1. Briefly describe Modularized Instruction, explaining its process and rationale.

2. List from memory five management aspects of Modularized Instruction. Describe how one should handle each of them.

    Aspects   *How to handle*

3. List and describe from memory six essential steps/components in preparing an instructional module.

    Steps/components   *Description*

4. Select a topic you think suitable for modularized instruction. Think through an instructional module that could be used with school students. Outline the module here. If your students cannot read, consider putting directions on tape.

You *may* be given credit for the module. If you do not pass the pretest, proceed with the remaining parts of the module.

At this point take the pretest on p. 114, unless you feel sure you can't pass it, in which case you may move directly into the module activities.

V. *Instructional objectives:* Upon completion of the learning alternatives suggested in this module, you will be able to:

A. Describe the process and rationale of modularized instruction.

B. List and describe six necessary steps/components in preparing an instructional module.

C. Describe how one attends to the following management details when using modularized instruction:
   1. Room arrangement
   2. Instructional materials
   3. Scheduling
   4. Tutoring
   5. Monitoring
   6. Conferencing
   7. Record keeping

D. Outline, in module form, a unit of instruction. Topic and age level will be selected by the student.

VI. *Enabling activities:*

A. The following activities support objective *A.* Select and complete any of them until you are sure you have reached the first objective.
   1. Read *Overview* paper on p. 116, which summarizes modularized instruction.
   2. Read the following pages in Block, *Mastery Learning,*[1] which explain much of the rationale upon which modularized instruction is based: pp. 2-3, 16-26, 95-97, 144-145.
   3. Examine a copy of a Florida B2 Teacher Education Module.[2] The introductory pages reveal process and rationale for modularized instruction.

4. Read p. 61 in the book by Nagel and Richman, *Competency Based Instruction.*[3] This page shows a good, concise example of a module.

5. Discuss modularized instruction with the instructor or with others who have had experience with it.

B. The following activities support objective *B.* Select and complete any of them until you are sure you have reached the second objective.
   1. Obtain a copy of one of the Florida B2 Teacher Education Modules. Read the introductory pages and any others you find worthwhile.
   2. Examine the sample San Diego State University Teacher Corps Module presented on pp. 117-118.
   3. Examine the module by Charles, "Crucial Ideas of Jean Piaget," presented on pp. 118-119.
   4. Examine the module on "Metric Linear Measurement," presented on pp. 120-146.

C. The following activities support objective *C.* Select and complete any of them until you are sure you have reached the third objective.
   1. Read Management paper, pp. 116-117.
   2. Compose a satisfactory plan for managing modularized instruction. Discuss this with another class member.

D. To reach objective *D,* carefully study the various modules presented in this chapter. Following their format, outline a module of your own. You choose the topic and age level. If your students can't read, consider putting directions on tape. You can work together with another person if you wish. Save the outline to include with the Postassessment.

VII. *Postassessment:* Take the posttest, which is the same as the pretest. The materials you

---

[1]Block, J., editor: Mastery learning, New York, 1971, Holt, Rinehart and Winston, Inc.
[2]Tallahassee, Florida, 1970, Florida Department of Education.

[3]Nagel, T., and Richman, P.: Competency based instruction, Columbus, 1972, Charles E. Merrill Publishing Co.

prepared for enabling activity 4 should be attached for item 4 on the test. Find the answer key and check your paper.

Hand your scored test paper to the instructor who will tell you what to do next, if anything.

You have completed this module. Thank you.

OVERVIEW

Modularized instruction is a way of organizing materials and activities so students:

1. Know what *specific objectives* they are supposed to reach
2. Have *optional activities*, from which they may choose, all enabling them to reach the objectives
3. Can *direct themselves* through learning activities, with minimum assistance from the teacher
4. Can *pace themselves*, that is, work at a rate of speed that suits each person
5. Have *check out procedures* that tell them when they have reached the objectives

The written form that shows this organization is called a "module." Modules, at their best, are concise, clear, and to the point. They suggest activity options that appeal to different students. For example, options might include reading, interviewing, discussing, observing, and using audiovisual media such as recordings, filmstrips, and motion pictures.

Well-prepared modules communicate clearly to students. They often include the following parts:

1. A short, interesting prospectus that introduces the topic, mentioning its importance and something about the general value that can be gained from it
2. Notation of special prerequisites, if any
3. Clearly specified instructional objectives, stated behaviorally
4. Alternative "enabling activities" that will enable students to reach objectives. This part describes the activities, necessary materials, how to use them, and what to do with completed work.

5. Pre- and posttests or other assessment devices that show attainment of objectives

MANAGEMENT

1. Room arrangement. The classroom should be arranged to facilitate modularized work, with special attention given to the location of work areas needed in the room. Typically included are an area for study, reading, writing, and other quiet activities, an audiovisual area, and a conference area. Noisy areas should be placed near each other and away from quiet areas.

2. Materials. Modularized instruction usually requires a quantity of printed and audiovisual materials. Teachers must be responsible for media and printed materials such as tests, books, and worksheets, but students can help obtain objects, pictures, and so forth.

Convenient storage facilities for materials include file cabinets, bookcases, tables, shelves, cupboards, cardboard boxes, packing crates, and shoe boxes.

The materials should be labeled or coded in some way so they can be easily secured and accurately returned to storage. Colors, numbers, and graphic symbols are useful in coding. Everything should be kept in its place when not in use.

3. Work periods. In modularized instruction students usually work at their tasks at a given time of the day. Modules contain all necessary directions, and once students become accustomed to them, they require little assistance from the teacher. Students may also work at module activities at other times of the day, designated by the teacher.

4. Instructing. Although modularized programs are set up so students can instruct themselves from materials provided, there may still be occasions that require individual or group instruction in some of the activities. This is especially true when skill development is involved. Teachers must demonstrate the skill, pinpoint student errors, and give remedial instruction as necessary. This function requires a scheduled time and place where instruction is given to those students who need it.

5. Monitoring. Teachers must watch over student work to ensure that:

Students are working purposefully.

Help is given when students encounter difficulties that stop progress.

Student errors in process or product are noted.

Students requiring special tutoring are identified.

Monitoring can be done with the teacher moving about the room or stationed at a central location from which the class can be observed while other work such as conferencing or checking is done.

6. Assessing performance. This function is performed in various ways at various times through:

Observing student work in progress and noting errors or difficulties in either process or product. Errors can be corrected individually when noted, or students can be called for small group tutoring at another time.

Analyzing products of student work such as completed worksheets to pinpoint errors or difficulties to be corrected later.

Testing, both diagnostic and criterion

Self checking by students

7. Conferencing. Conferencing with students should be done on a regular basis. Schedules can be set up so the teacher can confer with each student privately for about five minutes at least once per week. Conferences can be scheduled during unstructured times, such as free reading, project work, or at any time when individualized work is in progress. A pocket chart with name tags can be used for students to request conferences if needed at unscheduled times. Conferences should be used for discussing successes and pleasures, errors, difficulties, and plans for remedial work. Brief records should be kept of each conference.

8. Record keeping. Master checksheets are useful for recording modules that students have selected, begun, and completed and for keeping track of behavioral objectives reached. Student performance over a period should be charted to show progress; students can do this.

SAMPLE MODULES
Module: Interpersonal skills and techniques—adolescence[4]

I. *Prerequisites:* Modules on reinforcement, motivation, and adolescence, age of turmoil

II. *Estimated time:* 12 hours.

III. *Goal:* To provide prospective teachers with certain skills and techniques to deal with the problems of adolescence.

IV. *Prospectus:* A long time ago a man in trouble was told: "Trust in God. He will provide for you." "Yes," replied the man, "but what do I do until then?" Teachers ask similar questions and are often faced with problems that demand immediate attention. The crucial question often becomes: "How can I survive, here and now?" This module is designed to give the student a basic knowledge background for developing the skills and techniques to deal with adolescent behavioral problems and to demonstrate those skills and techniques within the school setting.

V. *Preassessment[5]:* Take pencil and paper preassessment for objectives *A* through *C* immediately following. Upon successful completion of the criteria for any one of these objectives, the student may opt out of further activities for that objective.

VI. *Instructional objectives[6]:* Upon completion of this module, the student will be able to:

A. List a minimum of ten adolescent attitudes toward schools and teachers and

---

[4]San Diego State University Teachers Corps Project, Dr. Morrow M. Stough, Director. Module prepared by Professor Hayden R. Smith, with contributions from Professors Joe Duckworth, Leone McCoy, Tom Nagel, Paul Richman, and Charlotte Yesselman. 1973.

[5]Preassessment measures not included here.

[6]Instructional objectives and alternatives abridged for the sake of brevity.

indicate for each whether these attitudes (in your opinion) were caused by effective or ineffective teachers, schools, administrators, or are a natural result of adolescent growth.

Criterion: Instructor judgment.

B. Identify, from a list of ten statements, those that show teachers at their worst in relationships with adolescents.

Criterion: 100% correct.

C. Identify, in eight classroom situations, whether the praise given by the teacher is evaluative or productive.

Criterion: Six of eight correct.

VII. *Instructional alternatives:*

A. The following activities support objective A.

1. *Read* three of the following articles, available in the Study Center.

   a. "Poll Shows Areas in Which Teachers, Students Disagree"

   b. "Frustration Rises, Academic Status Dips at Hamilton High"

   c. "Students Remember Their Teachers"

   d. "Reflections on the Early Adolescent"

2. *Observe* a junior or senior high school class.

3. *Design own activity*, if desired.

B. The following activities support objective B.

1. *Read* two of the following:

   a. "Primum Non Nocere"

   b. "Students Remember Their Teachers"

   c. Ginott, Haim: *Teacher and Child*, New York, 1972, The Macmillan Co., pp. 37-78.

2. *Observe* two classroom teachers and note effective and ineffective responses.

3. *Design own activity*, if desired.

C. The following learning activities support objective C.

1. *Read* one of the following:

   a. "Primum Non Nocere"

   b. Ginott, Haim: *Teacher and Child*, New York, 1972, The Macmillan Co., pp. 125-143.

VIII. *Module checklist* [7]: Check off items as you proceed through the module. Consult instructor when necessary.

IX. *Postassessment:* Take the posttest, turn it in to the instructor, and arrange for a conference with the instructor.

X. *Remediation:* If you fail all or part of the posttest, you and the instructor will agree on a remedial plan of study.

Module: Crucial ideas of Jean Piaget

Directions

1. Read the introduction.

2. Take the preassessment test, if you wish to do so. [8]

3. Undertake enabling activities, as necessary, listed below.

4. Take the posttest, when you feel prepared for it. [8]

5. Do remedial work, if necessary, by repeating the appropriate enabling activities.

6. Retake the posttest, if necessary.

Introduction

This module deals with the eminent Swiss psychologist Jean Piaget, and with his work and ideas. Piaget, now world famous, has spent a half century exploring the ways children develop intellectually. His findings and ideas provide many insights into the education of children, particularly during their elementary school years.

The module is designed to enable you to do the following things:

1. Describe several of the "educationally important" ideas of Piaget

2. Recognize and describe differences in the thought processes of children at different stages of mental development

3. Determine, through observation and testing, the intellectual stage(s) at which an individual child is operating

Objectives and enabling activities

OBJECTIVE A—State in writing ten generalizations drawn from Piaget's findings that have importance for teaching. (90%)

---

[7]This checklist not included here.

[8]Tests not included here.

Enabling activities:

1. Read Maier: *Three theories of Child Development*, New York, 1965, Harper & Row, Publishers, pp. 75-143.
2. Read Charles: *Teachers' Petit Piaget*, Belmont, Calif., 1974, Fearon Publishers.
3. Read Elkind: *Children and Adolescents: Interpretive Essays on Jean Piaget*, New York, 1974, Oxford University Press.

Assessment mode: Written exam.

OBJECTIVE B—State in writing one general characteristic of children's thought at each of the following states of mental development:

Intuitive thought

Concrete operations

Formal operations

Enabling activities:

1. Read Charles: *Teachers' Petit Piaget*, Belmont, Calif., 1974, Fearon Publishers.
2. Listen to tape "Piaget and Science Education."
3. Select your own procedures—articles, books, interviews, and so on.

Assessment mode: Written exam.

OBJECTIVE C—In writing, contrast the expected behaviors of children in the Intuitive Thought stage with children in the Concrete Operations stage with respect to language, play and work, rules, thinking and reasoning, classification, number, causality, authority and obedience, guilt and punishment.

Enabling activities:

1. Participate in lecture-discussion by instructor.
2. Read Ginsburg and Opper, *Piaget's Theory of Intellectual Development*, Englewood Cliffs, N.J., 1969, Prentice-Hall, Inc.

Assessment mode: Written exam.

OBJECTIVE D—Assemble materials and demonstrate procedures for testing children's ability to conserve *two* of the following: number, volume, area, length.

Enabling activities:

1. Participate in lecture-discussion by instructor.
2. Read either Piaget, *The Child's Conception of Number,* or Piaget, *The Child's Conception of Geometry.*
3. Read Chapter 1 in Weigand, *Implementing*

Teacher Competencies, Englewood Cliffs, N.J., 1977, Prentice-Hall, Inc.

4. View film "Testing for Piagetian Stages of Development."

Assessment mode: Students selected at random will demonstrate testing processes and materials for both group and instructor reaction.

OBJECTIVE E—Identify areas of probable difficulty for learners in first and second grade arithmetic books.

Enabling activity: Analyze first and second grade math books.

Assessment mode: Written report submitted to instructor.

OBJECTIVE F—Test a "normal" child's ability, at about age seven, to conserve one of the following: number, volume, area, length.

Enabling activity: Select child and test.

Assessment mode: Short written report, submitted to instructor.

OBJECTIVE G—Test an "academically retarded" child of about ten years of age on ability to conserve number, volume, area, length.

Enabling activity: Select child and test.

Assessment mode: Short written report, submitted to instructor.

Sample module for intermediate grades 4 through 8

The following module can be used for introducing metric measurement and the metric system in general. It will help students comprehend that the metric system is based on the decimal scale. It will also help them become accustomed to metric measurement and to begin thinking metric.

This module can be varied and adapted in many ways. It can be very useful in organizing activities for math laboratories or math learning centers. It can lead naturally into measurement of volume and mass. Although these materials are all printed, they require manipulable objects, in quantity and variety. You can also find good filmstrips and cassettes, such as those entitled "Introducing the Metric System" (BFA Educational Media), which can be incorporated into the module.

Module for metric linear measurement[9]

MISSION MEASUREMENT

INTRODUCTION

Just imagine what the world would be like if we didn't have ways to measure things. How different our lives would be!

People first began to measure long ago. They invented many different kinds of measuring units. After a time they found that a unit of measure is much more useful if people everywhere know exactly what it is and that it is always the same.

In France, in 1791, the *metric system* of measurement was invented. "Metric" means measurement in Latin. The metric system is very easy to use. As you will see, it is based on 10's, just like our decimal number system. To change from one metric unit to another, you multiply or divide by 10's.

The United States is in the process of changing to the metric system. We will be using *centimeters* instead of inches, *meters* instead of yards, *liters* instead of quarts, and *kilograms* instead of pounds.

This module will teach you how to do linear measurement, using centimeters, decimeters, and meters.

YOUR MISSION

Your mission is to discover some things about the metric system. To accomplish your mission you must follow the directions in this module. When your mission is accomplished, you will know how to do these things:
1. Measure things with "non-standard" units of measure
2. Use the standard unit of measurement called the *meter* and its parts—the *decimeter* and the *centimeter*
3. Measure with a ruler using metric units of measure
4. Estimate metric lengths before you measure
5. Measure surfaces that are not flat

CONTENTS OF THIS MODULE

Directions for all activities are given in the pages you have in your hand. *Think Sheets* for you to complete are in your yellow folder. *Other materials* you will need are in the Math Center.

YOUR INSTRUCTIONS

The instructions will tell you exactly what to do to accomplish your mission.

Sometimes you can choose which jobs you would like to do. You can mark ⊠ for the jobs you choose.

Each job you are still working on can be kept at your desk. When you finish a job, put it in the "In basket" at the Math Center.

---

[9] Based on materials arranged and submitted by Mrs. Sharon Rutledge, San Diego.

Some directions will say "*STOP* when you have turned this paper in and wait for new directions." You must follow these directions exactly to accomplish your mission! Check the "Out basket" the next day for your new directions.

In this module you will find some special symbols that will tell you how to do the jobs. Here is what they mean:

Do this job by yourself.   Work with a partner.   You can check your
                                                                own work. The answer keys
YOUR ASSIGNMENTS   are in the Math Center.

Do Think Sheet 1. It is in your yellow folder. When you have finished it, place it in the "In basket" and go on with your mission.

NOTE: Think sheets are included in these pages to facilitate your reading. They are kept separate when used in the classroom.

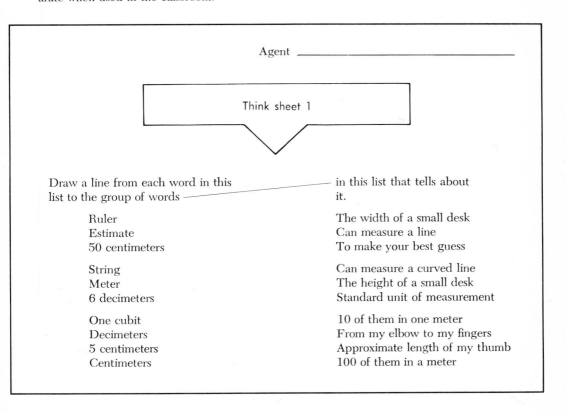

Agent _____

Think sheet 1

Draw a line from each word in this   in this list that tells about
list to the group of words   it.

    Ruler   The width of a small desk
    Estimate   Can measure a line
    50 centimeters   To make your best guess

    String   Can measure a curved line
    Meter   The height of a small desk
    6 decimeters   Standard unit of measurement

    One cubit   10 of them in one meter
    Decimeters   From my elbow to my fingers
    5 centimeters   Approximate length of my thumb
    Centimeters   100 of them in a meter

A long time ago people used parts of the body to measure things. Here are some of the parts of the body they used:

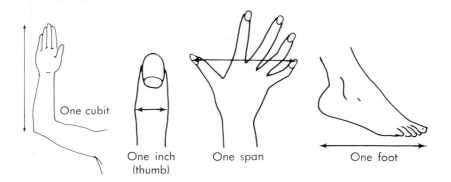

One cubit

One inch (thumb)

One span

One foot

Can you see that some people would have longer feet than others? Some people would have longer arms? Or a wider thumb?

Let's see how we measure this way. Choose *one* of the following jobs. Mark X on the job you choose. Write your answers on Think Sheet 2.

Job 1

Get one straw from the Math Center. Use it to measure the length of your desk. Record its length on Think Sheet 2.

Now use a pencil to measure the length of your desk. Record that length.

Choose three more things from the Linear Measures Box and measure the things on Think Sheet 2.

Job 2

At first an "inch" was as wide as a man's thumb. Measure your pencil with your thumb. How many thumb widths long is it? Record.

Now measure your pencil with a ruler having inches. Record that measurement.

Job 3

Long ago it was decided that a "foot" should be as long as a man's foot.

See how long our classroom is by measuring with your feet. Put your heel against your toe each time. Record how many "feet" long the room is.

Compare your measurement with a friend.

Job 4

Job four is for everyone to do. First, make your own ruler.

Choose a unit of measure from the Linear Measures Box, or use a part of your body such as your hand.

Next, get a strip of tagboard from the Math Center. Mark your unit on the tagboard to make yourself a ruler.

With your new ruler do Think Sheet 3.

Agent _____

> Think sheet 2

Job 1

Length of my desk in straws _____.

Length of my desk in pencils _____.

Measure each of these. Record your measurements.

Unit I measured with	Science book	Table leg	Width of window	Height of my desk

Were the units of measure you used good ones or poor ones? Why?

Job 2

My pencil is _____ thumb widths long when I measure it with my thumb.
When I measure it with a ruler, it is _____ inches long.

Which is larger, my thumb width or an inch? _____.

Job 3

Measured with my feet, the room is _____ feet long.

Measured with my friend's feet, the room is _____ feet long.
Is a person's foot a good standard of measurement? Why?

Agent _____

> Think sheet 3
> Job 4: Measurements around you

My unit of measurement is _____.

My measurements of these things: Measurements

    Length of my desk   _____

    Height of my desk   _____

    Length of my reading book   _____

    Height of the wastebasket   _____

    Width of a magazine   _____
Name five different things you could use to measure your height.

    1. _____

    2. _____

    3. _____

    4. _____

    5. _____
Explain what is meant by "standard unit of measurement."

STOP when you have turned this Think Sheet in. Wait for new directions.

The meter

You already know that a meter is a standard unit of linear measure. How long do you think a meter is?

Here is one way to find out how long a meter is.
This is a decimeter unit. The abbreviation *dm* means decimeter.

1 dm

Use your decimeter unit to measure string from the Math Center, 10 dm long.
Ten decimeters (dm) are the same length as one meter (m).
Cut the string so it is 1 meter (10 dm) long.
Check your meter string with the meter stick from the Math Center to see if they are the same length.

Check yourself

Use your decimeter to measure a strip of tagboard 10 dm long and 1 dm wide. Cut out your strip.

Write your answers to these questions on a separate sheet of paper.
You can check your own answers.
1. How long is a meter (m)? It is 10 _____.
2. Is the length of a meter closest to your foot, your arm, or your leg? Use your meter strip to find out. _____.
3. Divide your meter into 10 units of equal length. What is the name of each of the 10 units _____.
4. The Latin prefix "deci-" means one-tenth. We would write ¹⁄₁₀ like this: .1
   A _____ is .1 of a meter.
5. A meter is equal to _____ dm.

Measuring practice

Choose *one* of the following three jobs. The think sheets are in your yellow folder. You will need to use your meter tagboard strip.

Job 1

    Do Think Sheet 4.

Job 2

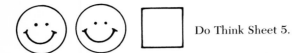

Do Think Sheet 5.

Job 3

Do Think Sheet 6.

Using your metric ruler

This metric ruler is 10 centimeters long.

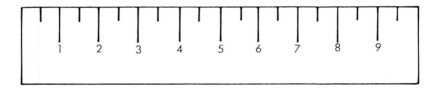

Use this ruler to mark the centimeters on your tagboard meter strip.

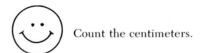

Count the centimeters.

Now do Think Sheet 7.

Do Think Sheet 8.

Think sheet 4

A race course

Patrick and Metric are off on a race to see who is faster. Each will start at their X's at the same time. If they go at exactly the same speed, who will get to the winner's circle

first? _____.

Was he really the faster? Give your answer and tell why.

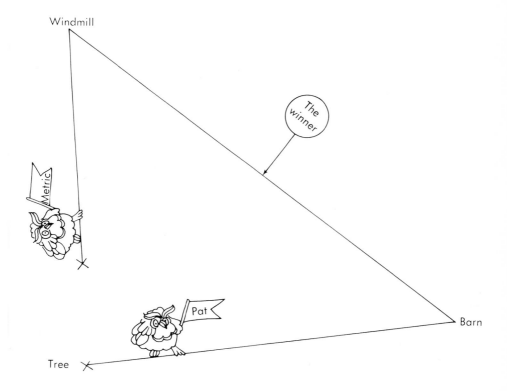

Hints: Metric's X to windmill _____ dm. Windmill to winner's circle _____ dm.

Pat's X to barn _____ dm. Barn to winner's circle _____ dm.

Agent _____

Partner _____

Think sheet 5

Use your meter strip to measure these distances:
From the classroom to the closest drinking fountain

_____ m   or   _____ dm
From our classroom to the nearest classroom

_____ m   or   _____ dm
The height of our classroom door

_____ m   or   _____ dm
The length of the chalkboard

_____ m   or   _____ dm

Agent _____

Partner _____

Think sheet 6

Use your meter strip to make these measurements.

Length of science table: _____ m   or   _____ dm

Width of Math Center table: _____ m   or   _____ dm

My height: _____ m   or   _____ dm

My partner is: _____ m   or   _____ dm

Find four other things in the classroom to measure:

1. _____ is _____ m   or   _____ dm

2. _____ is _____ m   or   _____ dm

3. _____ is _____ m   or   _____ dm

4. _____ is _____ m   or   _____ dm

Agent _____

Think sheet 7

How many centimeters did you count on your meter tagboard strip? _____ cm
The Latin prefix "centi-" means one hundredth. 1/100 can be written .01.
Find some objects that are about 1 centimeter (cm) long. Name them.

1. _____   4. _____   7. _____

2. _____   5. _____   8. _____

3. _____   6. _____   9. _____

About how wide is your little finger? _____ cm

Measure a paper clip at the Math Center. It is _____ cm long.

Find objects:

About 5 cm long.

1. _____

2. _____

3. _____

4. _____

About 10 cm long.

1. _____

2. _____

3. _____

4. _____

Agent _____

Here is a crossword puzzle for you. Your clues are at the bottom of the page.

Across

1. There are 100 in a meter.
3. Number of centimeters in one meter.
5. The _____ unit is the meter.

Down

2. One meter is equal to _____ decimeters.
4. Ten make one meter.
6. A ruler helps us _____ lengths.

STOP when you have turned in this paper. Wait for new directions.

Practice makes perfect

If you want to be able to measure accurately, you must practice measuring many things many times.

Here are four measuring jobs. You may choose to do any *three* of them.

But first you must make a 10 centimeter ruler. Mark it on a small strip of tagboard and cut it out.

Now do your three measuring jobs.

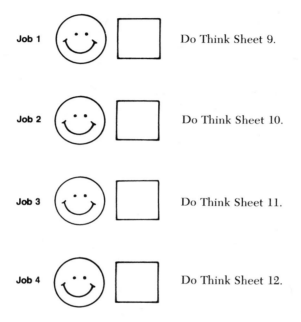

Job 1   Do Think Sheet 9.

Job 2   Do Think Sheet 10.

Job 3   Do Think Sheet 11.

Job 4   Do Think Sheet 12.

Build it

Builders must be able to measure very carefully. Try your hand at building something. Here is what you can do.

1. Go to the Build It Box.
2. Choose a pattern.
3. Measure the pattern to find the pieces you need.
4. "Build" the object on a piece of colored tagboard, following the pattern.

Do Think Sheet 13.

Build It Box

Boat

House

Rocket

Flower vase

Chair

Table

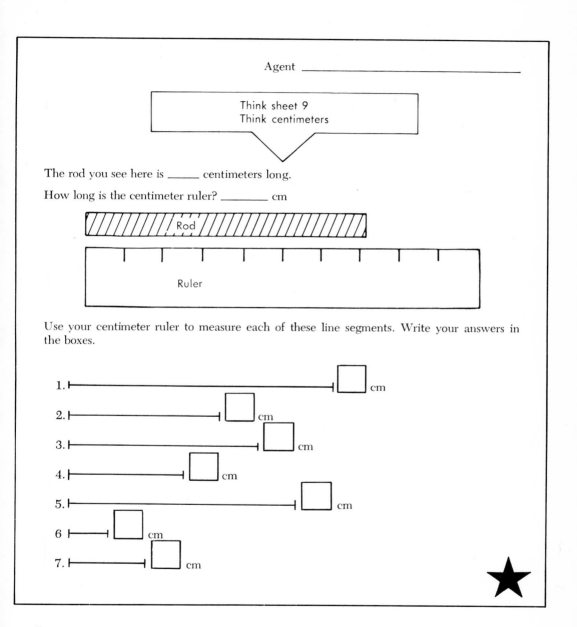

Agent _____

Think sheet 9
Think centimeters

The rod you see here is _____ centimeters long.

How long is the centimeter ruler? _____ cm

Rod

Ruler

Use your centimeter ruler to measure each of these line segments. Write your answers in the boxes.

1. ⊢————————————————⊣ [ ] cm

2. ⊢——————————⊣ [ ] cm

3. ⊢—————————————⊣ [ ] cm

4. ⊢—————————⊣ [ ] cm

5. ⊢———————————————⊣ [ ] cm

6 ⊢———⊣ [ ] cm

7. ⊢——————⊣ [ ] cm

Agent _____

Think sheet 10

With your ten centimeter ruler measure each of these line segments. Write your answers in the boxes.

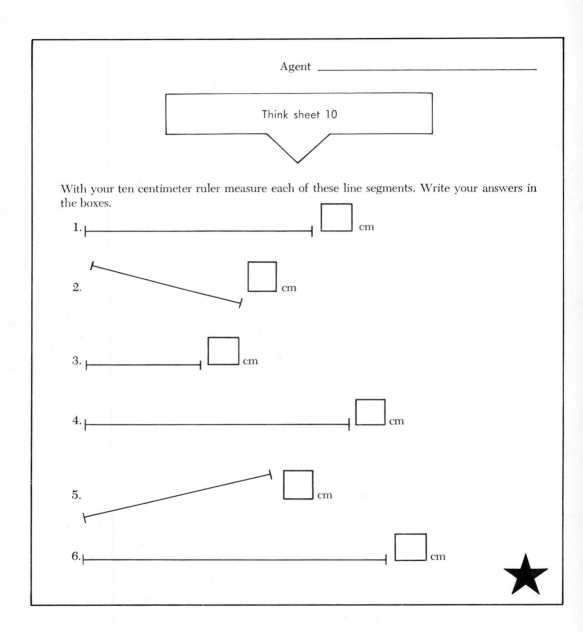

1. [ ] cm

2. [ ] cm

3. [ ] cm

4. [ ] cm

5. [ ] cm

6. [ ] cm

Agent _____

Think sheet 11

Use your 10 centimeter ruler to draw line segments with these lengths:

1. 2 centimeters long

2. 9 centimeters long

3. 7 centimeters long

4. 1 centimeter long

5. 10 centimeters long

6. 4 centimeters long

7. 6 centimeters long

8. 5 centimeters long

Agent _____

Measure each object. Write its length in each blank.

The spoon is _____ cm long.

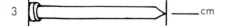

1 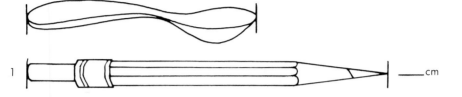 _____ cm

2 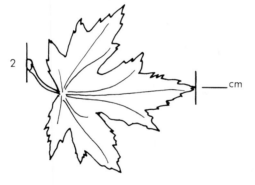 _____ cm

3 _____ cm

4  _____ cm

5  _____ cm

Agent _____

Think sheet 13

Measure each line segment. Write your answer in each blank.

A. |————————————————————————————| _____ cm

B. |————————————————————| _____ cm

      A is _____ cm longer than B.

A. |————————————————| _____ cm

B. |————————————————————| _____ cm

      A is _____ cm shorter than B.

A. |————————————| _____ cm

B. |————————| _____ cm

      A is _____ cm longer than B.

STOP when you turn in this paper. Wait for new directions.

Guess-timating

How good are you at guessing, or estimating? It is not always possible to measure. Sometimes you have to estimate.

Estimating means to make your best possible guess. You do that by comparing the thing, in your mind, with some unit of measure that you know.

 To practice estimating, do Think Sheet 14.

Now you may choose to do either *one* of these two jobs:

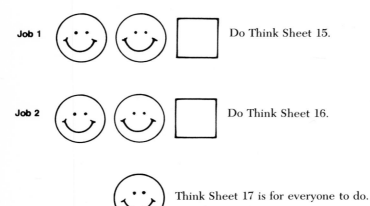

Job 1 Do Think Sheet 15.

Job 2 Do Think Sheet 16.

Think Sheet 17 is for everyone to do.

Agent _____

> Think sheet 14

Estimate how many times you think the width of your thumb will go across the top of this page. _____

Now check your guess by measuring with your thumb. Number of thumb widths: _____.

Use your thumb width as a unit of measure to find the lengths of:

Your nose _____

The palm of your hand _____

Your mouth _____

How does your thumb width compare with a centimeter? Measure your thumb width here:

Do you think your thumb would be useful for making estimates? Tell why.

Estimate how wide you think your index finger is: _____ cm.

Now measure it: _____ cm. Which one of your fingers has a width nearest one cm? _____. Use that finger to estimate these things:

	Estimate
Length of your desk	_____ cm
Width of reading book	_____ cm
Length of longest pencil	_____ cm

Agent _____

Partner _____

Think sheet 15

Choose five objects from the Guess and Prove It Box. Estimate the length of each. Then measure each object's length. Record both of these numbers.

Object	Estimate	Measurement proof

Estimate the length and then measure each of these line segments:

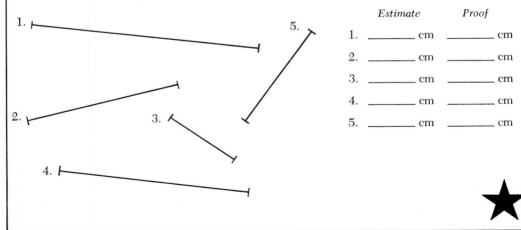

	Estimate	*Proof*
1.	_____ cm	_____ cm
2.	_____ cm	_____ cm
3.	_____ cm	_____ cm
4.	_____ cm	_____ cm
5.	_____ cm	_____ cm

Agent _____

Partner _____

Think sheet 16

Guess the measurements of these things. Then measure them with one of your metric rulers.

	Estimate	Measurement
Length of your desk	_____ cm	_____ cm
Height of your desk	_____ cm	_____ cm
Length of your reading book	_____ cm	_____ cm
Height of the waste basket	_____ cm	_____ cm

Estimate the length and then measure each of these line segments.

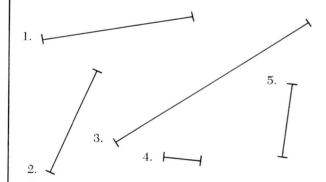

	Estimate	Proof
1.	_____ cm	_____ cm
2.	_____ cm	_____ cm
3.	_____ cm	_____ cm
4.	_____ cm	_____ cm
5.	_____ cm	_____ cm

Agent _____

Think sheet 17
Your guess is good

Estimate the length of each of these line segments in centimeters. Record your guess. Then measure each line segment and record that number.

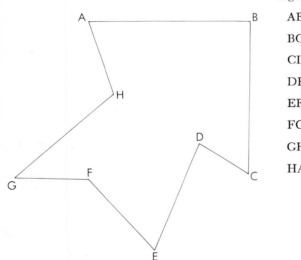

Segment	Estimate	Proof
AB	_____ cm	_____ cm
BC	_____ cm	_____ cm
CD	_____ cm	_____ cm
DE	_____ cm	_____ cm
EF	_____ cm	_____ cm
FG	_____ cm	_____ cm
GH	_____ cm	_____ cm
HA	_____ cm	_____ cm

STOP when you have turned in this paper. Wait for new directions.

So far we have been measuring straight lines. When we want to measure how long something is, we measure from the beginning to the end of it along a line. This is called linear measurement.

Do you suppose you could measure a round object such as a ball? How do you think you could do it? Experiment with measuring a ball at the Math Center.

You can measure any distance, as long as you have a place to start and a place to stop.

To practice measuring things that are not straight lines, you may choose to do either *one* of the following two jobs.

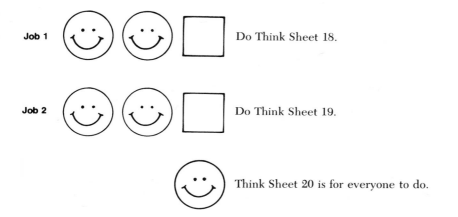

Job 1 Do Think Sheet 18.

Job 2 Do Think Sheet 19.

Think Sheet 20 is for everyone to do.

Agent _____

Partner _____

Think sheet 18

Measure each of the objects below, using your centimeter ruler.
To measure the curved lines, use a piece of string from the Math Center.
Measure the line with the string and then measure the string with your ruler.

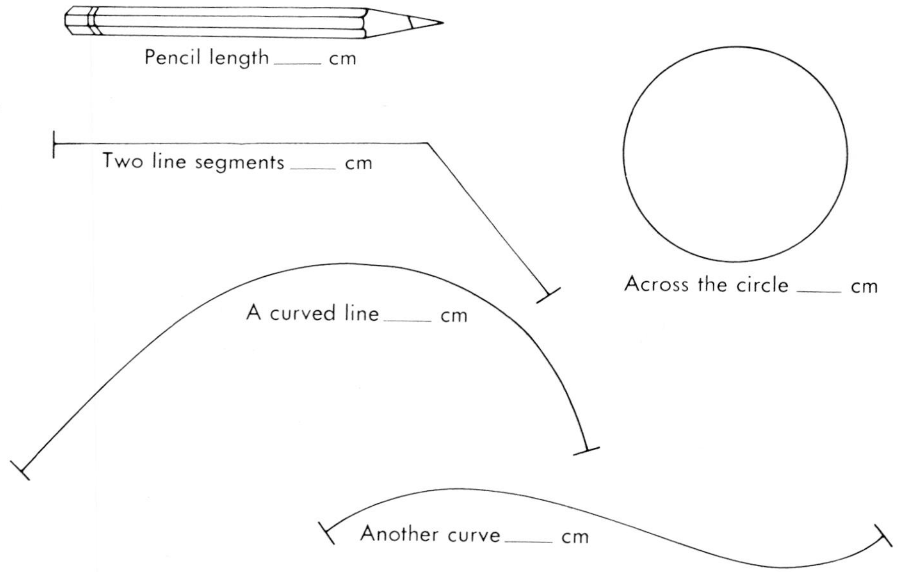

Pencil length _____ cm

Two line segments _____ cm

Across the circle _____ cm

A curved line _____ cm

Another curve _____ cm

Check answers twice.

Agent _____

Partner _____

Think sheet 19

Measure each of the objects below using your centimeter ruler.
To measure the curved lines, use a piece of string from the Math Center.
Measure the line with the string and then measure the string with your ruler.

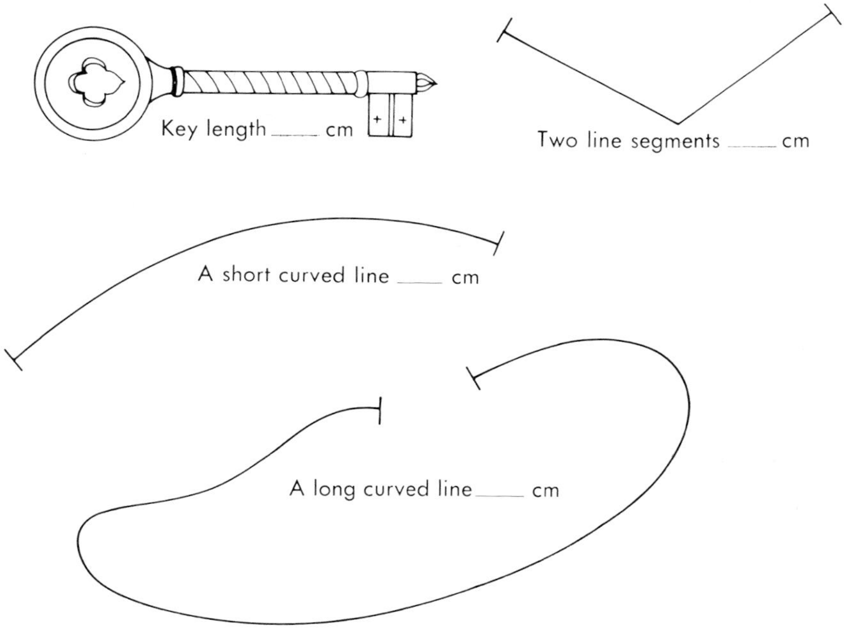

Key length _____ cm

Two line segments _____ cm

A short curved line _____ cm

A long curved line _____ cm

Check each answer twice.

Agent _____

Think sheet 20
Curves ahead

Measure each curved line very carefully. Double check your measurements!

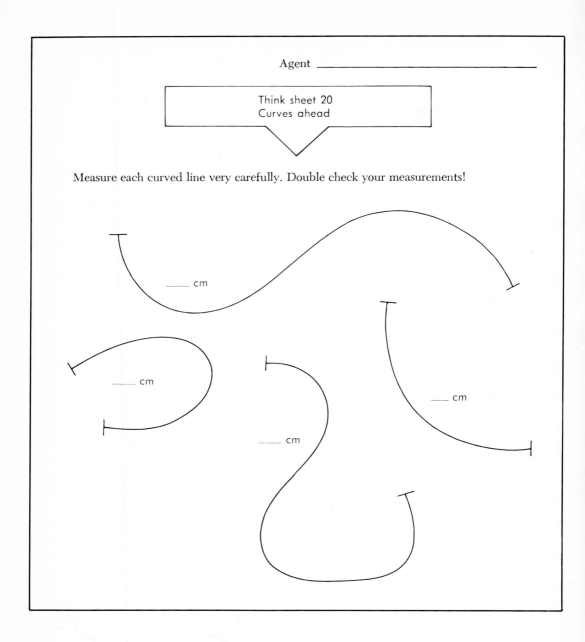

_____ cm

_____ cm

_____ cm

_____ cm

If you did this think sheet correctly, your mission is accomplished.

CONGRATULATIONS!

11

Nonformal basic programs

Here is your assignment for this chapter. If it suits you, fine. Have at it. If it doesn't suit you, explain why to your instructor, who will hopefully agree to a modification that better fits your needs.

Assignment

1. Find out what "nonformal basic program" means.

2. Explain, to your own satisfaction, why a teacher might want to use a nonformal basic program instead of diagnostic-prescriptive teaching, learning centers, modularized instruction, or open experience.

3. Select a topic of instruction in an area such as reading, mathematics, creative writing, biology, or whatever you prefer. Specify the kind of structure you would want if you constructed a nonformal basic program for teaching that topic. (Structure refers to the amount of control and direction over student activities and the range of student options in each. It includes such aspects as objectives, instruction, assignments, and evaluation.)

4. For your nonformal basic program, identify management details you would require. (Management details refer to grouping, scheduling, instructional times, conferencing, assessing performance, and keeping records.)

All information necessary for completing this assignment is included in the various sections that follow in this chapter.

OVERVIEW
Meaning

The name "nonformal basic program" needs some explaining. First, you have to recognize that this approach to individualizing instruction is teacher made; it can take many different formats and directions. If you accept this diversity of format and direction, you will find that the remaining descriptions of this approach fall naturally into place.

Now for the words in the name: "Nonformal" means that these programs do not have a precise, conventional form, or format. They differ greatly, from one to the other, in their organization, structure, and procedures. Nonformal does not mean the same as open experience. Nonformal programs do have structure. The structure needn't be as rigid as that of DPT or modularized instruction. Still, students know from the outset that they must work at certain specified topics, that they must complete certain amounts of work, that they must complete the work within time limits, and that the work must reach a certain level of quality before it will be accepted.

147

These programs, then, stipulate work to be done and how it will be evaluated. They allow students to pace themselves in meeting completion deadlines, but the deadlines must be met. They can allow a degree of choice among activity options, and they can allow different students to work at different topics, different levels of difficulty or sophistication, and branch out in different directions from the basic core.

"Basic" means that the topic is part of the "basic curriculum" of the school, as that term is generally used. That is, the topic comes from sciences, language, mathematics, and so forth and is not simply a pastime, extracurricular, or hobby type of activity.

Thus, nonformal basic programs are teacher-made programs of individualized instruction. They occur in basic curricular areas, and they do not have a predetermined format.

Why would a teacher want to use such an approach? Suppose you want to individualize fifth grade spelling or tenth grade biology. You don't think learning centers are appropriate for the topic; you don't believe in open experience; you think modules are too stuffy; you think DPT is too cut and dried. You want to individualize, but in a way that better suits you and your students. Therefore, you find ideas, activities, and materials from here and there, put them together in a way that suits your style, and together with the students you decide on how you will conduct your program in the classroom. What results from your attempts will fit into the approach category called nonformal basic.

Organization

When you begin to organize your nonformal basic program, you will find it helpful to proceed in this way:

1. Select the topic area.
2. Talk over the idea with students. Discuss their preferences, their willingness, their ideas for working and assembling materials.
3. Establish a few long-range goals. Within each of these goals, specify a few short-term objectives (behavioral, experience, or both).
4. Write out the objectives and post them. Check them off as they are reached.
5. Bring together the materials you need. They might include textbooks, reference books, audiovisual media, concrete objects, charts, maps, graphs, models, pictures, and so forth. Textbooks provide a convenient structure, as do curriculum guides.
6. Group the materials, shelve or display them, and clarify the ways they are to be used.
7. Decide on work procedures having to do with:
   a. Topics and tasks
   b. Times
   c. Materials
   d. Locations
   e. Clean-up details
   Write the directions briefly and post them in the room.
8. Consider diagnosis (if any) and how you will group and place your students.
9. Establish procedures for monitoring students and for checking their completed work.
10. Prepare a file containing a folder for each student. Keep records and samples of work in each folder.
11. Consider having a class meeting once or twice a week to discuss and iron out any problems that might arise.

STRUCTURE

Structure refers to the organizational detail that is built into an instructional program. We commonly speak of "structured" and "unstructured" programs, to differentiate between those that have greater and lesser degrees of teacher control. That's not very accurate, however, because all instructional programs have structure. We are really referring to the degree of structure they involve. For that reason, the terms "less structure" and "more structure" are used here to differentiate between programs that have less organizational detail and those that have more organizational detail.

Structure influences student performance in important ways. In more structured programs, students have relatively few options from which to choose. The teacher has planned everything for them in advance—objectives, activities, materials, procedures. Even when optional activities are allowed, each is carefully detailed.

More structured programs tend to have these characteristics:

1. Instruction aims at attainment of specified skills and concepts, selected by the teacher.
2. The teacher arranges details of instructional activities, procedures, and schedules.
3. Assessment aims primarily at determining whether objectives have been reached.

Less structured programs allow students a larger role in deciding what activities and materials they will use, in determining their work procedures, and in arranging their work schedules. This approach requires that students take responsibility for beginning, following through, and completing activities—tasks many students are not able to perform until they have had some experience with this type of program.

Less structured programs tend to have the following characteristics:

1. Instruction may aim at either provision of quality experiences, or the attainment of specific objectives, or both.
2. Students have greater freedom (and responsibility) in selecting their own activities, procedures, and schedules.
3. Assessment includes not only achievement but also students' self appraisal and their reactions to the activities they selected.

BEGINNING

You may have the feeling that preparing your own nonformal basic program is all too complicated, too difficult, too unwieldy. You don't see how you could ever break away from the approaches to which you are accustomed.

If you feel that way, you should read Schmidt's article "Individualization: Remaking the Reading Program."[1] Schmidt, a third grade teacher in Rochester, New York, wanted to move beyond the basal reader approach that had been traditionally used in his school. Keeping the best of the basal reader program, he moved slowly into an individualized program that he says took a substantial, though not overwhelming, amount of work. He built a new reading approach that included seven major aspects:

1. *Diagnosis,* to determine levels and difficulties of each student and to use a basis for further instruction. In diagnosing, he used informal reading inventories and group diagnostic tests.
2. *Individualized basal work,* to maintain sequence and to provide systematic skill development activities. He made study and answer cards that allowed students to work through the basal readers at their own rates.
3. *Multimedia stockpile,* including books, workbooks, phonics kits, flash cards, tape recorder, reading games, filmstrips, audio tapes, study cards, and answer keys.
4. *Self directing, self correcting activities,* to encourage students to proceed with as little teacher assistance as possible.
5. *Individual attention,* in the form of individual conferences, record keeping, and skill teaching. He kept track of comprehension, oral reading, and word recognition.
6. *Pupil teaming,* allowing students to work together in pairs, so the more capable help the less capable. Both students in the team profit from the experience.
7. *Scheduling and record keeping,* beginning with a schedule sheet on each Monday that shows activities and materials for each student for that week. Students check their schedule sheets at the beginning of each day to know what they are to do.

---

[1] Schmidt, T.: Individualization: Remaking the reading program, Teacher pp. 40-43, January 1974.

Students in Schmidt's class begin each reading period using one of the following:

Individual study cards, related to basal readers and workbooks
Self correcting materials, such as SRA Kits, worksheets with acetate overlay and answer keys
Programmed materials, such as the Sullivan Programmed Readers
Other materials, such as games and flashcards

The teacher's role is to set the environment, manage it, move about the room, help students when necessary, conference, teach special skill lessons, prepare the weekly schedules for students, and keep records.

Another example is a fifth grade teacher in California who decided to individualize her reading program. She went at the task in a different way than Schmidt, preferring to keep her students together in groups. She acquired quantities of reading materials and then set her room up to include four groups and five different kinds of activities. Her weekly organization looked like the accompanying chart positioned at the bottom of this page.[2]

---

[2] Reported in Charles, C.: Educational psychology: The instructional endeavor, St. Louis, 1976, The C. V. Mosby Co., p. 166.

ELEMENTS OF ORGANIZATION AND MANAGEMENT

As mentioned, nonformal basic programs vary greatly in form. For that reason it doesn't seem worthwhile to reproduce any particular program here. Instead, we will consider elements of organization and management necessary to any individualized program you might construct. We will also examine pieces of material that will give you ideas about how you might organize and manage your program. The elements we will consider are: objectives, diagnosis, scheduling, assigning, instructing, materials, follow-up activities, evaluation, and record keeping.

Objectives

If you use experience-referenced objectives, you must carefully think through the experiences you wish to provide for your students. Your interest is to make these experiences as stimulating, rich with materials, and worthwhile as possible. You hope they will open up new vistas for your students and get them started in new directions. You trust that given these kinds of experiences, students will pursue matters that are truly valuable for them. You don't believe you can validly predict what the outcomes will be, and you doubt that you should do so even if you could. Instead, you describe the experi-

	Group one	Group two	Group three	Group four
Monday	Conferences (read library books)	Skill session	Magazine reading	Project reading
Tuesday	Project reading	Conferences (read library books)	Skill session	Magazine reading
Wednesday	Magazine reading	Project reading	Conferences (read library books)	Skill session
Thursday	Skill session	Magazine reading	Project reading	Conferences (read library books)
Friday	Games, art, construction	Games, art, construction	Games, art, construction	Games, art, construction

ences fully, to be sure you have included what you want. Your objectives, then, are these descriptions of the experiences you intend to provide.

If you use behavior-referenced objectives, you proceed in quite a different way. You have in mind specific observable behaviors you hope your students will acquire. Those behaviors are your objectives. They, in turn, give direction to activities and materials used in learning and to the procedures to be used later in assessment and evaluation.

Behavior-referenced objectives are often used when development of specific skills and knowledge is desired. For example, behavioral objectives from an individualized program in measurement might include the following:

The student can:

Place objects in order according to height
Measure in feet, feet and inches, and inches
Demonstrate balance with varied fulcrums
Weigh objects to nearest pound
Read temperature on thermometer

At one time teachers had to compose such behavioral objectives for themselves if they wanted to use them in teaching. That task is easy, but time consuming. Nowadays, you don't have to compose your own objectives, although many teachers like to do so. You can find extensive and complete sets of ready-made, behavioral objectives in most schools and school district offices. Various publications also provide them in quantity. One of the best examples of published objectives comes from the Instructional Objectives Exchange (IOX) at the University of California at Los Angeles. This exchange sells several large volumes of objectives that cover most subject areas in considerable detail. Objectives for the affective domain are also available from IOX.

If you put together a nonformal basic program that emphasizes skill development, you will want to build it around behavior-referenced objectives.

Diagnosis

Diagnosis is used to find out two things: (1) what the present functioning level is for each student in a given topic area, and (2) what specific errors students make that might hinder their progress in those topics. In mathematics, for example, you need to know both these things about your students—what they can do in math and what specific errors they are making.

Diagnosis can be carried out using completed work turned in by students. More commonly, though, teachers use special tests that have been prepared to pinpoint certain skills and errors. We will examine parts of four diagnostic tests of the kind typically used in elementary schools. The first, from a primer-level test of word recognition, checks only achievement, not specific errors. The second, from a primary phonics test, checks for both achievement and specific errors. The third, from a spelling test, checks for specific errors, as does the fourth, from a math test.

Primer-level word recognition

Each student responds, individually, to words the teacher has written on flash cards. In this way students are checked on their ability to call the words correctly on a two-second exposure. The teacher keeps records of words with which students have difficulty. Later, each student receives special help with the words that gave difficulty.

Flash card words	2-second	10-second	Unable
1. Are	_____	_____	_____
2. Away	_____	_____	_____
3. Can	_____	_____	_____
4. For	_____	_____	_____
5. Kitten	_____	_____	_____
6. Me	_____	_____	_____
7. Red	_____	_____	_____

Primary phonics skills

This test serves the dual function of determining achievement and identifying specific errors. Notice that it uses nonsense syllables instead of real words to check students' use of phonics. Students are checked individually and only on the specific phonetic elements being tested, not the entire syllable.

	Skill needs
Element: Initial consonants bub dub fub pub hub jub kub yub lub mub	_____ _____
Element: Final consonants bub buc bud buf bug buh buj buk bum bun	_____ _____
Element: Consonant blends brub grub prub glub blub splub twub scub frub splub	_____ _____
Element: Digraphs shub phub bush chub buph thub buth buch	_____ _____

Spelling diagnosis

Diagnostic tests in spelling, such as the Webster-Kottmeyer Diagnostic Test, can show recurring error patterns. Tests like this can be given to groups. Here you see just a few examples of the sorts of items contained in these tests:

Element	Words used for testing
Short vowels	Closed syllable words with short vowel sounds, such as met, fit, cat, got, nut
"Le" endings	Words ending in le, such as little, kettle, nettle
Nonphonetic spelling	Words that don't follow phonetic spelling rules, such as one, would, rough
"Wh" beginnings	Words such as which, while, when
Doubling final consonant before "ing"	Words such as hitting, spitting, sitting
Dropping final e before "ing"	Words such as hoping, shaping, biting
Changing final y to i before adding ending	Words such as studies, parties, skies
Contractions	Words such as doesn't, wouldn't, can't
Silent gh	Words such as fight, might, night

Mathematics procedure diagnosis

Mathematics requires knowledge of procedure fully as much as knowledge of basic facts. The following examples show how various procedures can be checked to determine whether students have misconceptions that prevent their solving problems correctly even when they might know their basic facts.

Typical problems

Addition type

A. No carrying

$$\begin{array}{r} 34 \\ 23 \\ \hline \end{array} \qquad \begin{array}{r} 40 \\ 5 \\ \hline \end{array}$$

B. Carrying from 1's place

$$\begin{array}{r} 17 \\ 26 \\ \hline \end{array} \qquad \begin{array}{r} 18 \\ 3 \\ \hline \end{array}$$

C. Carrying from 10's place

$$\begin{array}{r} 243 \\ 192 \\ \hline \end{array} \qquad \begin{array}{r} 36 \\ 281 \\ \hline \end{array}$$

D. Carrying from consecutive places

$$\begin{array}{r} 174 \\ 168 \\ \hline \end{array} \qquad \begin{array}{r} 243 \\ 77 \\ \hline \end{array}$$

E. Carrying in alternate places

$$\begin{array}{r} 3675 \\ 2817 \\ \hline \end{array} \qquad \begin{array}{r} 47181 \\ 16378 \\ \hline \end{array}$$

Subtraction type

F. No regrouping

$$\begin{array}{r} 58 \\ -32 \\ \hline \end{array} \qquad \begin{array}{r} 398 \\ -174 \\ \hline \end{array}$$

G. Regrouping in 1's and 10's

$$\begin{array}{r} 37 \\ -18 \\ \hline \end{array} \qquad \begin{array}{r} 360 \\ -229 \\ \hline \end{array}$$

H. Regrouping in 10's and 100's

$$\begin{array}{r} 364 \\ -182 \\ \hline \end{array} \qquad \begin{array}{r} 400 \\ -60 \\ \hline \end{array}$$

I. Regrouping in consecutive places

$$\begin{array}{r} 437 \\ -148 \\ \hline \end{array} \qquad \begin{array}{r} 8124 \\ -7325 \\ \hline \end{array}$$

Multiplication type

J. No carrying

$$\begin{array}{r} 13 \\ \times 3 \\ \hline \end{array} \qquad \begin{array}{r} 22 \\ \times 4 \\ \hline \end{array}$$

K. Carrying from 1's to 10's

$$37 \times 2 \qquad 103 \times 4$$

L. Carrying from 10's to 100's

$$132 \times 4 \qquad 1030 \times 9$$

M. Carrying in consecutive places

$$183 \times 6 \qquad 3225 \times 7$$

N. Carrying in alternate places

$$1616 \times 4 \qquad 2705 \times 3$$

O. Multiplying by numbers ending in 0

$$17 \times 20 \qquad 326 \times 400$$

P. Multiplying by two and three place numbers

$$37 \times 13 \qquad 321 \times 413$$

The same approach can be used for division of whole numbers, fractions (addition, subtraction, multiplication, and division), decimals, and so forth.

Scheduling

Scheduling of activities was done in the programs reported on pp. 93 and 115. You can find many different ways for scheduling activities and work periods to your own plans. Some teachers like to have everyone work at the same subject, such as geography or science, during a given time of the day. Students may work individually during that time. Other teachers prefer allowing students to arrange their own work times during the day, so that some students might be working at one topic while others are working at others. This can be done easily in elementary schools, but not in secondary schools where students change classrooms for each subject.

Shown here are two daily and weekly schedules, for reading and for mathematics. Both occur during a fixed time of the day.

Reading schedule

Monday

Class does silent reading from basal readers,,library books, reference books, magazines, or newspapers.

Teacher conducts individual conferences with students and records materials read, difficulties noted, and suggestions for further reading.

Tuesday

Class does silent reading as on Monday.
Teacher calls individuals and small groups for oral reading and skill instruction, as determined necessary from the conferences.

Wednesday

Class selects individual work from options that include creative writing, project writing, reading games, and self checking seat work.
Teacher assigns worksheets as necessary and moves about the room, monitoring, assisting, and checking work in progress.

Thursday

Class works at activities selected from library books, reference books, magazines, newspapers, games, creative writing, or art related to reading and creative writing.
Teacher works at desk, planning and keeping records or circulates about the room, monitoring and helping.

Friday

Class selects freely from options that include games, art work, creative writing, and reading materials of all types. Students are allowed to work quietly in groups for drama activities.
Teacher calls selected individuals and groups for conferencing, assessing progress, and suggesting further work.

Math schedule: group work

Monday

Group: total class
Teacher introduces new concept/skill. Teacher demonstrates and asks students to demonstrate.
Class completes assigned activities in workbook or worksheets.

Tuesday

Group: total class
Teacher leads class discussion, reviewing the con-

cept/skill and exploring its application in real life situations.

Class completes assigned seatwork.

Wednesday

Groups: three small groups—slow, average, and fast

Teacher works with slow group, reviewing, manipulating objects, making simple applications.

Average group does worksheets that provide additional practice and works in pairs to drill.

Fast group, which shows mastery of the concept/skill, does worksheets involving advanced application to problem situations.

Thursday

Groups: three small groups—slow, average, fast

Teacher works with slow group on review, reinforcement, and continued application, then circulates among other groups.

Average group completes another worksheet on application of the concept/skill and then selects games, puzzles, and manipulatives from the math materials.

Fast group works on advanced application of the concept/skill, on individual projects, or on games, puzzles, and riddles from the math materials.

Friday

Group: total class

Teacher administers two-part exam. The first part is easier, the second more difficult. Both parts have to do with knowledge and application of the concept/skill.

Class takes the exam, each person doing as much as possible. After the exam, students select own activities from the math materials.

Math schedule: individual work

Example 1

Required of all

1. Take a direction sheet that introduces the concept or skill. (The direction sheets are illustrated to show step by step just what is involved in the task at hand.)

2. Do the corresponding worksheets that provide practice and application of the concept or skill. Give to the teacher when finished.

Options: select two

3. Worksheets to extend skill or concept through application, word problems, or problem solving

4. Math games, riddles, puzzles, manipulatives

5. Construction projects for making and using own math materials

6. Go on to new concept/skill topic.

Conferences will be required of all students. The teacher will call you for the conference.

Example 2

Contract work

Using contract, student selects work to be completed, which might include pages in textbook, workbook, worksheets, games, manipulatives, puzzles, or projects. If the teacher agrees, both sign the contract, which shows a probable completion date. When the work is completed, it is checked by the teacher. The student participates in the evaluation.

Assigning

Work assignments in individualized programs are made in two basic ways. Either teachers make assignments based on needs they believe students have, or students select the activities they will pursue from available options. Of course, both can be used together in nonformal basic programs, with teachers making some assignments while allowing students to select others.

When teachers make assignments, the procedure is fairly straightforward. They tell students what to do or direct them to materials that contain instructions. When students have a hand in selecting assignments, there is often need for some way of recording the selections, showing that teacher and student have agreed on them, and showing an indication of when the assignments are likely to be completed. One device commonly used for this purpose is the contract. Presently, we will look at a few contract forms. But first, let's note some forms teachers can use to give written directions to students.

1

Reading
(name of story
or book)

Workbook page_____

2

Writing
Practice these
letters:

_____

3

Math

4

Art

Clay center

5

Science

Film strip on
tide pools

6

Choice

— Listening post

— Coloring

— Puzzles

Primary written directions

Dear _____

Here is what you should do today.

Intermediate and upper reading

Directions

1. Go to library. Choose a book you would like to read.
2. Use the "rule of thumb" to see if the book is too hard.
3. Record this in your Reading Log:
   Title _____
   Author _____
4. Sign up for a conference with the teacher. When you are called for your conference, bring your Reading Log, your book, and any work you have completed.
5. As you read your book, or after you finish, do two of the following:
   Name the main characters and tell something about each of them.

Tell about the most exciting parts of the book.
Tell why you liked or disliked the book.
Tell how you felt as you read it.

Intermediate, upper, and secondary math

Name _____

Directions: Do the assignments shown on this sheet. When each is completed, bring it to the teacher for checking.

Date	Assignment	Percent correct

A few sample contract forms of the type commonly used in instructional programs are shown on pp. 156, 157, and 158.

High school English weekly contract

Name _____

My plans for the week beginning _____ are as follows:

Activity	Expected completion date	Preferred evaluation

Signed: _____
                      (student)

Signed: _____
                      (teacher)

Intermediate and upper weekly contract

Name _____

These are my work plans for the week beginning _____.
(Include those areas in which individualized work is done.)

Reading:

_____

Math:

_____

Language:

_____

Free choice:

_____

Signed: _____
(student)

Signed: _____
(teacher)

Intermediate and upper daily contract

Name _____   Teacher OK _____

Reading: Math:

I plan to use the   Notes:

_____ Library

_____ Tape recorder

_____ Filmstrip projector

_____ Record player

_____ Chalkboard

_____ Games

_____ Puzzles

_____ Reading center

_____ Math center

_____ Worksheets

_____ Reading or math kit

Instructing

Individualized programs depend on materials that "teach"—that provide information to students and help them know what to do and how to do it. Ideally, all materials should have high instructional value. The teacher is then freed to perform other tasks that materials can't do, such as interacting with the students.

Even the best individualized programs, however, don't reach this ideal state. Invariably, teachers find that students encounter difficulties, form misconceptions, or fail to understand procedures, so that direct teacher instruction becomes necessary. At that time the teacher must reassume a more traditional teaching role.

This role places the teacher in the position of providing direct verbal help to students. This help usually comes in one of these ways:

1. Specific suggestions about other resources, books, or media that will help students correct the difficulty
2. Leading questions that help students clear matters in their own minds
3. Expository teaching, where the teacher clarifies—explains—the matter that is causing the difficulty.

The third of these techniques—expository teaching—deserves attention here because it is so often called for in individualized instruction. Understand that the program itself draws students into other avenues of investigation, such as inquiry or problem solving. When students have difficulties with some part of one of these approaches, they seldom need more of the same from the teacher. What they need is direct help, quick and simple. They need someone to explain the matter to them so they can get on with their work.

Expository teaching does just that. It clarifies, makes plain, and comes directly to the point. When you use it, here's what you do:

1. You tell students the *what* of the matter, and if appropriate the *how* and the *why* as well.
2. You illustrate each what, how, and why with at least one example—concrete examples, if possible, that they can see, hear, or touch.
3. If a procedure is in question, demonstrate it, perhaps asking students to explain steps that are involved.
4. Give a practice example for students to perform that shows whether they have understood.

When you find it necessary to do this kind of teaching, remember one thing: Keep it short and directly to the point. Take just enough time to be sure the matter has been clarified in students' minds, then let them get back to their activities.

Materials

Instructional materials are the pièce de résistance of nonformal basic programs. They put muscle on the bone, meat in the broth, tiger in the tank. They determine, more than anything else, what students can do and what they will do. They attract. They stimulate. They direct. You can hardly overemphasize the role they play.

What do you look for in materials? What do you try to get? First and foremost, materials must teach, they must convey ideas and concepts. That much is essential. Beyond that, materials receive an extra plus for each of the following: color, interest, novelty, manipulability, diversity, and usability. They receive extra bits of credit if they are durable, storeable, and easy to assemble and display.

The possibilities are enormous when it comes to materials for individualized programs. If you put your mind to it and get help from your students, their parents, your local grocer and druggist and hardware dealer, and other teachers, and . . . and . . . , you will soon have more materials—good ones—than you ever dreamed possible.

These materials needn't cost you a fortune, either. A third grade teacher friend named Gina Morin has a fantastic collection of materials in her classroom. True, she does spend some of her own money to buy things for her room. But it's not as if she were spending it all on a sable rug for the reading circle or on a new set of *Britannica Junior*. She is (pardon me, Gina) a noble scavenger. She regularly makes the scene at those wonderful California flea markets called "swap meets." There she finds and buys such materials as complete sets of Audubon Nature Library books in mint condition, for pennies per book. A box of beautiful bits of abalone shell cost a dollar or so. Habitrails for her seven hamsters cost a small fraction of their retail store price. Coffee coasters with smiley faces cost a penny each at a local coffee shop. And so it goes, on and on. You would have to see it to believe it. Gina's kids always have fascinating things to do in that room.

Follow-up activities

Follow-up activities are those learning tasks students do after they have had initial basic instruction. They include tasks in practice, application, and problem solving. They include construction, art work, and projects of all sorts. They include games, contests, and puzzles—in short, all those activities we commonly call seatwork, enrichment, and extending activities.

Like instructional materials, the variety of follow-up activities is so immense, one hesitates to begin listing them. Nevertheless, we will look at a few examples of extending activities—those that take the student a bit beyond the initial instruction—and at a few examples of seatwork games, puzzles, and riddles.

Extending activities

First, here are a few kinds of things you can have students do in reading that will take them beyond the material read. Having read a book or story, the students are requested to do the following:

1. Read the first paragraphs of your book or story again. Try to find out:
   Where the story takes place
   When the story takes place
   What the problem situation seems to be
   Who the first characters are that are introduced
2. Make a list of the main characters in the story. Describe each of them with regard to:
   Appearance
   Personality
   Attitudes
3. Compare two of the characters in your story. How are they alike? How are they different?
4. Tell how these two characters helped or hurt each other in the story.
5. Choose your favorite character in the story. If you met that person, what kind of conversation do you think you would have? Write it out.
6. Choose a character from this story and one from another story you have read. Write a conversation between them.

Next, here is an activity worksheet in math, where students use beansticks to solve problems in subtraction:

Introduction: If you have 2 beansticks and 5 beans, and you take away 9 beans, how many beansticks and beans do you have left? Use your beansticks and beans and find the answer to this subtraction problem.

Now see if you can use your beansticks to find the answers to those problems:

25	27	24	24	26
− 8	− 9	− 4	− 5	− 9
22	22	42	42	52
− 8	−18	− 9	−19	−39
54	58	57	51	59
−13	−13	−44	−46	−19

When you finish, ask your teacher to look over the work. If you answer the problems correctly, you are ready for the next lesson in your arithmetic book.

The next example is a science observation data sheet that students fill out while doing observations.

Science observation data sheet

Name _____

DIRECTIONS: Go to the aquarium, terrarium, or specimen collection. Select an animal or plant to observe. Look at it carefully for several minutes. Then complete this data sheet.

Scientific drawing

Specimen identification

1. The specimen shown above is a(n) _____

2. This specimen is commonly found _____

_____

3. Three facts I know about the specimen:

   a. _____

   b. _____

   c. _____

4. Words I think best describe the appearance of this specimen:

_____

_____

Seatwork games, puzzles, and riddles

Games, puzzles, and riddles add cinnamon spice to the solid blandness of practice. They motivate to an astonishing degree, far beyond what we might expect. If you can find ways to make games of seatwork or add a touch of mystery, students will go at it eagerly and even seek it out as a preferred activity. Here are some examples. Be careful, or you will get caught up in them yourself.

MATH SECRET MESSAGE

Message: _____   _____   _____   _____   _____
         4-56-0   83-3-8   3-8-83-7-7-4   108-6-8-36-98-83-7   98-48

         _____   _____   _____   _____
         4-56-0   48-98-28-0-3-8   54-25-98-108   56-0-54.

Code:

A $= (9 \times 9) + 2$	_____	N $= 5 \times 7$	_____
B $= 8 \times 8$	_____	O $= 8 \times 7$	_____
C $= 4 \times 9$	_____	P $= 42 \div 7$	_____
D $= 90 \div 10$	_____	Q $= (14 \times 2) - 13$	_____
E $= 96 \div 12$	_____	R $= 39 \div 13$	_____
F $= 8 \times 6$	_____	S $= 12 \times 9$	_____
G $= (9 \times 3) + 1$	_____	T $= 9 \times 6$	_____
H $= 25$	_____	U $= 7 \times 0$	_____
I $= 14 \times 7$	_____	V $= 73 - 72$	_____
J $= 6 + 11$	_____	W $= 5 \times 2$	_____
K $= 32 \div 2$	_____	X $= 26 \div 13$	_____
L $= 28 \div 4$	_____	Y $= 36 \div 9$	_____
M $= 7 \times 6$	_____	Z $= 3 \times 7$	_____

CROSSNUMBER PUZZLE

Note: These crossnumber puzzles are easy to make.
Prepare *across* problems. Based on their answers, make up *down* problems that fit the answers.

a	b	c			d	e
f				g		
h			i			
		j				
k	l			m	n	
o			p			
q		r				

Across

a. 426 + 636 + 534 + 634
d. 10 + 9 + 25 + 17 + 28
f. 2222 − 1330
g. 113 + 225 + 210 + 89 + 218
h. 287 − 260
i. 5730 − 2810
j. 41 + 56 + 20 + 35 + 30 + 46
k. 2927 + 2142 + 1725 + 3084
m. 300 − 258
o. 61 + 147 + 186 + 420
p. 800 − 675
q. 13 + 16 + 63 − 20
r. 3012 − 1416

Down

a. 731 − 449
b. 919 − 624
c. 823 − 791
d. 130 + 86 + 42 + 194
e. 625 + 112 + 149 + 37 + 14 + 13
g. 187 + 264 + 219 + 228
i. 490 − 262
j. 4030 − 3744
k. 126 + 241 + 236 + 118 + 266
l. 1302 − 490
m. 35 + 71 + 92 + 60 + 98 + 73
n. 203 + 53
p. 696 − 681

Number magic

1. Write any three numerals so they decrease by one from left to right (example: 765). Reverse the number (example: 567). Subtract the smaller from the larger (example: 765 − 567 = 198). The answer will always be 198.
2. Write any numeral three times (example: 444). Add the three numerals (example: 4 + 4 + 4 = 12). Multiply by 37 (example: 12 × 37 = 444). The answer will always be the first three numerals you wrote.

Magic fifty

Trace the squares on a sheet of paper. Cut them out. Arrange them into a 4 × 4 square so that each row, vertical, horizontal, and diagonal, adds to 50. (Hint: the numbers 10, 11, 14, and 15 must go in the center.)

5	6	7	8
9	10	11	12
13	14	15	16
17	18	19	20

Target

There are several possibilities for this game. You can arrange them to suit yourself. Here is one possibility:

You must score exactly 100 points to win the dart game. How many darts must you use and which circles must they hit?

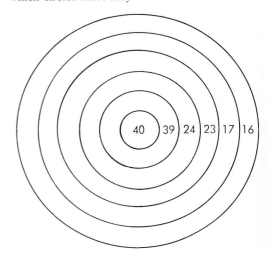

Number circles

Use the numbers 0 through 8. Place one number in each circle, so that the three numbers in each straight line add up to 12. (Do the same with the numbers 2 through 10 to equal 18, and the numbers 0, 2, 4, 5, 7, 9, 10, 12, and 14 to equal 21.)

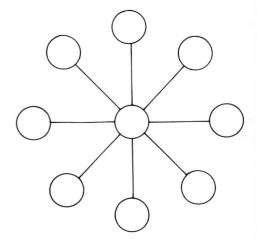

Count the squares

You know that squares are four-sided figures with all sides equal. See if you can find out the total number of squares in the figure shown.

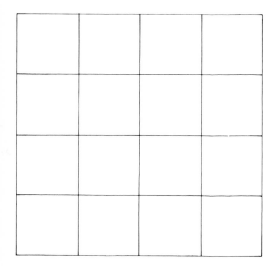

Math riddles

1. Suppose you went to bed at 8:00 at night. You set the alarm to wake you at 9:00 the next morning. How many hours sleep do you get?
2. If a doctor gave you 3 pills and told you to take one every 30 minutes, how long would it take you to use all three?
3. How many outs are there in one inning of baseball?
4. Suppose you have 20 sheep. All but 11 of them run away. How many do you have left?
5. Divide 40 by ½ and add 5. What is the answer?
6. You have 2 U.S. coins that total 55 cents. One of them is *not* a nickel. What are the two coins?

Dictionary game

Two teams compete. Each names a student to act as recorder. The teacher opens the dictionary at random, saying "I have opened the dictionary to a *pl* page." Each student team has 2 minutes to write all the words they can think of that begin with the letters pl.

Outer plains

Play individually or in teams. Teacher writes words on chalkboard that have many vowels and a few consonants, such as "outer plains" or "smoked bacon." Students see who can make the longest list of words in 5 minutes, using only the letters in those words.

Abbreviations

Make up a worksheet containing twenty words that have common abbreviations, such as pound, ounce, mister, doctor, street, Friday. Use timed or untimed sessions to see who can write the correct abbreviations for each word. Have students use the dictionary of abbreviations to make their own list of words.

• • •

We could go on almost indefinitely listing seatwork games, puzzles, and riddles. But the intent here was merely to illustrate. These examples should have given you many ideas for using such activities in your own nonformal basic programs.

Evaluation

Evaluation is the process of determining value or worth. We use it to decide whether a thing—an object, a product, a process, an attitude, or whatever—is good, adequate, or poor; worthwhile or not worthwhile; desirable or undesirable. It has, in essence, nothing to do with testing or measurement, although tests often furnish information used in evaluation. When you get to the heart of it, evaluation always involves one thing—making judgments about worth.

We make judgments about worth in both objective and subjective ways. Objective ways involve using evidence—evidence that is public—as the basis for judgments. They also use public criteria that show degrees of worth that everyone can understand. In objective evaluation of school work, then, we state criteria of worth that we weigh against samples of student work. This kind of evaluation plays a strong role in behavior-referenced instructional programs.

We also find it necessary to use evaluation that is subjective. Subjective evaluation uses evidence and criteria, too, but the evidence and criteria are not public. Such nonpublic evidence might include, for example, one's feelings about something. Feelings are very important, but they are essentially private. We can't really observe another's feelings. The criteria we use in judging are often—perhaps usually—private, as well. That is, we have not clarified them in our minds, nor have we stated them publicly. For example, we will often say that Susie is a good girl. We make that judgment because what Susie does matches up well against our hidden criteria of goodness. Other people might not think Susie so good, because they might hold different criteria of goodness.

Subjective evaluation plays an important role in experience-referenced programs. We strive to develop positive feelings and attitudes in our students, because such feelings so strongly influence their inclinations toward learning and their opinions of themselves and others. The only way we have for finding out what students feel is to ask them.

The kind of evaluation you use in your nonformal basic programs depends on your approach to teaching. If you believe in behavior-referenced instruction, you will use stated behavioral objectives and evaluation criteria. Then, as instruction progresses, you will obtain samples of student work that you will use as evidence on which to make judgments. If you believe in experience-referenced instruction, you will ask students to make subjective judgments about their classroom experiences—about whether the experiences were interesting, stimulating, valuable, efficient, and productive. You, too, will make judgments about the experiences you have provided, based on what you see students do during the instructional activi-

ties. And of course, if you combine behavior-referenced and experience-referenced approaches, you will use both types of evaluation.

We will not go into a detailed analysis of specific procedures used in objective and subjective evaluation. However, we should note the following:

Behavior-referenced evaluation (tends to be objective)

Begins with behaviorally stated objectives

Includes public criteria to be used in evaluation

Requires obtaining samples of student work, which are matched against objectives and criteria

The match-up between evidence, objectives, and criteria furnishes the basis for evaluative judgments.

Experience-referenced evaluation (tends to be subjective)

Begins with provision of quality learning experiences in which students engage

Calls on students to judge the experiences and, in particular, their reactions to them

Calls on teachers to judge the experiences based on their intentions and observed reactions of students

Final evaluative judgments are made in conferences between student and teacher, and they emphasize the personal meaning students have derived from the experiences.

Record keeping

As was the case with evaluation, record keeping also depends on the basic approach one takes toward instruction. If you are behavior oriented, you will want to keep records of behavioral objectives students have attempted, reached, and failed to reach. If you are experience oriented, you will want to keep records of experiences in which students have engaged, along with notations of outcomes and student reactions. Both approaches should incorporate conferences between student and teacher and should include samples of work produced by the students.

Whichever inclination you have—behavioral or experiential—you will want to keep a folder for each of your elementary students or an index file card for each of your secondary students. The purpose of keeping records in this way is to include as much written information on each student's work as you can conveniently process.

Elementary teachers can use file folders, kept in either a file cabinet or a cardboard box. Each student's folder can contain such items as copies of behavioral objectives, checksheets to show student progress, notes from individual conferences, and samples of student work.

Secondary teachers can use file folders, too, but sheer numbers make the process unwieldy. An index card system, in which student records are kept separated by class, can be used for keeping short written or coded records. So can spiral-bound notebooks, with a separate page for each student. The tradi-

CONFERENCE RECORD

Name _____

Date	Comments and notes

SCIENCE RECORD

Name _____ Topic _____

Date	Description	Drawing

DAILY WORK REPORT

					Very well	+	
Name _____				Code:	OK	0	
					Not so good	−	

	Mon	Tue	Wed	Th	Fri	Growth
1. I knew what I was supposed to do.	_____	_____	_____	_____	_____	_____
2. I got to work promptly.	_____	_____	_____	_____	_____	_____
3. I did not disturb others.	_____	_____	_____	_____	_____	_____
4. I finished my work on time.	_____	_____	_____	_____	_____	_____
5. How I feel about the quality of my work.	_____	_____	_____	_____	_____	_____

tional grade book is good for little, save recording scores and grades made on tests, projects, and various assignments. It offers no space for written comments from individual conferences regarding reactions, desires, and suggestions.

Ideally, each student should have a record folder. Inside the front cover, you can staple a checklist that students can use to chart their progress. This checklist can contain behavioral or experience objectives, or it can contain spaces to fill in names of books read, math processes mastered, and so forth.

Inside the back cover you can staple a conference record sheet, to be used for written comments from individual conferences. Such a record sheet might look like the one shown.

Inside the folder you can keep such things as contracts, test scores, samples of work, student self appraisals, and student kept record forms. An example of a form students can use to keep records is shown.

An example of a self appraisal form students can keep is shown.

ANNOTATED BIBLIOGRAPHY FOR SECONDARY CLASSROOMS

Most of the examples and illustrations we have considered suit elementary classrooms better than secondary. That may lead you to believe that nonformal basic programs can't be used at the secondary level. Such is not the case. Although much more individualized instruction has occurred at the elementary than at the secondary level, secondary teachers are increasingly finding ways to better adapt instruction to the needs and interests of their students.

To illustrate, this final section presents brief resumes of several recent articles describing individualized secondary instruction. The articles deal with four areas: general ideas, English, foreign language, and math and science.

Howard, E. R.: Developing sequential learning materials, *National Association of Secondary School Principals Bulletin* **54**:159-168, May 1970.

> The author suggests arranging the secondary classroom to create the following kinds of space:
> 1. Seminar area for discussions
> 2. Small project area
> 3. Individual study space
> 4. Informal reading space
> 5. Viewing-listening corner
> 6. Space for storage and dispensing of materials

Rinkel, M. E.: Multiplying the image; or a kaleidoscopic view of individualization (a working model for a busy teacher), *English Journal* **64**: 32-39, November 1975.

The author describes sixteen personalized strategies that proved effective in her high school English classes. Examples include:

Problem solving—using brainstorming, forced relationships, and group consensus

Role playing—for creative dramatics, sociodrama, pantomime

Tutoring—by selected student tutors

Individualized reading—student selected, using guidelines

Class projects—such as graffiti walls and word mobiles

Journal writing—used daily with or without specific directions

Independent study—students pick areas of study in accord with their own special interests

Learning activity packets—carefully developed sets of instructions and materials that allow students to work at their own pace

Shuman, R. Baird: English instruction can be individualized, *Peabody Journal of Education* **69**:307-313, July 1972.

The author acknowledges the difficulty of spending very much time each day person-to-person with some hundred plus students in English. He suggests substituting free student-to-student contact, with the class serving as a forum where student work is discussed by other students. Much free writing would be encouraged—not assigned themes or essays—but writing about things important to students in any form they want to try. The teacher would write along with students and share efforts equally.

Danielson, E. R., and others: The cassette tape: An aid to individualizing high school English, *English Journal* **62**:441-445, March 1973.

This article deals with building a cassette tape library and using it in the English program. The teacher introduces the topic, such as Hemingway, then directs students to the tapes, which serve as study guides and enrichment. The tapes are also used in many other ways:

As basis and beginning for student-led seminars

As guide to independent study

As inspiration for study and writing

To make evaluative comments on student papers. This saves much teacher writing and adds a personal touch.

Hawley, Robert C., and Hawley, Isabel L.: Scissors, glue, and English, too, *The Independent School Bulletin* **33**:41-43, October 1973.

The authors describe cut and glue activities for English classes that supplant the usual teacher-dominated style. They suggest using old magazines for making such things as:

Collages of words and pictures that represent ideas such as "your real self"

Poems made by cutting out and gluing together words, phrases, and sentences that are particularly interesting

"Self in five years" collages

Literature collages

Faces and captions

Story collages

The authors point out that these activities go far beyond the mere fun and games category. They stress organization and use of metaphor, connotation, imagery, balance, harmony, juxtaposition, phrasing, and grammar. They also help foster good self images.

Reimart, Harry: Practical guide to individualization, *Modern Language Journal* **55**:156-163, March 1971

This article tells how to arrange and manage individualized instruction in foreign language.

The class is divided into groups and placed in different areas of the room. One area is reserved for the tape recorder.

Activities and materials are arranged into packets, with written instructions. Students complete them and, when prepared, take quiz.

The teacher does nothing that can be handled by machines or the students themselves. This frees the teacher for conversation, clarification, and remedial work.

Some activities involve the entire class—songs, guests, films.

Fisher, Mary-Margaret: The nuts and bolts of individualization: Classroom management, *Modern Language Journal* **57**:179-185, Spring 1973.

The author details her experience in individualizing high school Spanish classes. She used instructional packets, containing all necessary materials and instructions. General announcements were made at the beginning of each class. Otherwise, students worked on their own. Records were kept of student progress, and periodic evaluation was made, based on student performance in class and mastery of materials.

Marusek, J.: A program providing highly individualized instruction for slow learning math and science students, *Science Education* **53**:217-219, April 1969.

The teacher sat in the middle of the classroom at a large table so he could readily help students. Study assignments were placed on a magazine rack. The room contained resource materials to accompany different study topics. Students completed assignments and turned them in at different times. The teacher looked over them at once, to give immediate feedback. Unacceptable work had to be redone. A progress chart was kept for each student.

Denton, Jon: Individualized chem-study, *School and Community* **56**:37, November 1969.

Each student received a guide consisting of course outline, contract grading system, and programmed materials for each chapter in the textbook. The class was divided into cells consisting of two or three students each. Each cell progressed at its own rate. Students were required to do homework, take tests, do lab reports, and do extra projects. A progress schedule listed the number of chapters completed during each evaluation period. Each student had to complete assignments before a grade card could be issued.

Kline, A. A.: Individualizing chemistry—A method used in an open high school, *Science Teacher* **39**:61-62, March 1972.

Students set their own goals with the help of the teacher. Class attendance is optional. There are no grades. The work is based on 15-minute modules, with a new schedule prepared daily. Some classes are teacher directed and are so designated. There are "concept days," "problem days," and "question days." The laboratory is open daily from 8:00 to 3:30. Students schedule their own use of the lab. They are given 60 investigations but are encouraged to do only those of particular interest. The teacher is always available as a resource. Student and teacher prepare joint written evaluation of each student's progress toward his own goals.

12

Learning centers

SERENDIPITY

Ser en dip' i ty: the faculty for making desirable discoveries by accident (Random House Dictionary).

Recently I taught a course called Classroom Management. Students in the course were first-semester beginners in elementary teacher education. They all had assignments in public school classrooms, where they worked for two hours each day, partly as teacher aides and partly as student teachers.

To help them get quickly into the swing of teaching, I decided to have each of them make a learning center, set it up in their classroom, and use it to instruct children. I had never done that before, but it turned out to be one of the smartest (well, OK—luckiest) assignments I ever made.

Making and using the learning centers did several remarkable things for my students:

1. It caused them to think of themselves as real teachers of real students.

2. It required them to take the initiative (and the responsibility) for conceptualizing and carrying out a significant instructional plan.

3. It caused them to think through carefully the outcomes they hoped to achieve with their students and ways they could de-termine whether the outcomes were reached.

4. It caused them to consider in detail the instructional value of the materials they included in their centers.

5. It caused them to organize those devilish management details, such as scheduling, conferencing, assessing performance, and keeping records. Much of this they learned by trial and error.

6. It caused them to take special note of students' reactions to activities and materials and to difficulties encountered with them.

7. It gave them status in the students' eyes, because the centers were something important, which belonged to the student teacher.

8. It gave them status in the teachers' eyes, because very few of their cooperating teachers had ever made or used learning centers.

9. It gave them status in other professionals' eyes. Literally hundreds of people—teachers, student teachers, school administrators, college professors, and occasional passersby from off the street—have seen those centers or photographs of them.

10. It *didn't* give them swelled heads—at least not noticeably so—because they all rec-

ognized that their centers had defects and limitations. For instance, they would have liked the centers to be more instructive, more individualized, more compelling, and easier to manage. They would have liked for more students to be able to use them at a given time. They wished the centers were easier to move, to store, and to keep. They wished they wouldn't get messed up so easily, that materials wouldn't ruin or disappear. Still, I believe that most of the students would say that making and using the learning centers was one of the most important things they did in their early training period.

CHAPTER FORMAT

I have tried to present this chapter in the form of a learning center, insofar as a learning center can be presented on printed pages. If the people at The C. V. Mosby Company (publisher of this book) were properly inventive, they would make pop-up pages, so that when the book were opened to this chapter, a miniature learning center would leap to three-dimensional life before your eyes. Oh well, I guess we have to live with our limitations. We will try to do the next best thing.

Fig. 5 is a photograph of a learning center.

Fig. 5. Learning center.

It is a learning center on "How to Make and Use Learning Centers." If you examine it carefully, you will see such components as directions, objectives, task cards, books, reports, informative papers, projector and slides, photographs, record keeping devices, scheduling device, storage boxes, and the portable container inside which everything fits.

Below you see a diagram of the same center, with numbered parts. Each of these parts is described and its function explained on the pages that follow. By the time you have gone through these pages, you will have gained the knowledge and skills necessary to make and use learning centers of your own.

COMPONENTS

This section names and describes the uses of various parts of this learning center. The component numbers correspond to numbers on the learning center diagram below.

1. Introduction. An introduction is a helpful, though not necessary, part of a learning center. Usually, it simply tells what can be done in the center. The introduction to this center is as follows:

In this center you can learn:
1. What learning centers are
2. What learning centers can do
3. Necessary components of a learning center
4. How to make learning centers
5. How to manage learning centers

2. Specific objectives. You can see that this learning center on learning centers is behavior oriented. That is, it is designed to enable you to reach specific, behaviorally stated objectives.

Learning centers don't have to use specific objectives. They can just as easily be experience referenced, if you prefer, providing a group of high quality experiences whose outcomes may be greatly diverse. Or, as is somewhat the case with this center, you may use a few behavioral objectives interwoven with a number of activities thought to be worthwhile for students.

The specific objectives included in this center are: After completing the activities in this center, students will be able to:

1. Explain what "learning center" means
2. List five instructional advantages of learning centers
3. List six desirable components of learning centers
4. List five essential points in managing learning centers
5. Make, set up, and successfully manage a classroom learning center

3. Directions for using this center. Clear, concise directions for using learning centers are indispensible. If students can read, directions should be written and posted in a conspicuous place. If students can't read, make a drawing that will remind them of each step. Then take them on repeated walk throughs of activities until they have sequence and procedures well in mind.

Directions for using this center are:

1. Observe the center. Note its parts and arrangements.
2. Complete the activities outlined on the task cards.
3. Work individually or in groups no larger than four.
4. Keep the center neat and orderly.
5. Record your progress on the record sheet.

4. Reminders. Depending on the topic, learning centers may need to include reminders to help students keep different possibilities in mind. This is especially true for experience-referenced or more open-ended types of learning centers, in which numerous kinds of activities are possible.

This learning center uses a reminder display to help students become aware of desirable features of learning centers. As you can see, the reminder display contains drawings and cut-outs, along with the words. A learning center should have color, things to look at, things to do, things to make, challenge, pictures, resource materials, variety, games, charts, puzzles, pictures, models, diagrams.

5. Slide viewing area. Learning centers can be made much more effective by incorporating auditory and visual media. This center contains a slide projector and three dozen slides on various kinds of centers and their components. A script accompanies the slides, describing each and drawing attention to specifics. Students quickly learn to operate the projector and care for the equipment properly.

6. Photographs. Photographs, diagrams, and models attract attention and have high instructional value. This learning center has several color photos, some mounted on the backdrop and some included in odds and ends component 14. They illustrate various kinds of centers and show students at work in them. The photographs in this center show learning centers on math, science, handwriting, and art.

7. Resource books. Resource materials add much to the quality of learning centers. These materials should be such that students can use them quickly and easily. It helps to mark pages for handy reference or include book markers with page numbers written on them.

The resource books included here have to do with learning centers and activities appropriate for them. Several good books on learning center construction and use are available. The six included here are well worth examining:

1. Godfrey, Lorraine L.: *Individualizing Through Learning Stations*, Menlo Park, California, 1972, Individualized Books Publishing Co.
2. Gurske, Barbara, and Cote, Bernard T.: *Learning Center Guide*, Sunnyvale, California, 1972, CTM.
3. Kaplan, Sandra, and others: *Change For Children: Ideas and Activities for Individualizing Learning*, Pacific Palisades, California, 1973, Goodyear Publishing Co.
4. King, Pat H.: *Individualized Instruction: 50 Games That Teach*, Encino, California, 1971, International Center for Educational Development.
5. Point associates (Charles, C., ed.): *Learning Centers That Teach*, Washington, D.C., 1977, University Press of America.
6. Voight, Ralph C.: *Invitation To Learning 2: Center Teaching with Instructional Depth*, Washington, 1974, Acropolis Books, Ltd.

8. Student reports. One of the most interesting and helpful things you can include in a learning center is a sampling of work done by previous students. Student work seems to have a very good effect on other students. It gives them a feeling of confidence, it shows them examples of well done work, and it stimulates them to produce something a little better than what they see in the sample.

This learning center contains reports made by college students who built and used learning centers in student teaching. The reports detail learning centers in math, science, and puppetry and describe the results of using the centers. These three reports are included on pp. 181 to 193 of this chapter.

9. Informative papers. Sometimes you can't find short, concise material that explains a particular topic, concept, or activity you want to include in your learning center. When that happens, you may want to prepare and duplicate such papers yourself. That's what I

did for this learning center. I prepared three brief informative papers entitled:

Paper 1. "Learning Center Overview"
Paper 2. "How to Make a Learning Center"
Paper 3. "Managing Learning Centers"

These papers are included on pp. 178 to 181 of this chapter.

10. Scheduling device. Most learning centers can accommodate only a few students at a time. Therefore, you must devise a way of scheduling students into the center or into various centers if you have more than one. Common ways of scheduling include:

1. *Teacher assignments.* Students are scheduled into the center by the teacher on the basis of need.
2. *Self selection.* Students schedule themselves into the center during free times. A pocket chart with students' names on strips of paper serves well, or students can write their names on the chalkboard.
3. *Contracts.* Students arrange activities and times with the teacher using written "contracts."
4. *Rotation.* This way of scheduling uses a paper wheel that turns against a fixed background, showing which group is allowed to work in the center at a given time. That type of device was used in this learning center. You can see how it works in the photograph.

11. Record keeping device. You probably won't enjoy keeping records, but the importance of doing so can hardly be overstressed. They supply a permanent record of who did what, along with indications of success, failure, difficulties, and pleasures. For students, they chart a trail of accomplishment—tangible proof of progress and success. For parents, they show at a glance what a son or daughter has done and become able to do.

The record keeping device used in this center is a master checksheet. Students' names are recorded down the left-hand side. Across the top are columns for each of the seven task card activities (to be explained presently) and for each of the six behavioral objectives listed for the center. As students complete each of them, checkmarks are placed in the appropriate places.

12. **Task cards.** Assigned work in learning centers can be made in a variety of ways. One of the most convenient ways is to write required assignments on task cards, which are kept in the center. Students can select task cards, read the directions, and complete the activities assigned.

This learning center uses seven task cards. They are presented here:

Task card 1

1. Examine the learning center. Notice the parts it contains and how they are arranged.
2. Take a sheet of paper. Diagram and explain at least one change in the center that you think would improve it—that is, make it more attractive, more usable, more interesting, or whatever. You may do this work individually or in a group.
3. When you have finished this work, place your paper in the starred box on the table. Then put a check on the record sheet for task card 1.

Task card 2

1. From the green box get a copy of Paper 1, "Learning Center Overview."
2. Read the paper. Quietly discuss the following points with another student, until you both think they are clear:
   a. Meaning of "learning center"
   b. Instructional advantages of learning centers
   c. Characteristics of learning centers
   d. Components of learning centers
3. When you have finished, return Paper 1 to the green box. Check the record sheet for task card 2.

Task card 3

1. Use the slide projector to view random slides of learning centers. The typescript in the blue cover explains each slide.
2. Look carefully at the photographs mounted on the backdrop.
3. If you have questions about them, ask the instructor.

4. When finished, check the record for task card 3.

Task card 4

1. On the table you will find several books on learning centers. Scan through them. They can be purchased in college bookstores.
2. When you have finished, check the record sheet for task card 4.

Task card 5

1. Go to the red box and get a copy of Paper 2, "How to Make Learning Centers."
2. Read the paper. Discuss it quietly with another student if you wish. You may keep the paper.
3. When you have finished reading it, check the record sheet for task card 5.

Task card 6

1. Go to the orange box and get a copy of Paper 3, "Managing Learning Centers."
2. Read the paper. Discuss it quietly with another student if you wish. You may keep the paper.
3. When you have finished reading it, check the record sheet for task card 6.

Task card 7

1. Look in the Learning Center Report Box. There you will find some reports on learning centers that college students have prepared.
2. Examine one or more of the reports.
3. When you have finished, return the reports to the box. Check the record sheet for task card 7.

13. **Receptacle for student work.** When students complete worksheets and other materials, they should have a designated place in the center to put them. Some teachers use in-baskets and out-baskets. I used four coded boxes in this center. The red, green, and orange boxes hold informative papers for students to use. The starred box is used as a receptacle for completed student work.

14. **Odds and ends.** This learning center contains one large sheet of green tagboard with ideas, suggestions, and pointers on it. I call it an odds and ends component. It shows clear and opaque contact paper for covering boxes and protecting materials such as task cards. It

has some sample task cards from other centers, ideas about color schemes that make centers more attractive, and additional photographs of learning centers used in classrooms by student teachers.

INFORMATIVE PAPERS

The following three papers, "Learning Center Overview," "How to Make a Learning Center," and "Managing Learning Centers," were included in this learning center for students to read.

Paper 1. Learning center overview
Meaning of learning center

The name learning center worries some people at first. They fear it stands for something new, mysterious, and esoteric. It doesn't. Learning centers are refinements and improvements of the familiar interest centers, science corners, book nooks, project areas, and other approaches that teachers have used for years.

The refinements are very important, though. Learning centers emphasize instruction and learning, not pastimes or busy work or hobbies. They expand teachers' effectiveness in many ways. For example, they help students instruct themselves, they bring together and coordinate materials for quality instructional activities, and they allow students to schedule much of their own work.

Learning centers are compactly arranged sets of materials and directions that fit easily into different areas of the classroom. Corners serve as good locations for learning centers because they furnish extra wall space. Other favored locations include areas near shelves, bookcases, cabinet tops, and bulletin boards. Almost any center needs places for storing materials, completing activities, and displaying completed work.

Instructional advantages

Learning centers enhance instruction in several ways. Some of these include:

1. They bring materials and activities together into a compact, highly organized cluster.
2. They encourage students to take initiative in scheduling, beginning, and completing learning activities.
3. They lend themselves to multimedia use in learning.
4. They can provide basic instruction, application activities, and enrichment activities.
5. They provide a balanced combination of structure and student freedom.
6. They can be organized around a large variety of topics.

Component parts

Component parts of learning centers vary according to the type of center, the topic, and the teachers' philosophy about learning and teaching. Most centers, however, require at least these basic components:

1. Objectives. Few teachers like to go to the trouble of making explicit statements of their instructional intents. Yet, objectives always affect instruction in two ways. First, they give direction to the selection and sequence of experiences thought desirable for learners. Second, they come into play in evaluation, since they are the criteria against which student performance is judged.

Thus, implicit objectives, which lie fuzzily in the back of the mind, should be made explicit and clear. When clarified, they can assume two different forms. One form is what we call behavioral statements—they tell what we intend that learners become able to do. Another form is what we call experience statements—they describe in detail the experiences we make available to students.

When you put together a learning center, you should write out either behavioral objectives or experience objectives. Make them so clear that anyone who can read them will understand what they mean.

2. Directions. Students should know quickly, easily, and clearly, the following things about the learning center:

a. What they can do
b. What you expect them to do
c. How they should proceed
d. How and where they obtain materials
e. What they do with completed work
f. How they participate in evaluation

3. **Task cards.** Task cards provide necessary instructions for students on how to carry out various learning activities.

4. **Samples and models.** It helps to include samples of work other students have done. These samples, which serve as models, encourage productive work and provide examples of possibilities. If you include examples, you should stress that they represent individual instances of good work and that students should try to do something a bit different or better.

5. **Media.** Multimedia give learning centers special value and appeal. When possible, media include quantities of objects to manipulate, pictures, resource materials, projectors and recorders, and materials for games, construction, and creative activities.

6. **Scheduling devices.** Scheduling of students into learning centers can be managed easily by preparing a device that shows which students are to be working in the center at a particular time. You can find examples of several devices such as wheels, pocket charts, and clothespin boards in the books on learning centers.

7. **Record keeping devices.** One difficulty in using learning centers is keeping track of what students have attempted and completed. You can avoid this difficulty by preparing a master checksheet that shows names, activities, and objectives. Use your own code marks to show which activities were started and which were completed at a satisfactory level.

Evaluation

If you use experience types of objectives, you and the students make judgments about the learning activities themselves—about their appeal, their difficulty, their value, and needed modifications.

If you use behavior types of objectives, you look to see whether students can perform the acts specified in the objectives. You can do this by observing students at work, analyzing their completed products, or giving them tests.

Regular conferences should be held with individual students, and annotated records of those conferences should be kept. These records can be kept in student folders, along with samples of student work.

Paper 2. How to make a learning center

All learning centers, regardless of topic or age level, have certain elements in common. If you decide to make a learning center, follow the steps outlined here. Doing so will ensure that you include the necessary basics.

Step 1 : Select topic

When you select your topic or subject area, keep in mind that the topic must be one that can be effectively handled in a learning center.

Step 2: Specify objectives

Specify objectives, either experience or behavioral, that clarify the activities, skills, and concepts you want to stress in the center.

Step 3 : Identify experiences

Based on your objectives, spell out activities for the center. Include a variety of activities attuned to different levels of student ability.

Step 4: Collect materials

Obtain and organize materials needed for the activities. Use inexpensive items. Old discarded furniture, cupboards, and cement block shelves, make fine storage areas. Coffee cans with plastic lids, shoe boxes, egg cartons, wood and fabric scraps, and other such odds and ends are invaluable. You don't have to spend a lot of money to make a rich learning center.

Step 5: Prepare activities

As you prepare activities for your center try to include such things as:

Clearly written directions, placed on or near each activity

Eye catchers—decorations such as pictures, charts, funny faces, lettering, cartoons, graphs, models, and so on

Task cards (if used) placed in an area made specifically for them, so they won't get lost in the shuffle

All worksheets, student record charts, folders, samples, completed work, and resource materials

If you make your center colorful and attractive enough, you will have no trouble getting students to use it.

Step 6: Make schedules

Be sure you have a method for scheduling students into the center. For example, you might use a pocket chart that shows who should be using the center at what time. You can find such methods in *Change For Children*[1] by Kaplan and others, available in college book stores.

Step 7: Prepare records

Prepare record forms that show who has used the center and what the results have been. These forms should be quick and easy to use, but accurate. Several such forms can be found in *Change For Children*.

Paper 3. Managing learning centers

This paper outlines details you must give attention to if you want your learning center to be used efficiently and effectively.

Introducing the center

The way you introduce the learning center sets its tone for several days. Be enthusiastic about it. Act as though you consider it something special. Be thoroughly prepared to explain every aspect. Give special attention to:

1. What we can do in the center
2. How we do each activity
3. Where we keep the materials
4. How we take the materials out, use them, and replace them
5. Where we put finished work
6. How we keep records

You will also need to discuss scheduling, responsibilities, and rules of behavior for working in the center.

Scheduling

After you have introduced the center and students have had an opportunity to walk through it, you are ready to schedule work periods in it. Basically, you need to devise a way to show who is to work in the center at specified times. Teachers usually allow students to choose to work in the center during free times. They also assign students to the center as needed. It helps if you provide a schedule that everyone can see. You might want to make scheduling devices such as circular charts, pocket charts, clothespin boards, contracts, simple chalkboard notes, or even "postcards" from you to students.

Sometimes you will probably want students to work individually in the center. At other times they can work in groups. The schedule should provide equal and ample time for all students.

Materials

To begin, you will need to bring together most of the instructional materials. As students get acclimated to the center, they will be able to add activities and materials of their own.

---

[1]Kaplan, S., and others: Change for children: Ideas and activities for individualizing learning, Pacific Palisades, California, 1973, Goodyear Publishing Co. Inc.

Students should clearly understand the following things about materials:

1. Where materials are stored and how to get them
2. How to use the materials and where to use them
3. What to do with materials when finished
4. How to care for the materials

Instructing

Despite your best planning, students will occasionally encounter difficulties with instructional activities. You must be ready to instruct them as needed, either in the center or elsewhere. Try to work in the center with students as much as you can.

Monitoring

Especially in the early stages of using the center, you will need to keep careful watch over what goes on there. Position the center so you can see it as you move about the room, work at your desk, or work with groups of students.

Assessing performance

You will want to know several things about students' work and progress in the center.

1. Which activities they complete
2. How well they perform the learning tasks
3. What skills and information they acquire
4. How willing and eager they are to use the center
5. Which activities are most popular and which seem to teach most

You obtain this information by observing students at work, noting their interest in going to the center, examining work they have completed, conferencing with them informally, and occasionally if you wish by testing them over the content of the center.

Record keeping

Try your best to keep accurate records of what has transpired in the center.

Checksheets can be used to keep track of who does what—who begins activities, who completes them, and who reaches various objectives.

Completed work can be examined and analyzed.

Conferences can (and should) be held periodically to find out what students especially like and dislike about the center and what they think they have learned.

Tests can be used, if you think them desirable, to determine acquisition of knowledge or skills.

Folders should be kept for each student to hold samples of work and notes from individual conferences.

DESCRIPTIONS OF THREE LEARNING CENTERS

The following pages describe three learning centers that were made by teachers and used in their classrooms. Although they were developed for certain grade levels, you can readily see that they could be adapted to a range of different grades. The sixth grade center on electricity could even be used in junior or senior high school.

Example 1. Primary learning center on puppetry[2]

This learning center on puppetry was planned and used in a kindergarten–first grade classroom. It represents a type of combination strategy, using both behavioral and experience objectives.

Objectives

Objectives were established for the following instructional emphases: attitude/value development, skill development, knowledge acquisition, knowledge application, aesthetic

---

[2] Based on materials planned and submitted by Juanita Bergey and Marilyn Evenson, Crockett School, San Diego, California.

OBJECTIVES	ACTIVITIES	MATERIALS
1. Manipulate puppets	Practice with puppets to show actions, emotions	Puppets
2. Self expression through role playing	Short play	Puppets, stage, scenery
3. Retell story in sequence	Hear story on tape; retell using puppets	Tape recorded story
4. Anticipate outcomes	Give play; audience guesses ending	Taped story without ending
5. Compose own endings	Hear story without ending; compose ending for story	Taped story without ending
6. Discuss ideas in story	Discussion involving players and audience	Puppets and stage
7. Identify feelings	Show feelings through puppets' actions	Puppets and stage
8. Create puppets	Use materials to make various kinds of puppets	Socks, velcron eyes, etc.
9. Demonstrate art of puppetry	Manipulate puppets to show mood, emotion, action	Puppets
10. Create stage scenery	Make scenery for selected play	Paper, crayons, cloth, as needed

experience, and creative production. Activities and materials appropriate to those objectives are presented above.

Room arrangement

Fig. 6 shows one corner of the classroom where the puppet center will be located.

Materials

The following materials will be needed for carrying out the activities planned for the puppet center.

1. Puppet stage (teacher furnishes)
2. Stage scenery (children make)
3. Puppets. A few should be ready made. Children make others, using socks of different colors and bags with different types of eyes, mouths, noses, wigs, moustaches, and hats.
4. Table on which to place the stage
5. Chairs for the audience
6. Bookcase for holding materials
7. Listening post with tape recorder and tapes of stories such as "Chicken Little," "Little Red Riding Hood," and "Jack and the Beanstalk"
8. Story sequence cards
9. Seatwork papers

Materials storage and retrieval

Materials are stored on the bookcase. Students obtain their own materials there and return them to the bookcase when finished. The stage folds. Scenery slides into holders on each side of the stage.

Scheduling and assignments

1. All students will use the learning center on a rotating basis.
2. Children will be divided into groups of four. Two will give the play while the other two act as an audience.
3. Graph sign-in paper must be kept so each child has an equal chance to use the center.

Sequence of activities

1. Children listen to tape of story.
2. Children put sequence cards of story in order.
3. Teacher chooses children to give play.

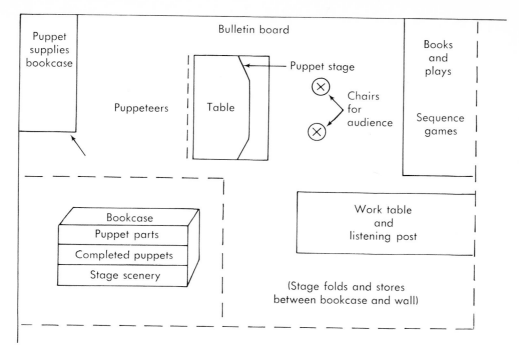

Fig. 6. One corner of the classroom.

4. Children decide which puppets to use.
5. Children put up stage with proper scenery.
6. Children present play.
7. Audience and puppeteers trade places.

Tutoring/instructing

1. Teacher shows children how to make puppets.
2. Teacher shows children how to manipulate puppets.
3. Teacher shows children how to make scenery.
4. When children are just beginning to work on a play, the teacher should check to be sure children understand story and check sequence work.

Assessing student performance

When a group presents its play to the entire class, observe the performance to check on the following:

1. Did the students use the right puppets to represent the characters?
2. Did they present the story in sequence?

3. Did they manipulate the puppets properly to show actions and emotions?
4. How do they seem to feel about their performance?

Progress report on results of puppet center

(The following report was presented approximately one week after the puppet learning center was initiated in the classroom.)

We have just begun setting up the puppetry learning center in our classroom. To get things going, I brought a stage and puppets for the children to use. Meanwhile, the children are beginning to make their own puppets and scenery, and I am getting our own puppet stage ready for the room.

Using the borrowed stage and puppets, I discussed the learning center with the children. They were eager and everyone wanted "first turn." We decided everyone will have a turn on a rotated basis. We also decided that each child must keep his own progress record.

We began in this way: I chose a simple story—"Little Duck Takes a Walk"—and read it aloud to the class. I showed pictures as I read the story. We discussed the characters and how Little Duck couldn't get any friends to take a walk with him. At last he finds a little old man who had the time and interest to walk with him.

I had a "funny bird" puppet. We discussed the fact that the play was fictional and we had to use our imaginations. The children were quick to accept the "funny bird" as a duck. I played the duck, and different children were chosen to be the other characters. We talked through the play, and we had our problems. For example, the first child agreed to go for a walk with the duck. We had to stop and remember that the story didn't go like that and what we wanted to do was follow the story. To do that, the children would have to remember the play and follow it.

Sure enough, the next child forgot the reason for not going on a walk with the duck. We decided that any reason was all right as long as it did not spoil the plot and sequence. Then we talked about making up lines if they couldn't remember the exact words. That turned out well, since exact words were not too important in the story.

Then I showed them the other puppets I had. I had an old man puppet, but the rest were wrong for their parts. That was no problem. The children were quick to see how a butterfly puppet could be a bird, a mouse puppet could be a squirrel, and a frog puppet could be a rabbit. Some children suggested we add more puppets and make the play longer. We did, making the play longer but leaving the plot about the same.

Then I chose children to be the puppeteers, and they went to a practice area. I placed the stage in the reading circle, which was the only area large enough for the rest of the class to be an audience.

As the puppeteers presented the first play, they all wanted to be on stage at the same time, but their voices were so quiet, they could hardly be heard. Nonetheless, the audience enjoyed the presentation immensely.

Following the play, we had a discussion about it. We discussed why characters had to take turns to keep the sequence in order. We also agreed that soft voices were nice because they wouldn't disturb the rest of the class when the center was being used later on. We decided if children did a really good play, they could tape record it, and they could also invite children from other rooms to come see it.

The next day a group was allowed to use the center on their own. They listened to a tape of the story at the listening post and put picture cards of the story in order. This helped them review the story. They decided who would be the different characters. They were instructed to mark the graph if they completed the play and the audience enjoyed it. I told them that if they didn't finish the play, they could work on it more the next day.

The first few days have gone very well. Fortunately I have a volunteer parent to work in the center and keep things running smoothly. The more mature children have found the plays easier to perform. Some children have suggested their own plays. The children are also choosing to use the center during free time before school starts.

Example 2. Third-fourth grade math center[3]

To put it bluntly, my third and fourth graders hated math. Their attitude was that math wasn't fun and never could be. They struggled along with it, all right, but their faces showed only two emotions—boredom and frustration. When I decided to develop a

---

[3] Based on materials arranged and submitted by Sharon Cherry, Crest School, El Cajon, California.

math learning center, my first aim was to break that mold. I wanted to create something that would let students learn and enjoy themselves at the same time.

I knew that to appeal to all students I would have to include a range of activities. I knew I would have to present the math center as a "fun thing." I knew I would have to eliminate the scary feelings associated with math. I thought it might help to call the center the "Math Shop" and let it belong to the class instead of me.

To spark interest among the students, I decided to make the shop look as inviting as possible. At the same time I decided it should be more or less all in one piece, ready to use. I decided to make it appear overnight. On Friday the students left the auditorium (our classroom). When they returned on Monday, the first thing they saw was the Math Shop—something new, bright, colorful, different, and inviting. The students' reactions fulfilled all my hopes. I could hardly keep them away from the center.

Before I opened the shop for business (ahem—classroom shop talk), I took small groups through orientation tours. During this time I explained each activity and went over rules and directions. They asked several questions, and I let them try one of the activities. After students had the tour, they placed their names on the progress ladder.

We started by letting groups work in the shop for equal amounts of time during the week. We found better ways, though, as time passed. Now I may assign a different group each day and let others use the shop during their free time. Sometimes they can use it instead of worksheets. Some students go there every day to reinforce skills in which they are particularly weak.

The shop is set up so students can direct themselves. They can choose activities with the idea that the more they do, the higher they climb on the progress ladder. Any activity may be repeated. Some activities are drill types and do not necessarily require checking. Other activities have to be shown to me, or I check the students during work to see if they have understood the activity. A few students sometimes help me check completed work. When a student completes everything in the shop (which is not easy), he may add an activity if he wishes. I check out students who think they have learned everything in the Math Shop by assigning worksheets and games and then conferencing with them. This procedure works well.

I keep accurate records of the work that has been completed, and I keep notes concerning additional work or conferences that might be necessary. I use a notebook with pocket pages. That way I can store papers for discussions with students, along with quiz sheets and other materials of this sort. To be sure that I conference with each student, I use a chart with each child's name and a series of squares. The squares are marked so I know at a glance with which students I am to talk. A student who wants to talk with me about problems in the shop can make an appointment by singing his name on a card kept inside a little book. This is called the "Can I Talk To You?" book. It has been very helpful, and students seem to like the idea of making appointments.

I have been quite pleased with the results of the math shop. It has added greatly to the math program. It is especially helpful when a student becomes frustrated with an assignment he does not understand. Most importantly though, the center has reached my main objective. The students can work in the shop, learn new skills and concepts, and still enjoy what they are doing. They are learning through pleasurable and successful experiences.

You might be interested in seeing a few comments from students concerning their feelings about the Math Shop:

"I like dynamite shack. I also like the games cards."

"What I like is learning about fun stuff to do."
"When I finish work I can go to the shop."
"Over the ranebow game is fun."
"I like the work sheets."
"The dynamite shak is the roof that comes off and the cards go all on the grod."

Activities

Here is a list of the activities available for students in the Math Shop. I printed them on a reinforced sheet of red tagboard, around a center display of traffic signs: yield, dead end, one way, detour, stop, railroad crossing, speed limit, traffic signal, highway sign, and others. I wrote:

That's right! Stop . . . Look . . . Listen . . . and then Try These Things:

The Dynamite Shack	"Whiz"
Game cards	"Multiplication
Cupboard-top count-	Bingo"
ing	Cuisenaire rods
Tic Tac Toe	Bean sticks
Magic puzzle	"Callah"
"Equivalents"	"Factor to Win"
"Fifty"	"Multiplication
"What × What"	Rock Tape"
"Number Trail"	"What ÷ What"

"Marble Drop Maze"
"Objective"
Flash cards
Still More! . . .
"Fraction Discs"
"Match It"
"Math Canasta"
"Lonesome George" (easy)
"Lonesome George" (hard)
Timed time-tables
"Fact Path"
You may like to add a game you know.
You may like to make up your own fun-sheet.
You may want to measure how long things are.

"What Time Is It"
"Fun Sheets"
"Stuff Counting"
You may have some nice work you would like to put on display.
You have a chance to earn a nice award with your name on it.
You may earn something from the pot of gold at the end of the rainbow.
Do you like secrets? There are a few in your Math Shop. Can you find them?

As you can see, there were many activities in the Math Shop. I will briefly describe just a few of them:

The Dynamite Shack (Fig. 7). This was one of the most popular activities, and it could be used in a number of different ways. For drilling on basic facts, for example, you would use it this way: Place the flash cards on top of the

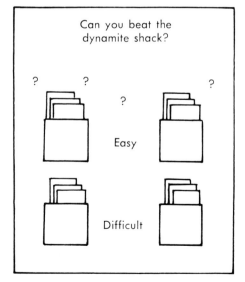

Covered with colored contact paper

Pockets made of envelopes hold flash cards of varying levels of difficulty

Fig. 7. The Dynamite Shack.

Dynamite Shack. Turn on the timer and begin picking cards one at a time off the roof, answering each one. You try to beat the timer. If you don't, the roof of the shack pops off along with any remaining cards. I used the display shown in Fig. 7 with the Dynamite Shack, and I changed the fact cards periodically.

Game cards. I made five individual game cards, which were used for reinforcement of various math skills. The student would select one of the cards and follow the directions printed on it. Work is done on the card with easy-off crayon. Upon completion, the student received a "reward." Fig. 8 is a sample of one of the game cards.

Other individual games. I prepared a number of games that can be played individually. I placed them in cigar boxes covered with contact paper. One example is a game called "equivalents." (Fig. 9). You play it by putting together problems and answers that are equivalents.

Worksheets. I keep five different kinds of

worksheets in the cupboard, and I change them periodically. These worksheets are all fun to do; students can find secret messages and so forth. Students can display completed worksheets, if they wish.

Extra activities. I keep a number of extra activities available for students who want to try something different. An example is the "magic puzzle" (Fig. 10). The task is to arrange

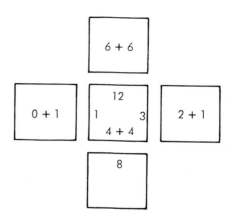

Fig. 9. Math game, "Equivalents." Make cards as shown, of several combinations.

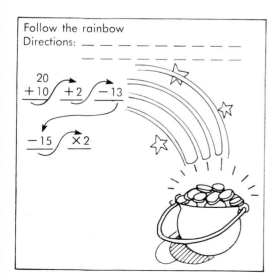

Fig. 8. Card game for reinforcement of math skills.

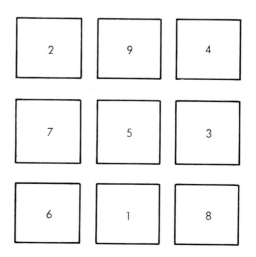

Fig. 10. "Magic puzzle." These are very quick and easy to make.

nine numbers so that each of the rows, columns, and diagonals has the same sum. There is one possible solution.

• • •

These were just a few examples of the activities available in the Math Shop. Periodic addition of new activities to the Math Shop kept the students' interest alive for several months.

Example 3. Sixth grade learning center on electricity[4]

This learning center, developed around the E.S.S. unit "Batteries and Bulbs," provided several weeks' interesting work for students in a sixth grade class. It is a combination strategy. Behavioral objectives stipulate several desired outcomes. The open-ended activities, however, place emphasis on the quality of experience rather than on predetermined outcomes.

Learning emphases

Inquiry skills
Observation skills
Knowledge about what's inside light bulbs, how simple circuits work, series and parallel circuits, conductors and nonconductors, and how people use electricity
Ability to follow directions
Working cooperatively with others
Construction of simple, series, and parallel circuits
Vocabulary enlargement

Behavioral objectives

1. The learners will be able to name five conductors and five nonconductors of electricity.
2. The learners will be able to describe and diagram the following:
   Contents of bulbs
   Simple circuit showing switch

---

[4]Based on materials arranged and submitted by Lucinda McLaughlin, Flying Hills School, El Cajon, California.

Parallel circuit
Series circuit
3. Learners will be able to explain the differences between and the uses of parallel and series circuits.
4. The learners will be able to explain how a fuse works and why it is desirable in a circuit.
5. Given batteries, bulbs, and wires, learners will be able to build simple, parallel, and series circuits.

Introducing and scheduling

I introduced the learning center by having a science lesson on electricity. The lesson was a prototype of activities contained in the learning center. I asked the children to arrange themselves into groups of four. This gave us eight groups. Each group received a coffee can containing two batteries, two flashlight bulbs, and two wires. Thus, there was a bulb, battery, and wire for every two learners. They also received cards called "scientific data cards." I said, "How many different ways can you make the bulb light? Find out what you can and write your findings on the scientific data card."

When the lesson ended, I told the children they would stay in the same groups and I would assign them to turns in the learning center. Each group had a number, one through eight. I placed a time schedule in the learning center. It had half-hour sessions for each group. Two groups participated each day, and the sessions ran Tuesday through Friday. This allowed each student to participate once a week.

Science boxes

I included ten different activities in the learning center. All were, in part, open ended: Students manipulated, observed, experimented, and recorded what they observed or concluded. Eight of these activities were placed in "science boxes," which were clear plastic shoe boxes. I made duplicates, two of each box. This allowed twice as many

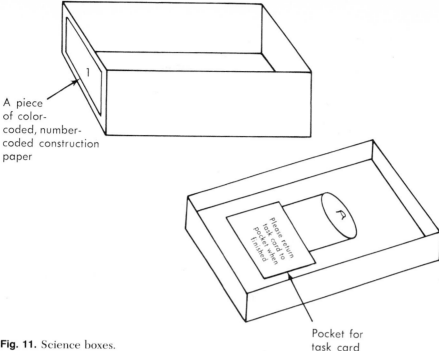

A piece of color-coded, number-coded construction paper

Please return task card to pocket when finished

Pocket for task card

Fig. 11. Science boxes.

children to use the center. Fig. 11 shows what the science boxes looked like.

Books and filmstrips

In addition to the eight science boxes, I included one group of activities having to do with reading science books and another having to do with viewing science filmstrips. I included the following books, which I obtained from the school library, parents, other teachers, and the university library:

The How and Why Book of Electricity (Grosset and Dunlap)
Junior Science Book of Electricity (The Garrard Press)
A First Electrical Book for Boys (Charles Scribner's Sons)
Electricity in Your Life (John Day Co.)
All About Electricity (Random House)
Basic Science Education Series: Electricity (Row Peterson)

Electricity (American Book Co.)
Electricity and How it is Made (Webster)

I included the following filmstrips, which I obtained from the school library and from the district office library:

The Electric Cell (The Jam Handy Organization)
Current Electricity (The Jam Handy Organization)
How Water Power Makes Electricity (Pat Dowling Pictures)
How is Electricity Used in the Home? (The Jam Handy Organization)
Using Electricity Safely (The Jam Handy Organization)

Scientific data cards

The scientific data cards that I mentioned earlier served to help students organize their thoughts and to help keep records of work that each had completed. I made them from

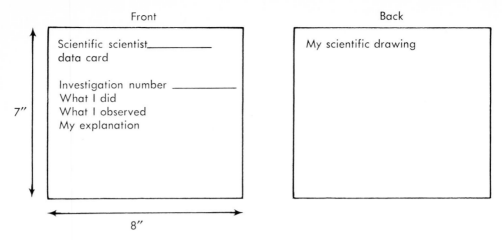

Fig. 12. Scientific data cards.

manila tag that I cut into 7 by 8 inch pieces. See Fig. 12.

Task cards

I made task cards to provide instructions for completing the ten different groups of activities. Each science box contained a task card, fitted into a pocket attached to the inside of the lid of each box. See Fig. 13.

Here is a description of the contents of each task card.

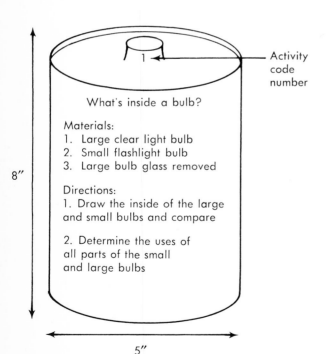

Fig. 13. Task cards.

Task card 1. What's inside a bulb?

MATERIALS
  1. A large, intact, clear light bulb
  2. A small, intact flashlight bulb
  3. A household bulb with glass removed
DIRECTIONS
  1. Draw the inside of the large and small bulbs, then compare.
  2. Determine the uses of all parts of the large and small bulbs.

Task card 2. What's inside a bulb?

MATERIALS
  1. A household light bulb
  2. A sink or dishpan
  3. A triangular file

DIRECTIONS: Put an unbroken household bulb under water in a sink or dishpan. File along the line that divides the glass from the base, until water enters the glass. What do you think is happening?

Task card 3. Beginning circuits

MATERIALS: Wires, flashlight bulb, flashlight battery

DIRECTIONS: Try to light the bulb using a piece of wire and a battery. See how many different ways you can make the bulb light. It will help if you will make sketches of your different attempts, including those that do not work.

Task card 4. Making a circuit

MATERIALS
1. Bulb holder and bulb
2. Switch
3. Battery holder and battery
4. Wires

DIRECTIONS: See if you can light the bulb in its holder using a switch, wires, and battery in its holder.

Task card 5. More on circuits

MATERIALS
1. Two small flashlight bulbs and bulb holders
2. One battery and battery holder
3. Wires

DIRECTIONS
1. Can you make the bulbs light in two different ways?
2. Show your two ways in a scientific drawing.

Task card 6. Series circuit

MATERIALS
1. Flashlight battery
2. Battery holder
3. Switch
4. Flashlight bulbs
5. Bulb holder
6. Wires
7. Two diagrams of series circuits

DIRECTIONS
1. Build a circuit like diagram 1 and see what happens.
2. Build a circuit like diagram 2 and see what happens.

3. What happens in circuit number 2 if you unscrew one of the bulbs? Can you explain why this happens?

Task card 7. Parallel circuit

MATERIALS
1. Two bulbs and bulb holders
2. One battery and battery holder
3. Switch
4. Wires
5. Diagrams of two parallel circuits

DIRECTIONS
1. Build a circuit like diagram 1 and see what happens.
2. Build a circuit like diagram 2 and see what happens.
3. What happens when you unscrew one of the bulbs in number one and number two? Can you explain why this happens?

Task card 8. Conductors and nonconductors

MATERIALS: Flashlight battery, light bulb and holder, insulated copper wire, scrap pieces of cloth, paper, rubber

DIRECTIONS
1. Connect the battery and the light bulb, but leave a gap between the two pieces of wire.
2. Hold each of the materials listed above against the ends of the wires at the gap.
3. What makes the bulb light? Can you explain why?

Task card 9. Books

MATERIALS: Science books having to do with electricity (listed previously)

DIRECTIONS: Select a book from the table and read a section that interests you. Write or draw what you learned on a scientific data card.

Task card 10. Filmstrips

MATERIALS: Filmstrips, listed previously, and viewer

DIRECTIONS: Select a filmstrip and view it. Write or draw what you learned on a data card.

Scientific data card file

I used tagboard, construction paper, and clear contact paper to make these file boxes for scientific data cards (Fig. 14).

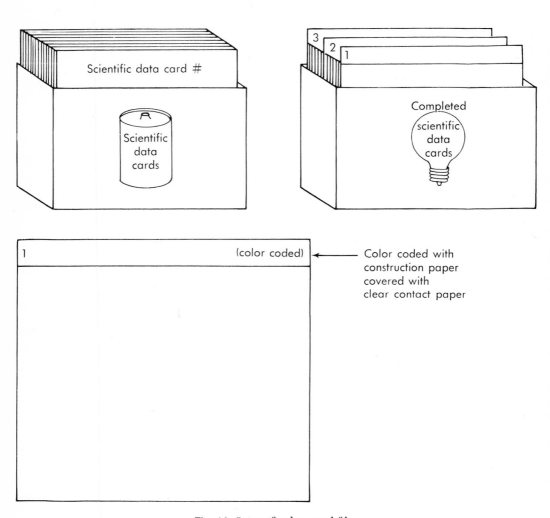

Fig. 14. Scientific data card file.

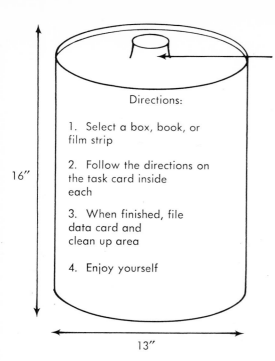

Directions:

1. Select a box, book, or film strip

2. Follow the directions on the task card inside each

3. When finished, file data card and clean up area

4. Enjoy yourself

16″

13″

Fig. 15. Directions for using the center.

Directions for using the center

I made the following device for giving directions for using the center. I drew and lettered it on a piece of tagboard, then cut it in the shape of a battery. I posted it at the center in a conspicuous place (Fig. 15).

Evaluation and record keeping

All records were kept on the scientific data cards, which showed activities undertaken, completed, and the quality of the completed work.

I held a conference with each group every two weeks. I asked the children questions about the tasks—which they liked best, what they thought they had learned, and so on.

Hints

Wire can be obtained free from the telephone company.

Sometimes dry cells can be obtained free from the telephone company. If you buy your own, buy flashlight batteries. Shop around. The prices vary quite a bit.

Flashlight bulbs vary in price from store to store. Shop for comparative prices.

Coffee cans covered with contact paper are very good for keeping extra wire, batteries, and bulbs.

Bookcases are good for holding the science boxes. You can also make storage facilities easily by getting cardboard apple boxes from the supermarket produce department. You can cover them with colored butcher paper.

13

Open experience

We began our search into individualizing instruction with the recognition that students have learning styles that differ, one from the other. We noted that some students require structure and guidance in their learning activities. Later, we considered behavior-referenced programs of instruction appropriate for them. Diagnostic-prescriptive teaching and modularized instruction were examined as two approaches typical of behavior-referenced instruction.

We also noted that some students require more freedom in their learning endeavors. They can initiate activities, direct themselves, find their own rewards in learning— in short, take responsibility for their learning. These students function well in experience-referenced programs of instruction, where emphasis is placed on quality optional learning experiences rather than on prespecified outcomes of those experiences.

For students of this second type, we should consider providing "open experience" activities. Presently, we will examine the open experience approach in some detail. But first, let's see what has caused the recent interest in open experience and open education.

ACID TONGUES

We teachers have taken our scoldings in the last few years. Of course, we got them before, too, but we used to shrug them off, telling ourselves they came from a few crackpots, ne'er do wells, and sour grape vendors. We can't do that any more. The criticisms come too often from authorities, from scholars who have done their homework. We can't ignore them any longer. They not only tell us what's wrong; they also tell us what would make things right. And we have to admit that many of them are true in what they say.

But just what do they say? Let's note the opinions of three of the best known critics. What they say reflects pretty accurately the tenor of today's criticisms of teaching and schooling.

A. S. Neill[1]: Education's job is to bestow happiness. It can do this simply, by abolishing authority. Students don't need to be lectured. They don't need to be coerced. They don't need to be forced. Instead, they need to be allowed to be themselves, to determine what it is they want to learn, to be free from punishment and hostility.

[1] See especially, Neill, A.: Summerhill: A radical approach to child rearing, New York, 1960, Hart Publishing Co., Inc.

194

Charles E. Silberman[2]: Schooling is preoccupied with control and order. It is regulated by the clock. It fosters docility. It fails to spark initiative, interest, delight, or productive effort. It stultifies learners, leaving them without self direction or responsibility. Students learn only to give teachers what they want, to cheat, to pretend, to fantasize, to conform.

Herbert Kohl[3]: Schools are supposed to help the young live better lives now and help them live better lives in the future. They do neither. What they do is heap on authority and boredom. They allow no opportunity for making decisions or taking on responsibility. The teacher's main function is to control. Schooling is overwhelmingly authoritarian and oppressive. What happens to students? They learn to hate. They show their hate through defiance, unruliness, mockery, belligerence, apathy, and truancy.

These three critics don't stop at saying what's wrong with schooling. They give their remedies for the ills as well. The remedies vary somewhat, but they all stress student freedom, self direction, and purposefulness. Neill would have youth direct their own lives as students, deciding what and when they want to learn. Silberman would have teachers free the psychological climates of their classrooms, doing away with rigid, abusive teacher behavior while allowing students much more freedom in selecting their learning activities. Kohl would free the classroom climate by allowing students to delve into virtually any activities of interest available in school, so long as the students don't do damage to property or each other.

All these proposed remedies touch on the concept of "open education," which rests on the belief that learning is a personal matter for each student, that different students find different things worth learning, that different students learn at different rates, that teachers promote significant learning to the extent they take students seriously as human beings and attempt to facilitate their learning rather than direct and force it. In open education it is considered necessary that students initiate learning activities, that they direct themselves, and that they take responsibility for what they do. This concept of teaching aims at capitalizing on learners' curiosity, imagination, and concern.

MEANING OF OPEN EXPERIENCE

As used in this chapter, open experience means much the same as open education. The only difference between them is that open education implies a total-day, total-year psychological freedom in teaching and learning, whereas open experience refers to shorter episodes of such freedom, occurring at various times within an overall program that is somewhat more structured.

Since the key word in both is "open," we had best take a moment to consider what that word means.

People often confuse the labels "open space" and "open experience," assuming they refer to the same concept. They don't. Open space describes a type of school building construction that has no interior walls to separate one classroom from another. Many students and several teachers work within this open space area. It affords the chief advantage of flexible grouping, allowing teachers to work with large and small groups simultaneously.

"Openness" in the psychological sense has nothing at all to do with physical space. Instead, it describes a state of mind, a way of personal interaction, a social-emotional climate that pervades the classroom. Although difficult to define in a sentence or two, a classroom that is psychologically open will have most of these characteristics:

---

[2] See Silberman, C.: Crisis in the classroom, New York, 1970, Random House, Inc.
[3] Kohl, H.: The open classroom, New York, 1969, Random House, Inc. (A New York Review Book).

1. Students play a strong role in planning—in deciding what topics they will pursue, how and when they will pursue them, and what materials and resources they will need.
2. Students direct their own learning activities, to a large extent. They take the initiative instead of waiting for the teacher to tell them what to do.
3. The teacher helps and encourages students in warm, positive, personal ways. Punishment and sarcasm are not used. A spirit of personal acceptance runs through the teacher-student relationships.
4. Feelings, emotions, attitudes, and values receive strong attention, along with traditional knowledge and skill acquisition.
5. Evaluation occurs as students judge their own progress and the personal meaning their learnings have for themselves. Teachers seldom evaluate unless asked to do so by the students.

The open experience approach to individualizing instruction has, as its single most important quality, this psychological openness. Openness is there and evident. Though the open experience episodes may be brief and though they may occur infrequently, students know that during those times they have responsibility to direct themselves in ways they feel most appropriate, as long as they do not limit those same possibilities for other students.

ORIGINS

There is nothing new under the sun, they say, and you learn to believe that when you try to trace the origins of ideas. Every time you think you've discovered something unique, you find that somebody else thought of the idea much earlier, though maybe in a slightly different form. So it is with what we now call open education.

Let it suffice to make mention of a few thinkers whose writings have given form to the open education movement: Rousseau, Pestalozzi, Froebel, Montessori, Dewey, and Piaget. Many others have made impor-

tant contributions; we have already noted ideas of Neill, Silberman, and Kohl. Jerome Bruner, Joseph Featherstone, Jonathan Kozol, and many others deserve mention, too. In the interests of time and space, however, we will limit ourselves to the small sampling listed here.

We will begin with a brief mention of **Jean Jacques Rousseau,** whose ideas were, as is always the case, elaborations on thoughts of others who influenced him. Remember how his fictional Emile received the most informal, direct experience with nature-centered education. Emile's character was stoutly formed by the exercise of freedom and, we must note, by avoidance of contact with society, which Rousseau considered a debasing influence.

Then **Johann Heinrich Pestalozzi,** with roots in Swiss peasantry, held sway. Describing how Gertrude taught her children as they hovered close about her skirts, he drew attention to warmth and concern and kindness in teaching. Pestalozzi, in his quiet bumbling way, championed the cause of the common people, seeking to raise them from poverty and degradation. He saw charity as a total failure, because it did nothing to help people help themselves, and he thought little better of current education, which at that time (he lived from 1746 to 1827) was harsh intellectual training imposed from without. Pestalozzi believed people had qualities that would allow them to rise above their downtrodden state, and he thought a new kind of education would enhance and release those qualities.

Pestalozzi saw within children a rich store of feelings, emotions, and abilities. He believed that if education could begin within children, rather than come from without, these dormant qualities could be nourished and brought to fruition. The child, he said, not subject matter, should be the central focus of education. Natural growth and natural development of potentialities were far more important than memorization of facts. Education could facilitate this normal growth process by supplying stimulation and guidance, incorporating:

Respect for children's individuality

Exercises, progressing from simple to complex, in harmony with natural growth, to enhance natural abilities

Discipline based on love and acceptance instead of punishment and rejection

After struggling for many years, Pestalozzi at last received assistance from a group of people interested in seeing his educational ideas furthered. He began operating a school in Burgdorf, which he later moved to Yverdon. His school attracted attention of scholars from all over Europe. So impressive were his new ideas that the Pestalozzi method was soon disseminated to many other countries, including France, Germany, Holland, and the United States.

Following Pestalozzi, who influenced him greatly, **Friedrich Wilhelm Froebel** (1782-1852) gave form and impetus to the kindergarten movement. In fact, he coined the name "kindergarten" himself. He was, some might say, a romantic about the nature of children. He believed that every educational principle came directly from the child; the teacher was merely to follow wherever the child led, not teaching in the sense of imparting knowledge, but encouraging children in their own activities. Through this avenue Froebel showed the value of spontaneous play and cooperation among children.

The educational program Froebel established for his kindergarteners consisted of three parts—the use of "gifts," singing of songs, and the playing of educational games in the play circle. "Gifts" were blocks or other materials arranged in a box, to be taken out by children, played with, and then replaced. The materials could be used as the child desired, though ordinarily some could

be used for making geometrical patterns, while others were for sewing, drawing, and coloring. Play songs were sets of pictures with accompanying verse and music that encouraged children to participate actively through rhythms and pantomimes. Play circles, popularized by Froebel for kindergarten use, involved the children's holding hands and playing various kinds of educational games, including stories and dramatizations.

Maria Montessori, the first woman medical doctor in Italy, identified natural learning tendencies in children and built an elaborate system of instruction to capitalize on those natural tendencies. She found that children have a very strong tendency to work spontaneously. They want to do this work unhindered and undisturbed. When allowed to work this way, children become (or remain) "normalized"—they show concentration, cooperation, initiative, self discipline, joy, and love for order.

However, when children are thwarted in their natural inclinations to work—that is, when adults impose their rules on them, or inhibit their movements, or do not provide them direction and guidance—undesirable deviations crop up in children's behavior. They begin to lie, quarrel, and disobey. They become timid and fearful. When they do these things, the fault lies not with them, but with the school.

Montessori made detailed descriptions of ways children differ from adults intellectually. She concluded that children pass through three different stages of intellectual development. In effect, they have three different "minds" as they move through these stages.

Montessori called the first stage "the absorbent mind." This stage occupies the years from birth to about age six. In the first half of this stage the mind constantly absorbs impressions from the environment without thinking about doing so. In the second half, the mind continues to absorb, but activities come under conscious control, with will and intent.

The second stage, during the approximate years six to twelve, is a stage of "uniform growth." Children are robust and serene, daring and venturesome. They rapidly become able to reason. They want to act independently, yet they feel a growing need to be with others.

The third stage, "transformation," occurs between the approximate ages of twelve to eighteen. In contrast with the uniform growth stage, this period sees great physical and emotional change. Individuals become highly sensitive about themselves—about their bodies, their abilities, their appearance. They are filled with self doubt, hesitation, discouragement. Yet, they show heightened creativity, idealism, and adult-like thought.

Montessori believed it necessary that schools be constituted to enhance normal, healthy development at each of these three stages. She believes this could best be done through preparing special learning environments that would allow students to do what their best natural inclinations led them to do. They should be free to experiment, run risks, and make mistakes, all in a supportive atmosphere. The environment and its materials must be kept always orderly, neat, and clean. Montessori believes that insistence on neatness and orderliness developed responsibility, prevented frustration, and conserved mental energy.

Teachers have a clearly defined role in Montessori's scheme. They behave in clam, unhurried, respectful ways. They never lecture students or tell them how to do activities. Instead, they give hints, through demonstration and example, about how to perform activities and use materials. They show but don't tell. They help when called and are forever watchful. They always show care,

gentleness, and patience. In these ways teachers serve children in their quest for responsible freedom.

John Dewey, probably the greatest American educational philosopher, saw experience and education as synonymous terms. He stressed the necessity for students to be active manipulators of experience rather than passive receivers. All types of experience, however, are not equally worthwhile. Dewey stressed experiences that fostered democracy, which for him had meaning far beyond that of political processes or form of government. He considered democracy a way of life, a way of relating to others, a way of transacting business with one's environment.

Dewey believed schools could foster democracy, as he conceived it, by integrating the schools into community life, by allowing students to interact in a wide range of shared interests, and by training students to evaluate their experiences. He would make schools a part of the community at large by setting up reciprocal interactions between shcool and home, business, industry, universities, libraries, museums, and so on. He would also have students' in-school experiences always related to matters of daily life, so they might have the greatest practicality possible.

Dewey would provide shared interests for students within the school by first arranging learning environments to capitalize on the normal interests of students. He would then bring students into the goal-setting processes, so they could help set goals that were truly their own, rather than the school's. Students would engage in activities and topics that had meaning and significance to them, that really mattered. Still, they would be urged to pursue interests in depth, not shallowly as passing fancies, emphasizing the ways they related to other persons, places, and events.

Students would be trained to evaluate

their experiences and outcomes along lines such as:

Whether they enhance constructive communication
Whether they open up further experiences
Whether they encourage personal commitment to a course of action

Jean Piaget is a modern Swiss psychologist, born in 1896, who continues his incredibly productive investigations into the way children think. He has clearly shown that children don't think in the same ways adults do—that in fact they are incapable of adult-like thought until somewhere between the approximate ages of twelve to fifteen. He has found that children pass through progressive stages of intellectual development, not at fixed ages, but always in fixed sequence.

Three of the stages Piaget has identified are especially important in education. The first of these is the stage of *intuitive thought,* which begins at the approximate age of four and ends at about age seven. In this stage children do not use adult logic. Instead, they operate on the basis of intuitions or hunches. They can neither understand nor learn on the basis of order of events, cause-effect relationships, or number relationships. They have difficulty remembering rules or even understanding other speakers accurately.

The second of these three stages is the stage of *concrete operations,* which begins at an approximate age of seven and ends at an approximate age of eleven. Students have now developed the ability to make relationships and to understand and follow sequences and rules. They can think through problems mentally, but they think in terms of concrete objects, not abstract ideas.

The third of these three stages is the stage of *formal operations.* Students can now engage in abstract, adult thought. They can form theories and carry out mental experiments.

These findings have had immense influence on educational thought. Materials and activities for learning are being developed with an eye toward students' intellectual abilities instead of the intentions of adults.

OPEN EDUCATION TODAY

Open education has no required form, no preset structure. It flows, reforming itself in accord with needs of learners. Yet it has consistent traits that make it identifiable and distinguishable from traditionally structured approaches. Those traits include the intended results in learners, and they include the nature of the teaching-learning environments.

Open education's purpose is to produce learners who come to show the following traits:

1. They initiate activities, direct themselves, and assume responsibility for their own learning.
2. They face uncertainty with equanimity and cope routinely with change.
3. They behave openly, honestly, and with respect for themselves and others.

To produce these results, open education relies on teaching-learning environments that reflect these characteristics:[4]

1. The classroom contains an abundance of materials and possibilities for activities.
2. Room space is arranged into attractive, inviting activity areas.
3. Students have freedom to select and devise their own learning activities and to move about the classroom.
4. Students are allowed to work individually or in groups that form naturally.
5. The total group is brought together periodically to discuss matters of group concern.
6. Creative expression in all forms is valued.
7. Teachers consider themselves learners along

---

[4] For an excellent, concise description of open education, see Kohn, S.: North Dakota's quiet revolution and Vito Perrone, National Elementary Principal **52:**49-57, November 1972.

with the students. They continually explore new ideas and new possibilities. They exemplify the active learner role for students.

8. Teachers work alongside students, helping, encouraging, and supporting as necessary.

9. Teachers strive to maximize effective communication among all members of the group, including themselves as members. They seek opportunities to talk at length with individual students.

10. Teachers try to help students evaluate their own work.

But will open education really work? Will it allow students to make desired growth in both cognitive and affective areas? The answer seems to be yes, though some questions about its effectiveness remain.

Day and Brice studied six year olds in various types of classrooms. They found that students in open classrooms performed as well as others in academic achievement and self image, while being judged more task oriented and less easily distracted.[5]

Halsted, Bober, and Streit caution that open education may not be for everyone. They identify basic assumptions about open education:

1. Children are innately curious.

2. Children will explore their environment if it is not threatening.

3. Children have the competence and the right to make significant decisions concerning their own learning.

4. Children who learn something of importance to themselves wish to share it with others.

Even if these assumptions are valid, some students may not be suited to open education. Halsted, Bober, and Streit conclude that students with the best chance for success in open education are those with strong *inter-*

nal locus of control, which means they see their actions and the consequences of those actions as being under their personal control.[6]

BEGINNINGS

Who wouldn't like to help students become self starting, self directing, and responsible? Every one of us would if we could. And if it would ensure success, we would all strive to establish teaching-learning environments with characteristics like those just listed. But saying it is easier than doing it. What's worse, students have to get used to the whole thing, too. Even if we could miraculously remake our structured teaching styles into open ones overnight, we'd have two and a half strikes against us, because our students probably couldn't handle the abrupt change.

So what can we do? How can we start? Kohl suggested beginning with open experience ten minutes per day.[7] Blitz suggested the same thing, plus two other ways for gradually giving up some teacher control. They were allowing students to work individually within group assignments and allowing students to choose their own activities within a topic area.[8] Nault also strongly advocates a gradualist approach.[9] He contends that gradually moving from more structure to less has a twofold effect. It permits teachers to contend more easily with unexpected occurrences, and it gives students a chance to progressively develop the decision and planning abilities they need for success in the open

[5] Day, B., and Brice, R.: Academic achievement, self concept development, and behavior patterns of six-year-old children in open classrooms, Elementary School Journal 78(2):132-139, November 1977.

[6] Halsted, D. L., Bober, A. M., and Streit, F.: Open classroom: A panacea?" The Educational Forum 41(4): 487-491, May 1977.

[7] Kohl, H., *op cit.*, p. 71.

[8] Blitz, B.: The open classroom: Making it work, Boston, 1973, Allyn & Bacon.

[9] Nault, R.: Open education—A gradualist approach, The Elementary School Journal 73:107-111, November 1972.

classroom. Nault suggests moving toward openness in a way that gives students decision-making responsibilities first within single lessons, then within subjects, and finally within large segments of the day.

Geiser suggests a similar approach in his article "If I'm Not at the Center of Things—Where am I?."[10] He describes how teachers must be architects of the classroom, facilitators, and supporters of learning.

Cramer goes into more detail.[11] She describes how teachers can begin by forgetting the schedule for one day a week and allowing students to select their own tasks and work procedures. She uses Thursdays for "free time learning," preceded by a planning period on Wednesday afternoon, during which students list the activities they would like to do the next day. What do her fourth grade children like to do? Cramer says their favorite activities are:

Discussions, on topics such as "kid's lib" and "parent-son problems." They often tape their discussions.

Art, where students teach each other various techniques in arts and crafts

Peer tutoring, where more advanced students help less advanced ones

Review and practice, with students working together on basic curricular topics

Independent work, such as writing letters, using the typewriter, and drawing

Discovery centers, with open-ended, science-related activities such as optics and aquarium observation

Game centers, where numbers of language arts and math games are kept

What do teachers do during this time? They have the major responsibility for setting up the materials and activities in the classroom. They coordinate activities. They observe and help when needed. They chat with individuals and work groups, finding that once under way not much supervision is required. They come to know each student much more intimately. When necessary, they bring some of the students back into more structured activities. The end result of this style of teaching finds the teacher, as well as the students, happier and better satisfied with both process and results.

Rogers goes at the matter in a more direct way. The best thing to do, he says, is to forget you are a teacher.[12] Instead of remembering and relying on teaching skills acquired over the years, you would become a "facilitator of learning." Instead of planning in advance what you think students should learn and how you think they should learn it, you would do these things:

1. Find out what things interest your students, puzzle them, concern them, excite them.
2. Search out ways to help your students find answers to their questions. Help them find resources, people, books, and materials that will let them learn what they want to know.
3. Foster a psychological climate that allows students to behave spontaneously, to make mistakes, to be secure, and to learn from a variety of sources.
4. Show in your own behavior the personal traits of genuineness, empathetic understanding, and valuing of the learners' feelings and opinions.

Most of the example programs we have considered so far have been carried out at the elementary level. You may think that open experience is all right for little kids, but that adolescents and adults don't go for such open, free-wheeling stuff. If you think that, you are wrong. True, most of the recent attention given to open education has focused

[10] Geiser, R.: If I'm not at the center of things—Where am I? Teacher p. 18, February 1974.

[11] Cramer, R.: The best things in school are free, Teacher pp. 44-47, February 1974.

[12] Rogers, C.: Forget you are a teacher, Instructor **81:** 65-66, August-September 1971.

on elementary education. But it works every bit as well—maybe even better—at the secondary and university levels.

For example, Cohen, feeling great pressure, frustration, and discontent with her traditional way of teaching one hundred eleventh grade students in English, decided to try the open classroom in her traditional high school.[13] She accumulated a large supply of secondhand paperbacks from students, from her own collection, and from used book stores. She let students use the audiovisual catalog to decide which films and recordings they would like to use. Those were ordered. She hung up suggestions around the room for individual and group activities—suggestions about topics, authors, styles, creative work, and so forth.

Students were given a week to explore the room and its possibilities. Then they prepared short written plans for how they intended to use their time. Students entered progress reports three times per week in their personal journals, which were kept filed in the classroom and which the teacher read weekly.

Cohen reports that her own role was somewhat as follows: With some difficulty, she gave up lecturing, directing lecture-related discussions, and formal testing. Instead, she talked with students, suggested ideas and possibilities, and read work they had completed. Perhaps most important, she continually worked with students to help each clarify exactly what was expected in the way of activities and procedures. She found no discipline problems, and almost all the students produced something worthwhile.

At the university level, I recently taught a graduate class in advanced educational psychology using an open approach. Twenty-five

students attended the class. A number of interested visitors also attended from time to time. I began by briefly describing ideas and the works of thinkers I considered especially influential in matters of learning process and procedure. I showed books and articles from my own collection, and I discussed a couple of topics about which I was then thinking and writing. I told the students I considered them professionals and I wanted to work along with them on topics important in their personal or professional lives. I also told them they could work individually or in whatever kinds of groups they wanted to form. I would talk with individuals and groups, explore promising leads, suggest useful materials, and generally do what I could to help.

The class was one of the best I ever had. Students quickly assumed responsibility and began working. We put a good deal of wear and tear on my personal library, and we spent hours and hours talking. I required that the students submit four short papers, outlining work completed and plans for future work. They also had to make two short oral reports to the class about their work. Otherwise they were free to pursue their activities however they wished, as long as they checked in with me at the beginning of each class. Those students did some of the finest work I have seen. Their reactions were extremely positive, and I was very pleased with the entire effort.

STRUCTURE

A great deal has been said about the desirability of moving away from the rigid structure of traditional classrooms. That may have caused you to believe that open experience reaches its maximum effectiveness when structure disappears completely from the classroom. Such is not the case. Open experience requires structure. Students need the assurance of boundaries, however broad.

[13]Cohen, B.: An open classroom in a traditional high school, NJEA Review **66**:58-59, September 1972.

They need to know what things are acceptable and what are not. They need to know something about possibilities, about what things have been tried before, about other students' interests, attempts, and results.

Moreover, when you arrange activities and materials for those activities, you are providing structure. You are setting patterns, possibilities, and limitations for what can be done. But this kind of structure is far different from that which exists in many traditional classrooms, where teachers plan all topics, activities, and evaluation procedures in advance, and all students go through them together under the direction of the teacher. This type of rigid structure does not permit students to do what we strive for in open experience, which is to plan their activities, initiate and sustain them, and take responsibility for the entire procedure.

RESULTS OF OPEN EDUCATION

Few empirical studies have been conducted to show how open education compares, in its results, with traditional education. We truly don't know, as yet, whether it produces the laudable effects in learners that we intend. This lack of evidence is partly the result of a lack of appropriate measuring devices. We simply can't measure, in an objective way, the degree to which a given student is independent, trusting, responsible, considerate, and critical of thought.

One outcome has been observed, however, in both England and the United States. Given traditional standardized tests of scholastic achievement, students in open classrooms have scored as well as students in traditional classrooms. As Perrone says, even that is impressive.[14] The fact is that curricula in traditional classes tend to be directed toward tests, and the students have had the opportunity to become more test wise.

SYNTHESIS

If we were to pull together the ideas about open education that we have noted so far, we would see a striking parallel between them and what Postman and Weingartner list as characteristics of a good school.[15] Evidently, their biases lie in the direction of open education, for the characteristics they list include the following:

1. *Time structuring*, that does not follow arbitrary sequences, that allows students different amounts of time to complete activities, and that allows students to organize their own time, at least to a degree
2. *Activity structuring*, that allows different students to do different things, according to their own interests and judgments, and that allows them to plan and engage in activities in their own ways, not simply in response to teacher dictates
3. *Valuing* of inquiry, independence, self knowledge, self direction, responsibility, and practicality
4. *Evaluation*, that emphasizes reinforcing responses, mastery learning in which only success is recorded—not failure, humanistic procedures in which students take part in making judgments about their efforts.
5. *Teacher-student relations*, that are collaborative, mutually supportive, and not antagonistic, in which students assume responsibility for their own actions
6. *Teacher behavior*, that is student centered, facilitative, and exemplary of the value of continual learning

In conclusion, perhaps we can say that more than anything else, open experience

---

[14] For an excellent, brief treatment of open education, see Perrone, V.: Open education: Promise and problems, Bloomington, Indiana: 1972, The Phi Delta Kappa Educational Foundation.

[15] Postman, N., and Weingartner, C.: How to recognize a good school, Bloomington, Indiana: 1973, The Phi Delta Kappa Educational Foundation, pp. 28-42.

and the humanistic movement aim at living life to its fullest and most enjoyable extent. Heschel, in some of his most compelling words, spoke of life as something more than absurdity:

And above all, remember that the meaning of life is to build a life as if it were a work of art. . . . What's really important is life as a celebration.[16]

OPEN EXPERIENCE CASES

Misgivings—sometimes moderate, sometimes strong—invariably beset teachers who would make their teaching more open. They fear students won't learn, won't progress on schedule, or won't study important things. They fear parents and administrators and other teachers will criticize them. They fear and mistrust their own abilities to bring it off, to prepare properly, to facilitate students' learning. Most of all, they fear the unknown, the different, the unpredictable.

But once they have tried open experience, most teachers (though in truth not all of them) find their fears unfounded. Students don't just fool around—not when very interesting activities and materials sit before them. In fact, many teachers find their students work harder, with more interest and less disruption, than ever before. They find that they, for the first time, have an opportunity to talk with individual students, to work alongside them, or just move about, ready to assist when needed, but also willing to keep a respectful distance when not.

As for parents and administrators, both will rally to your side, or at least will not actively oppose you, if you take it upon yourself to explain carefully what it is you have in mind—what you intend to do, why, and how you will go about it. Most parents will want

assurance, and rightfully so, that their children will get the "basics," which usually means the fundamental skills of reading, communication, and mathematics. The principal's blessing, which you must strive to get, not only facilitates your work in school but also provides an essential buffer between your work and the sometimes hostile opinions of parents and other teachers.

Maybe these precautionary notes weaken your resolve to try open experience. Don't let that happen. You will probably encounter no difficulties whatsoever. Knowing the worst that might happen should give you courage to try.

Recently, I taught a class of forty-five experienced elementary and junior high school teachers, none of whom had ever tried using an open experience approach. I strongly urged that they all try. Forty-three of them did. Of the forty-three, one teacher quickly abandoned open experience, saying that things soon went from bad to worse. All the rest of the teachers made mild to glowing reports of the results of open experience in their classrooms.

These teachers went into open experience slowly. Some started, as Kohl suggested, by allowing ten minutes per day for the students to do whatever they chose to do (so long as they didn't do physical damage to materials, furniture, themselves, or others).[17] He included the right to do nothing at all. They found they were soon able to increase the amount of time. In fact, students often requested it.

Others started with a free choice time before school. They opened their classrooms thirty to forty-five minutes earlier than usual and let the students come in to work or play at activities they chose. They found that large

---

[16] Stern, C.: Abraham Joshua Heschel: last words, Intellectual Digest, June 1973.

[17] Kohl, H., *op. cit.*, p. 71.

numbers of students, best described as recalcitrant during the "required" part of the day, began coming early to school, and their improved attitudes seemed to carry over into the remainder of the day as well.

Still other teachers began by modifying existing structure somewhat, in ways similar to those suggested by Blitz.[18] One of these ways is to make group assignments, as usual, but allow individual students to pace themselves and move into some related topics on their own. As Blitz points out, you give up some intellectual control over your students, but you can still keep your seating arrangements, routines, and overall classroom organization.

Blitz suggests another approach that allows students to select their own activities within a given topic area. In social studies, for example, each student selects, from a range of options, an area of investigation. They seek out whatever materials, references, or resource people they need for completing the tasks they have set for themselves. This approach also allows you to move gradually from a more structured to a less structured environment in the classroom.

Whatever your inclinations or misgivings about open experience, you won't be able to grasp its possibilities until you try it in one form or another. That was the unanimous opinion of the many teachers I mentioned. To illustrate, here are reports from two of the teachers who tried open experience for the first time.

Before school free choice[19]

This report describes an open experience approach that was used with a fourth-fifth

grade combination class, from 8:15 to 8:40 daily.

Overview

My open experience program started the day after the two ladies spoke to our class about the success of the free choice time in their district. The next day was a minimum day for my school, with a half day set aside for parent-teacher conferences. The children had to come to school a little earlier than usual and would leave school two hours earlier. I thought this would be a good time to see just what would happen if I let the children spend about twenty minutes doing something of their own choosing.

I came to school early and quickly put out various materials. When the children arrived, I told them I had a very important announcement to make when they had entered the room quietly. They were quite curious about it. My announcement was as follows:

You have approximately twenty minutes to choose and engage in some activity that you will find set out around the room. If you choose to just sit, you may. In either case, the one rule is that you may not bother anyone except to get help. This includes me! Go!

The children immediately began looking for something that they would like to do. Luckily, I had made enough options available so that there were no real problems. After twenty minutes, I called for a clean up and put away period. I told groups of children where to put the materials that they had been using. In about five minutes all were back in their seats.

I asked the class if they would like to do this kind of thing two or three times each week, even if it meant coming to school a little earlier. This would, of course, be voluntary. Most of them said yes. I told them I would get some plans and materials together

[18] Blitz, B., *op. cit.*
[19] This report is based on materials prepared and submitted by Mr. John Callahan, Valencia Park Elementary School, San Diego, California.

over the weekend and we would start on Wednesday of the next week.

I returned to school on Monday with my plans completed and began to gather materials. On Monday afternoon, my instructional aide took the boys out for PE while I kept the girls in and gave them their orientation about the free time that would start on Wednesday. They wanted to start the very next morning, but I told them it would not be quite fair to the boys, and they understood.

Tuesday afternoon, I kept the boys in and gave them the same orientation as the girls. They seemed very receptive to the few ground rules I gave them.

On Wednesday morning, most of the class came early. We reviewed what had been discussed previously. We then had a short period for signing up for activities. Again, there were enough activities to accommodate the children. Things went pretty well. I had to remind a couple of people that we did have some standards that they had already agreed to follow. I helped a few of the children with some of the activities. At the end of the period, we briefly discussed how the morning went. I believe we were all satisfied with the beginning. As the program continues, most of the children come early. Some have already asked if they might bring things from home to play with. To me, this is a significant step.

I believe that the finest result of the free period has been the willingness of the children to come to school early and participate in activities with other children. I also see some improved attitudes as the children move from free time into the regular lessons. This fact alone makes the whole program worthwhile. There is another bonus, too: I am getting to know some of my children a little better in this unstructured time. Perhaps we both see each other in a different way. Maybe that's the crux of the whole matter. I'm really glad I have added this to my daily program.

Options during free choice

The following is a brief listing of the options I made available to my students during the free choice time before school.

1. A learning center on maps.
2. A cassette tape recorder, with blank tapes, for children to record while reading, singing, or just talking.
3. A one-cylinder lawn mower engine for dismantling, examining, putting back together, and general exploration. I furnished tools from my own collection.
4. Art activities. Children use available materials as they see fit at a designated table. The materials, limited because of the mess up and clean up factors, include drawing paper, crayons, pencils, pastel crayons, scissors, glue, paste, clipboard, rulers, magazines, and tissue paper.
5. Reading games. This is a set of commercially prepared reading games to develop reading skills without extensive teacher involvement.
6. Filmstrip viewing area. In a darkened alcove I set up the projector and provided a set of fiction strips, which I change on a weekly basis.
7. A chalkboard area for practicing spelling, while working with a partner.
8. A chalkboard area for working on math, either alone or with a partner.
9. A chalkboard area for drawing, practicing handwriting, doodling, and other such things children enjoy doing on a chalkboard.
10. A specially designated area in a corner for putting together jigsaw puzzles, which may be left uncompleted in that special place.

Ground rules

Here are the ground rules I established with the children before we began the open experience activities. They worked very well.

1. If you come, you participate.
2. Follow rules.
3. Don't bother others.
4. Clean up after yourself.
5. Try before asking for help.

6. Be ready for regular lessons when choosing ends at 8:40.

Introducing the program

In the afternoon I had my instructional aide take the boys out for regular PE activity. I kept the girls in and introduced the program to this smaller group. The following day I kept the boys while the girls went out.

I told them about the options available and gave them a brief walk through and explanation of the sign-up procedures. I went over general standards of behavior, clean up procedures, and times for choosing.

Regarding my role, I told the students I would watch and help them as necessary, but that during this time I didn't want to be the "teacher." This time was to be a period for independent exploration and fun, without any heavy stuff. I told them I would watch to see that they always had a good supply of materials with which to work.

Conclusion

As I mentioned earlier, this daily period of free choice has added much to my class. The students come eagerly before school starts, and they seem to have a much better attitude toward school in general. Surprisingly, I like it, too.

In-school academic work[20]

This report describes a structured teacher's attempt to loosen up the academic learning activities of his elementary school students.

Overview

Open experience has, for me and in my way, been quite successful. However, as you will see in this report, my way is still a rather structured kind of open experience. The materials I have in my classroom are basically for academic goals. I could not feel comfortable—at least not yet—in working in a totally open classroom with hamsters, nails, finger paints, and ducks. The students have plenty of free time, but it is used in academically oriented ways.

I believe my room environment can be judged a success by measuring it through the actions of those who are the most important critics—the students themselves. School starts at 8:55, but they start coming into the classroom about 7:45. By "they" I don't just mean children from my room. They come from other rooms, too. And they stay after school, sometimes until 4:30 or later. The students enjoy using the learning centers or playing chess in the club I started. I had worried about losing my materials, but despite the numbers of students passing through my room each day, not one thing has been stolen or purposely damaged. The students leave the room looking just as clean as when the custodian swept it.

I do not have any paid aides or parent volunteers working with me in the room. I have found that most parents mean well but can't relate to different types of children and they are unreliable about showing up to help because of other commitments. I found the best teacher aides to be other children and consequently I use a number of cross-age tutors in my room, which fits in well with the open experience idea.

As for record keeping, it is a chore but one that has to be done. There is no way a teacher can really understand the problems of a child thoroughly if someone else corrects the student's work. Errors in certain academic areas do not always have a pattern at first, and a teacher who doesn't correct the paper might miss the error and the subsequent building of a pattern of error. As you know, it is pretty difficult to break a habit.

---

[20]This report is based on materials prepared and submitted by Mr. Eugene M. Dean, Jr., San Diego Schools, San Diego, California.

In summary, the open experience, through experimentation and evaluation, has arrived at the state my report mentions. While certainly not the open classroom, it is a far cry from the straight rows and teaching the same subject to the whole class, which I did as a first-year teacher. Free time is great if you have something the children want to do and see a purpose in doing. If they go along with your sales pitch, you will seldom have trouble and learning has a better chance of taking place. And that, my friend, is the name of the game.

Experience options

In outline form, my program looks like this:

Topics (options)	Grade level	Day	Time
Math	2—Jr. high	M—F	Anytime
Social studies	2—6	M—F	Anytime
Reading	2—Jr. high	M—F	Anytime
Language arts	2—5	M,W,F	11:00-11:40

Here is a listing of the materials available to students in each of the topic option areas:

Math

1. Flash cards on basic facts in addition, subtraction, multiplication, and division
2. Teacher-made and commercial worksheets for basic facts plus fractions, telling time, number lines, set theory, decimals, and units of measurement
3. Checkers, colored and numbered in base 10 and base 5. Activities involve multiplication, addition, and subtraction, besides knowing how to play checkers.
4. Teacher-made hand clocks for telling time
5. Teacher-made number wheels for learning multiplication and addition
6. Commercial math puzzles
7. Scholastic math kit covering all math topics in elementary grades
8. Tapes on math drills of basic facts
9. Filmstrips on various math concepts
10. Math enrichment books and workbooks
11. Library books and science books dealing with math

Social studies

1. Library books, encyclopedias, and Time-Life books
2. Filmstrips and soundstrips on concepts being studied
3. Collection of famous Blacks in America and their contributions to our country, including pictures, cards, and books
4. Map puzzles of the United States and continents of the world
5. Teacher-made transparencies of various kinds
6. Slide rule knowledge game in which children are given a social science objective with controlled variables. Example: River—Mississippi—Country. The slide ruler can cover any one of the variables. Example: River—Mississippi—United States.
7. Teacher-made worksheets on various research projects, reports, and social science concepts being studied at that time
8. Student-owned books, puzzles, and materials
9. Tapes and recordings of famous people and events in history

Reading

1. Library books chosen by students and teacher
2. Students' books from home
3. Magazines and comic books
4. Basic reading texts
5. Filmstrips on reading concepts geared to individual children
   Example: filmstrip on consonant blends
6. Children's magazines
7. Newspapers
8. Children's short stories and poems
9. SRA and Scholastic reading kits
10. Time-Life books and other related social studies material

Language arts

1. Team teaching with a fellow teacher on Monday, Wednesday, and Friday from 11:00 to 11:40. Otherwise my students have access to the language arts learning center anytime.
2. Study prints for creative writing
3. Tapes, filmstrips, and soundstrips used as supplement to creative writing and grammar
4. Teacher-made transparencies for grammar, sentence structure, and punctuation

5. Teacher-made and commercial worksheets for grammar, sentence structure, and punctuation
6. Teacher-made charts for creative writing and poetry
7. Children's creative writing stories and poetry

Ground rules

Free time—the "open experience"—is an all-day affair with the children meeting as a whole group only for the flag salute, school business, and physical education. Students are taught at grade, cluster, and individual levels, so there is a considerable amount of time during which they function alone or in small groups. They are to use the learning centers only as supplements to basic instruction. The only other rule is that the students are responsible for keeping the learning centers neat and clean.

Introducing the program

I introduced the open approach by describing how the class would be structured and what learning options would be available. I told them that at least in the beginning the class structure would be like this:

1. The whole class would meet together for the purpose of introducing new concepts or for having discussions of matters pertinent to the entire class.
2. The class would be split into third and fourth grade levels for basic instruction.
3. The class would be further divided into clusters of six for intensive work in subject matter fields.
4. The class, grades, and clusters would be further broken down to the individual level to facilitate individualizing instruction.

After describing the structure, I introduced the learning options, following this procedure:

1. All topics were introduced to the class as a whole. I gave special attention to the purposes of the topics and to the concept of open experience.
2. Specific topics were again discussed in the grade level groups. Certain materials in the learning centers were to be used only by students in one grade or the other until I had time to use diagnostic tests to break the class structure down on the basis of individual needs.
3. At the cluster level, we discussed how the materials were to be used, for example, how to use the math kit or how to use the tape recorder.
4. I encouraged students to ask questions and discuss possibilities they saw.

I also discussed what I considered my role to be in the open experience approach and how I intended to keep records. I told the students I intended to work very hard to help them and keep things going smoothly, but that it would not look like the teaching they were used to seeing. For example, I would hold reading conferences, teach math concepts as needed, and conduct small group discussions. At any given time during the day I might be working with one student, with ten, or with the entire group.

With regard to record keeping, I do keep records of each student's work at each topic level and learning center; however, I do not keep detailed records of all the materials they use in the centers. I like to let them work at some things without always having to feel accountable to me. For specific topics, I keep these kinds of records:

Reading. I keep records of individual conferences I hold with each student on the books they read, and I keep track of what they do with remedial materials I prescribe for them.

Math. I keep records of what the students do with the math kit and with the materials I supply them for specific purposes.

Language arts. I keep records of the worksheets students use for grammar, sentence structure, and punctuation, as well as their creative stories and poetry if they are related to the subject matter being taught at that particular time.

Social studies. I keep records of grade level projects being carried out, along with supplementary work they do in the learning center.

Conclusion

Though my instructional program may appear rather structured, it nevertheless represents a significant movement for me away from structure and toward openness. I am very well pleased with it so far, as are my students. As I mentioned, they work eagerly in the classroom before school, during the school day, and after school. I think their eagerness speaks better than anything else about the effectiveness of the program.

14

Commercial programs and materials

When people mention the value of individualized instruction, they are usually referring to its educational advantages. There are exceptions, however. Several enterprising companies have recognized its dollar value, and they have poured ready-made programs into what must be a fertile market. For a few dollars per student, any one of several publishers will place in your hands a thoroughly impressive array of plans, procedures, materials, record forms, and most anything else you need for individualizing instruction in your classroom.

Some of these programs are nothing short of awesome. They give you, in neatly compact compartments, collections of fascinating instructional materials that might take you weeks or months to assemble on your own. Detailed instructions and management systems tie the materials together. They tell how students begin and how they work on their own; they explain how progress is determined and recorded and how evaluation is carried out. They describe the teacher's role in the whole affair. They have been put to the test of practice before coming on the market. You could hardly go wrong using them, though you would be hard pressed to find

any single program that suits your philosophy about structure, control, content, and sequence and at the same time suits the various interests, abilities, and cognitive styles of all your students. Still, some of these programs are truly outstanding. They can also cost you a couple hundred dollars or more—much more.

Other commercial programs are not so great, hardly worth more than the paper they're printed on. Even with today's inflation that's not much. You can find several that are called "individualized," but their only claim to that name is that they contain instructions so students can work on their own. Otherwise, everyone does the same activities, using the same materials that lead to the same objectives.

This chapter presents notations and descriptions of some of the commercial programs that are useful in individualizing classroom instruction. To begin, we will take note of three elaborate (and expensive) programs for individualizing instruction. They are Individually Guided Education (IGE), Individually Prescribed Instruction (IPI), and Program for Learning in Accordance with Needs (PLAN). Though they are fine programs, their cost puts them beyond the reach of most classrooms and schools. Then we will take note of a representative number of smaller, less costly programs, whose use in normal classrooms is far more likely.

ELABORATE PROGRAMS

So you will recognize the names of a few of the large-scale commercial programs for individualizing instruction, brief descriptions of three such programs are presented here. These three programs are designed for implementation on a school-wide basis. They require a total school commitment, and many personnel, materials, and facility modifications must be made to implement them. The three programs we will consider are Individually Guided Education (IGE), Individually Prescribed Instruction (IPI), and Program for Learning in Accordance with Needs (PLAN).

Individually Guided Education

Individually Guided Education (IGE) was developed under the direction of the Wisconsin Research and Development Center for Cognitive Learning. It provides instruction individualized for each student by making variations in objectives, activities, and time allocations. The program is behavior referenced. It uses specific behavioral objectives, selected for each student in accord with personal characteristics and school program.

In IGE, students work independently, in small groups, and in large groups. They receive much one-to-one help from teachers, aides, and other students. Each student's program is determined jointly by the instructional staff and the student.

The following provisions must be made to implement IGE.[1] You can see that they

---

[1] Klausmeier, H., and Ripple, R.: Learning and human abilities, New York, 1971, Harper & Row, Publishers, pp. 229-236.

represent significant departures from traditional school practices.

Entering behavior assessment. All students are checked for functional ability levels in the various curricular areas.

Objectives. Overall objectives are established on a school-wide basis. Specific instructional objectives are established for each student.

Curriculum content and sequence. Scope and sequence of the curriculum are established by the instructional staff of each school.

Instructional materials. IGE requires a large quantity of graphic and audiovisual materials. These materials are selected by the school's instructional staff.

Instructional staff. Teaching teams consist of lead teachers, staff teachers, first-year teachers, intern teachers, and teacher aides. The lead teacher coordinates the activities of the various team members. Decisions about duties and functions are made by the team unit, based on experience, preparation, and interests of team members.

Instructional procedures. Instruction begins in nongraded "instruction and research" (I & R) units of 75 to 150 students. These I & R units meet each week to plan activities. Students then receive instruction individually or in small or large groups as necessary. The program emphasizes continuous progress of each student within the nongraded organization.

Continual assessment. Careful assessment is made of students' entering abilities, progress, and attainment of objectives. Computer assisted management facilitates record keeping.

School facility requirements. IGE requires grouping flexibility, which requires the following space provisions:

1. A large flexible space, such as a gymnasium, for large group noisy activities
2. A large central resource center, for computer terminals, audiovisual equipment, library, and instructional materials
3. Room spaces of varying size, to accommodate one-to-one, small group, large group, and total group activities

IGE is a quasi-commercial program. Materials, directions, and so forth do not have to be purchased. However, training and consulting costs represent a considerable financial outlay, not to mention the costs of computer service. IGE is commercial in the sense that professional services almost certainly have to be purchased before the program can be put into effect in a school.

Individually Prescribed Instruction

Individually Prescribed Instruction (IPI) was developed by the Learning Research and Development Center at the University of Pittsburgh. The program, designed for elementary school instruction, covers the areas of mathematics, reading, science, spelling, social studies, and handwriting. The IPI curriculum is not set by grade levels. Rather, each subject area is divided into levels. Each level contains a number of specific behavioral objectives.

Each curriculum area in IPI uses the same instructional strategy. That strategy involves the following steps:

1. Students take a pretest to see which behavioral objectives they can (and cannot) reach.
2. Based on the results of the pretest, the teacher prescribes learning activities for students individually.
3. The student goes to an aide for help in obtaining materials for the activities in the prescription. Those materials are kept in large storage areas in the room where the class work is being done.
4. The student completes the prescribed work.
5. The student then takes a posttest to see whether the objective related to the prescription has been reached.

The teacher administers and scores pretests and posttests. Prescriptions are a part of the prepared program, and they come ready-made. The teacher simply selects the appropriate prescriptions for each student. The prescriptions include a "Standard Teaching Sequence" and perhaps worksheets and workbook pages for students to complete.

Teachers also conduct small group instructional sessions as they become necessary.

Program for Learning in Accordance with Needs

Program for Learning in Accordance with Needs (PLAN) was developed by the American Institute for Research in the Behavioral Sciences. It is a sophisticated, modularized instruction approach that uses a computer for scoring, record keeping, and matching students with appropriate module activities.

Aside from the functions performed by the computer, PLAN's modules have the same essential format as the modules with which you are already familiar. Each module contains four to six behavioral objectives. Related to each module are various optional learning approaches, called "Teaching Learning Units" (TLU). Individual students select the TLU they find most appealing. Features of TLU's include examples of the types of questions one should become able to answer, a list of learning activities, and a list of instructional materials to be used with the activities.

The teachers' main role is to organize the classroom and facilitate students' individual work. They help students select and arrange programs of study, and they tutor and serve as resource persons when necessary.

REPRESENTATIVE KITS

Most of the smaller, less elaborate commercial programs come in kit form. The kits vary in size from boxes smaller than a loaf of bread to groups of three or four largish boxes. All, however, are compact enough to be placed on a table or a shelf; they require little classroom space.

The kits described in this section represent only a fraction of the number now available. New materials are appearing regularly, and they number far more than we could properly give attention in these pages. Don't conclude that the kits described here are necessarily the most effective or efficient that you can find. Every program could not be included here, and some excellent ones are not described. Still, these kits are representative of what is available on the market. They show differing formats, yet they all promote work that is individualized in one way or another.

You will see that the kits reported here deal with the areas of reading and mathematics. Most available kits fall into those areas. Individualized kits in science and social science do exist, though they are relatively few in number. Numerous kits are available that provide multimedia packages and enrich-

ment activities for entire groups, rather than for individualized work.

Reading/language kits
The Power Reading System

Winston Press
25 Groveland Terrace
Minneapolis, Minn. 55403

Level: Grades 1 through 11

This program is designed for the development of basic reading skills. It can be used effectively in skill development phases of primary through high school reading programs.

The Power Reading System is a diagnostic-

Study Skills — Use of Reference
Newspapers, Major Sections
Lesson Plan

Objective
Given examples of writing from newspaper editorials, feature articles, and news articles, the student will be able to distinguish between fact and opinion and determine which type of newspaper article stresses which kind of writing.

Materials
- Newspapers for each student in the class
- Worksheet "Newspapers, Major Sections" (two pages)

Directions
Note: Before presenting this lesson you may want to look at Lesson 69, "Newspapers, Index," and Lesson 43, "Distinguishing Fact from Opinion."

Write the following words on the board:
news articles
feature articles
editorials

Pass out the newspapers to the students. Initiate a discussion on the major sections of a newspaper. Explain to the students that they are going to look at three major sections which are included in almost all newspapers, especially daily newspapers in major cities. Point out that these three categories are written on the board. Read the three aloud. Ask if anyone knows the major differences between these three kinds of articles. (News articles generally present the facts of a story. They may quote people with opinions, but the writers are generally careful to document all information given in the story. Feature articles combine the use of fact and opinion to pre-

sent a story which is often based on a cause, an individual's activities, or a local or national trend. Editorials, although relying on the facts reporters have gathered, always represent the opinion of the newspaper, the local editor, or a syndicated editorial columnist on a certain issue.)

Tell the students that often, but not always, news articles appear on the front pages of the paper. Feature articles generally appear in sections about family living, travel, contemporary life, entertainment, which are usually in the second or third section of the newspaper. Editorials appear on editorial pages.

Have the students page through the newspaper and look at the headlines and first paragraphs of stories. Ask them to list two or three short articles they think fit into each major category. Write several titles for each major category beneath the category title on the board.

Mention that there are many other parts of a newspaper other than news, features, and editorials. Advertising, both commercial and classified, comprises a large portion of the newspaper. There are local calendars of events, weather reports and forecasts, and other announcements that cannot properly be called news articles. There is usually a sports section and a business section also. Articles in these two sections can be classified as news articles, feature articles, or editorials.

Ask the students if they can think of another newspaper category that appears everyday, which is designed both to entertain and to influence readers. (The cartoons.) Explain that there are basically two kinds of cartoons: the one-panel cartoons, often appearing on the editorial page, which comment on current local or national issues — often political; and the multipanelled cartoons, appearing on the "funny" pages, which often represent opinions in the form of humor, but their main purpose is to entertain.

Write the words *fact* and *opinion* above the words already on the board like this:

	fact	opinion
news articles		
(article titles)		
feature articles		
(article titles)		
editorials		
(article titles)		

Choose one of the news articles listed on the board and have the students read it. Begin discussion of the article by asking the students to relate the stated facts. As they relate the major facts of the story, write them on the board under the *fact* column. Ask if anyone found an opinion in the news article. Was it quoted from another source or reported as fact?

Repeat this procedure with a feature article and an editorial. Have the students pick out facts and opinions they find in the feature and opinions they find in the editorial. (They should also attempt to pick out the facts on which the editorial opinions are based.) Repeat the above procedure until the students can distinguish the three main categories and can also distinguish fact from opinion.

After you have finished this group exercise, pass out the worksheet "Newspapers, Major Sections." Instruct the students to complete it. Go over the answers in class to make sure that each student is able to distinguish between fact and opinion in the articles given.

The Power Reading System
Copyright 1975. Winston Press. Inc

Fig. 16. Power Reading System. (Reprinted from Power Reading I, copyright © 1974, Winston Press, Minneapolis, Minnesota. Used with permission.)

prescriptive program. All activities are keyed to items on the Reading Survey Test contained in the program. Prepared lesson plans detail procedures and materials for carrying out learning activities. Criterion tests then serve to indicate whether students have mastered the skill objectives around which the program is built.

The Power Reading System is compact, efficient, and easy to use. It consists of three kits that contain instructional units on word recognition, comprehension, and study skills. Specific behavioral objectives undergird the units. It uses a file drawer method or organization. Records are kept on a master checklist, included in the program. Individual checklists for students also come with the materials. Fig. 16 shows a sample of a lesson plan included in the program.

SRA Reading Laboratory Series

Science Research Associates, Inc.
155 North Wacker Dr.
Chicago, Ill. 60606

Level:
Grades 1 through 3 (Kits I, Ia, Ib, Ic)
Grades 4 through 6 (Kits IIa, IIb, IIc)
Grades 7 through 12 (Kits IIIa, IIIb, IVa)

One of the first kits, widely used and comprehensive, the SRA kits continue to be very popular. Each kit spans a number of different grade levels. Materials are designed to place each student at the appropriate level of reading ability and foster individual progress.

Materials are color coded to show reading levels. Students select materials and work through on their own. They also check their own work. Teachers do only occasional spot checking. The kits contain:

Power Builders, reading selections that develop vocabulary, comprehension, and word attack skills. The selections cover a variety of topics. Answer keys are provided for students.
Listening Skill Builders, selections that are read to students, to help them learn to understand and remember what they hear

Rate Builders, short reading selections intended to develop reading speed with comprehension
Student Record Books, books that explain procedures for using the kit materials. Students write responses to exercises in them.
Teacher's Handbook, a handbook that contains skill builders and explanations of procedures in using the kits.

The new SRA Mark II Kits (1978) include cassette tapes and contemporary stories.

Individualized Reading From Scholastic

Scholastic Book Services
904 Sylvan Avenue
Englewood Cliffs, N.J. 07632

Level: Primary elementary through secondary

The Scholastic Individualized Reading Program exemplifies the degree to which commercial programs have been made comprehensive, attractive, and useful. The publishers emphasize that the program is for teachers who want to individualize reading but who don't have the necessary time or materials to prepare their own program.

This program emphasizes reading skills, good literature, and interesting learning activities. Each elementary unit (grade) includes 100 paperback books, with wide ranges of readability and age interests. Along with the paperbacks come materials students can use on their own: general activity cards, skill activity games, discussion cards, individual student reading logs, records, and a flannel board with cutouts.

Materials teachers use to manage the program include informal reading inventory cards, a conference notebook, and a master worksheet book. An explicit teacher's guide describes ways to begin the program, how to organize it, how to conduct conferences, how to group students, how to evaluate progress, and possible problems that might occur.

The secondary programs show even more diversity than the elementary. The *Action* and *Double Action* kits contain a large variety of attractive and useful materials including the following:

Unibooks—groups of very short stories followed by practice exercises
Short stories
Plays
Scripts (for acting out)
Records

Figs. 17 to 19 show a portion of an alphabetizing game, the cover from a teaching guide, and instructions on reading a one-act play.

Personalized Reading Center

Xerox Corporation
245 Long Hill Road
Middletown, Conn. 43216

Level: Primary through junior high

Like the Scholastic Program, the Personalized Reading Center contains selected paperback books for students to read. There are seventy-five "core" books, plus twenty-five "enrichment" books. Activities related to them stress comprehension, vocabulary, and literature skills. The program provides for student selection of books and related activities and allows them to work at their own pace.

Contents of the Personalized Reading Center are: books, story cards, creative activity cards, reading placement survey card, wall chart of procedures, pupil's logs, teacher's log, reading placement survey, and answer keys.

In using the program, the teacher follows these steps:

1. Give placement test.
2. Based on test, suggest appropriate core collection (books) for each student.
3. Allow students to select own books from suggested core.
4. Students begin with story cards.
5. Students complete exercises in logs.
6. Students score own exercises.
7. Students read selected paperbacks.
8. Students select creative activity cards.
9. Conference between teacher and student.

From the student's perspective, procedures go like this:

1. Use pupil's log to find out about books your teacher suggests.
2. Read about the books and look at the pictures. (The pupil's log has illustrations and brief comments about each book.)
3. Choose the book you want to read. Remember its number.
4. Get the four story cards with the same number.
5. Answer the questions on the answer sheet in your log. Correct your own answers.
6. Read the book you have chosen.
7. Get the creative activities card with the same number. Choose your activity.
8. Have a conference with your teacher. Tell her about the book you have read and the activity you have chosen.

In Fig. 20, *A*, you can see an example of a story card. In Fig. 20, *B* you see story card answer sheets and a book review.

Springboards: Reading Motivation

Noble & Noble Publishers, Inc.
750 Third Avenue
New York, N.Y. 10017

Level: Upper intermediate and secondary

This program is especially well suited for junior high school reading and for high school remedial programs. Most of the activities require reading abilities at the fourth and fifth grade levels. None is above sixth grade level. However, the characters and plots have high interest for secondary students.

Springboards consists of four separate programs, which are housed together in one kit. There are twenty separate lessons in each program. The four programs are:

1. The American History Program
2. The Negro in American History
3. Viewpoints in Fiction
4. The World History Program

Each Springboard serves as a motivational lesson and provides remedial reading and vocabulary building exercises. Some of them look like newspapers, others like magazines.

Text continued on p. 221.

Fig. 17. An alphabetizing game. (Scholastic Magazine.)

Episode 7   **INSIDE STORY, page 23**

Aim: To have students write, discuss, and, if necessary, revise their own first sentences.

Story Line: After the discussion of opening sentences (Episode 6), the two story editors, still in the Book Worm, decide to try writing first sentences of their own. They comment on each other's first sentences. After returning home, the story editor takes a second look at his sentence and, based on his own evaluation of it, either revises it or lets it stand.

Comments: Although this episode builds on the work in Episodes 5 and 6, it is a departure from the student's preceding work. Here the student is asked to write something original, a first sentence of his own.

There is no harm in the student's modeling his opening sentence on one of those he selected in Episodes 5 and 6; emulation is a legitimate way to start original writing.

The student should carefully consider his student-colleague's criticisms and suggestions, but he is free to accept or reject them. Both a too hasty acceptance and a too hasty rejection of criticism are to be avoided. Similarly, while the student should give some thought to revising his sentence, he may well decide that the first version is the best. So be it.

Summary of Student Tasks:

1. Write an opening sentence for a story.
2. Discuss each other's first sentences with another student.
3. Either revise or don't revise the sentence.

Fig. 18. The cover and a page of a teaching guide. (Scholastic Magazine.)

READING A ONE-ACT PLAY

The final section of the *Drama* lessons tests the students' ability to utilize what they have learned about how to read a play. The lesson is based on another Chekhov play titled *The Bear*. Make the reading assignment as follows:

ON PAGES 83-87 IN YOUR BOOKS THERE IS A SHORT-ENED VERSION OF ANOTHER ONE-ACT PLAY BY CHEK-HOV CALLED THE BEAR. *I WANT YOU TO READ IT CARE-FULLY AND BE READY TO ANSWER SOME QUESTIONS ABOUT IT. THIS WILL BE A TEST, AND I WILL ASK QUES-TIONS LIKE THOSE WE HAVE BEEN TRYING TO ANSWER ABOUT* THE MARRIAGE PROPOSAL.

Before the class begins reading, you might mention that the title of this play in Russian is properly translated as *The Bear*. However, in many American anthologies it is translated as *The Boor* because a boorish person in Russia is often called a bear.

READING A ONE-ACT PLAY

The following scene is adapted from a one-act play by Chekhov called *The Bear*. Popova, a pretty young widow, still in mourning after seven months, is the owner of a large farm. Smirnov is a big, muscular ex-soldier who owns a neighboring farm. Popova's late husband had owed Smirnov a large amount of money for oats, and Smirnov has pushed his way into Popova's house and demanded she pay him his interest on the loan. Popova has said she will pay him the day after tomorrow, and they have argued. Smirnov has been shouting, stomping around the room, and bullying Luka (Popova's elderly servant), while insulting women in general and Popova in particular. Popova has finally gotten angry and is trying to get Smirnov out of the house.

THE BEAR

Smirnov: Don't you shout at me!

Popova: I'm not the one who's shouting. You're shouting! Please go away.

Smirnov: Pay me and I'll go.

Popova: I won't give you any money!

Smirnov: Oh, yes you will!

2 – **Popova:** Just to spite you, I won't pay you anything.

Smirnov: I'm not lucky enough to be either your husband or your fiancé. So I don't have to put up with your temper. *(He sits down.)* I don't like scenes.

Popova *(enraged):* You're sitting down?

Smirnov: Yes. I am.

Popova: Get out.

Smirnov: Give me my money.

3 – **Popova:** You impudent clod. Get out of here. *(Pause.)* You're not going?

Smirnov: No.

Popova: No?

Smirnov: No.

83

Popova: You're an ignorant peasant. You're a crude bear! *(Smirnov stands.)* A brute! A monster!

Smirnov *(advancing toward her):* What right do you have to insult me?

Popova: I am insulting you! So what! I'm not afraid of you.

4 – **Smirnov:** You think that because you're a woman you can insult me and get away with it! You're wrong. I challenge you.

5 – **Luka:** Oh, Lord in Heaven!

Smirnov: Pistols!

Popova: You think that because you have big fists and bellow like a bull that I'm afraid of you.

Smirnov: I challenge you! Nobody gets away with insulting me! I don't care if you are a woman!

Popova: Bear, idiot, peasant, bully!

Smirnov: If women want to be equal, they should behave as equals! Let's fight!

Popova: You want to fight!

Smirnov: Right now!

Popova: This minute! My husband had some pistols. *(She goes out and returns a second later.)* What a pleasure it will be to put a bullet through that thick head of yours! *(She goes out again.)*

6 – **Smirnov:** I'll shoot her down like a bird! I'm not one of these sentimentalists. Women are just like anyone else to me.

Luka: Oh Heavens. *(He kneels.)* Kind sir. Have pity on an old man and go away. You've frightened the lady half to death already and now you're going to shoot her.

Smirnov *(not listening):* If she fights me it will mean she really believes the sexes are equal! I'll shoot her like a chicken! But what a woman! *(He imitates her.)* "What a pleasure it will be to put a bullet through that thick head of yours!" What a woman! How her eyes flashed . . . she accepted my challenge! I've never seen a woman like that!

Luka: Dear sir, please go away! I'll pray for your soul as long as I live.

Smirnov: That's a real woman for you! A woman like that I

84

Fig. 19. Instructions on reading a one-act play. (Scholastic Magazine.)

round and round on its reel.

At the same moment, there was a small sound near the door where Walt usually sat. Walt drew his gun, snapped off the flashlight, and edged silently down the dark hall. Then he aimed his flashlight at the sound and switched it on.

"Don't move," he said. "I've got you covered." In the beam of light stood two of the museum's daytime guards. They were holding an album of valuable stamps.

"They planted the tape recorder inside the mummy case," Walt explained to the director the next day. "They would turn it on by remote control. As soon as I left the door to check the Egyptian room, they would slip into the museum."

"What were they doing with the stamps?"

"They were lifting stamps off the album pages and replacing them with fakes," Walt said. "They would change as many stamps as they could. Then, as soon as they heard me coming back to the door, they would leave. Last night they almost finished the job."

"Walt," said the director, "you're a fine watchman. I owe you an apology—and a raise."

A
_____

In the book The Incredible Detectives *mysterious things happen inside a museum. This story is also about a museum mystery.*

Choose the best ending for each of these sentences and write the letters in your log:

1. When the crooks put the tape recorder into the mummy case, the mummy probably felt
   a. cold inside.
   b. angry about it.
   c. nothing at all.
2. When Walt first heard the mysterious voice, he probably thought

a. he was going crazy.
b. someone was in the museum.
c. he would lose his job.
3. When Walt first reported that the mummy was talking, the director probably felt
   a. sorry for Walt.
   b. proud of Walt.
   c. afraid of the mummy.
4. When the tape recorder broke, the crooks probably
   a. didn't know it was broken.
   b. thought Walt had broken it.
   c. knew they would get caught.

BOOK NO. 28

After their mother dies, Julie and her brother live with their stuffy aunt. Then Chris goes away to school and her father remarries. It seems that no one has time for Julie.

B

card a	card b
number correct	number correct

card c	card d
number correct	number correct

20

Fig. 20. A, Story card. **B,** Story card answer sheets and book review. (Xerox Education Publications.)

Each is a four page folder, with exercises following the lead stories.

Fig. 21, *A* shows the first page of one of the Springboards. Fig. 21, *B* shows the exercises that follow the reading sections.

The Literature Sampler (1964)

Learning Research Association
1501 Broadway
New York, N.Y. 10030

Level:
Elementary (Junior edition)
Secondary (Secondary edition)

The Literature Sampler uses selected samples from existing literature and is designed to supplement the regular reading program. The Junior Sampler, for example, contains 120 book previews, distributed through the areas of "Tales of Courage and Daring," "Sports," "People," "Animals," "Fun For All," and "Mystery." The primary objective of the program is to increase reading interest, enjoyment, and comprehension.

Students select materials that interest them, complete associated activities, check their own work, and keep their own records. They pace themselves. Materials are stratified as easy, average, and difficult, within each grade level.

Activities include such things as completing reading aids, working through discus-

FICTION REVISED   SPRINGBOARDS ®

LUIS AND MARY O'TOOLE

WHAT DO YOU REMEMBER?
(Do not write on this sheet unless instructed by your teacher.)

Part I: Write the letter of the answer you think is correct in the space at the right.

1. Luis warned his friend about (a) girls' parents; (b) pizza; (c) sports.
2. Mary O'Toole had (a) blond hair and blue eyes; (b) red hair and blue eyes; (c) black hair and dark eyes.
3. Mary O'Toole said that Luis (a) was the worst pizza cook in Philadelphia; (b) was very stupid; (c) was the best pizza cook in town.
4. She asked Luis (a) to go bowling with her; (b) to go to the movies; (c) to meet her parents.
5. Mary's father (a) was very tall; (b) was fat; (c) was small and thin.
6. Luis played the following sports with Mary's father: (a) badminton, bowling, and table tennis; (b) water polo, boxing, and football; (c) weightlifting, softball, and hockey.
7. Mary's father (a) was not good at sports; (b) was very good at sports; (c) hated sports.
8. Luis decided to stop dating Mary O'Toole because (a) her father exhausted him; (b) he didn't like her; (c) he couldn't get along with her mother.
9. Before Luis asked Angela Scolotti for a date, he (a) asked if she liked to dance; (b) asked if she had money; (c) asked about her father's hobbies.
10. Angela's father's idea of exercise was (a) fishing; (b) checkers; (c) tennis.

Part II: What's another way of saying it? Put in the space at the right the statement that best fits the first statement.

1. Luis confused me: (a) I didn't quite understand what Luis was talking about; (b) Luis made me very happy; (c) Luis made me sad.
2. Mary's mother was plump: (a) Mary's mother was very short; (b) Mary's mother was very thin; (c) Mary's mother was a little fat.
3. This is fascinating: (a) This is silly; (b) This is very interesting; (c) This is boring.
4. He hit me accidentally: (a) He meant to hit me; (b) He hit me, but he didn't mean to; (c) He hit me very hard.
5. He entered the room like an elephant: (a) He made a lot of noise when he entered the room; (b) He came into the room on his hands and knees; (c) He came into the room quietly.
6. I like to play a game called badminton: (a) I like a game that is played with a big ball you throw into a basket; (b) I like a game that is played with a heavy ball you roll down an alley; (c) I like a game that is played with small rackets and a net.
7. When I bowled with him, he told me my style was wrong: (a) He told me the way I bowled was wrong; (b) He told me my ball was wrong; (c) He told me I didn't speak well.
8. She is my big romance: (a) I don't like her; (b) She doesn't like me; (c) I love her!
9. I was shocked: (a) I was very happy; (b) I was very surprised; (c) I was very sad.
10. He never spoke in a normal voice: (a) He didn't know how to speak; (b) He never spoke loudly; (c) He didn't speak like other people.

Give yourself five points for each correct answer.

GENERAL CONSULTANTS: Abraham Kavadlo, Adjunct Associate Professor, Sociology Department, Hunter College; Peter G. Kontos, President, Educational Dimensions, Inc.; John P. Gallagher, Language Arts Coordinator, K-12, Lindenhurst Public Schools, Lindenhurst, Long Island.

ADVISOR: Marjorie Drabkin, English Language Arts Curriculum Specialist, Grades 5-12, New York City Board of Education.

PHOTO CREDIT: Wallace C. Vogt.

NOBLE AND NOBLE, Publishers, Inc.   750 THIRD AVENUE, NEW YORK, N. Y. 10017   Z2272-5

B

Fig. 21. A, First page of one of the Springboards. **B,** Exercises that follow the reading sections. (Noble and Noble Publishers, Inc.)

sions, and following up on suggested library use. Many such activities are detailed in the teacher's guide that accompanies the program.

SVE Basic Reading Skills Modules

Society for Visual Education, Inc.
1345 Diversey Parkway
Chicago, Ill. 60614

Level: Kindergarten through grade 3

Individualized supplementary reading program in kit form. Separate kits for reading readiness, vowel sounds, consonant sounds, and base words. Each kit contains sound filmstrips, manipulatives, games, activity cards, diagnostic materials, checksheets, worksheets, and sample letters to parents.

Bell and Howell's Reading Game Sound System

Audio-Visual Products Division
1909 E. Cornell
Peoria, Ill. 61616

Level: Kindergarten through grade 6

Materials for teaching reading readiness and word attack skills through advanced phonics. Students see, hear, and practice the reading skills orally and in writing until the skill is mastered. Materials include teacher's manual, color-coded skill packets, posttests, and worksheets.

Individualized Directions in Reading (IDR)

Steck-Vaughn Co.
807 Brazos
Austin, Tex. 78767

Level: Kindergarten through grade 6

A diagnostic-prescriptive program for individualized work. The program uses criterion-referenced inventories and prescriptive-learning materials intended to correct reading skills deficiencies and emphasizes phonics, structural analysis, and comprehension.

Hoffman Instructional Reading Kits

4423 Arden Drive
El Monte, Cal. 91731

Level: Grades 1 through 9 (developmental)
Grades 3 through 12 (remedial)

Diagnostic-prescriptive materials that focus on the specific skills of decoding and comprehension. The kits are intended to supplement the basic reading program.

Skillbooster

Modern Curriculum Press
13900 Prospect Road
Cleveland, Ohio 44136

Level: Grades 4 through 6

Contains specific skill-building exercises in Building Word Power, Increasing Comprehension, Working with Facts and Details, Organizing Information, and Using References.

BFA Kits

2211 Michigan Ave.
Santa Monica, Cal. 90404

Level: Kindergarten through grade 12

BFA produces a number of kits for all grade levels. Examples include the Comprehension Skills Laboratory Series, Power Reading, and the Reading Vocabulary Laboratory.

Skills Box (Language)

Holt, Rinehart and Winston, Inc.
383 Madison Avenue
New York, N.Y. 10017

Level: Grades 7 through 9

The Skills Box is a junior high and high school level program that stresses the development of language skills. Emphasis is placed on the following:

Vocabulary: prefixes, suffixes, figures of speech, context clues

Punctuation: sentence punctuation, commas, semicolons and dashes, quotations and titles
Spelling: capitalization, apostrophes, ie and ei, plurals, homonyms, prefixes and suffixes
Usage: subject verb agreement, irregular verb forms, personal pronouns, who and whom
Dictionary: locating words, spelling and pronunciation, definitions

Procedures are as follows:

1. To begin, the teacher administers the diagnostic tests in the student record book.
2. On the basis of the test results, students are told which materials to obtain from the Skills Box. Individual students obtain the material and work through it at their own speed.
3. Students check own work, using the answer key.
4. Students check which lesson has been completed on the Progress Plotter.
5. Students take achievement tests related to materials used. Each student scores own test, or the teacher can score them.

Tutorgram

ERCA
Dept. 20
Iron Ridge, Wis. 53035

Level: Grade 4 through junior high

Individualized self teaching systems for learning nouns, verbs, adjectives, adverbs, capitalization, punctuation, synonyms, antonyms, and homonyms.

Keys to Good Language; Keys to English Mastery

The Economy Co.
P.O. Box 25308
1901 North Walnut
Oklahoma City, Ok. 73125

Level: Grade 4 through junior high

Nongraded, individualized materials for teaching essentials in speaking, writing, and thinking with emphasis on grammar, vocabulary, spelling, dictionary skills, and reference skills.

Continuous Progress in Spelling

The Economy Co.
P.O. Box 25308
1901 North Walnut
Oklahoma City, Ok. 73125

Level: Grades 3 through 8

Kits for individualized spelling, using a test-study-test approach in combination with peer teaching. Duplicating masters are available.

Wordcraft

Communacad
Dept. IM, Box 541
Wilton, Conn. 06897

Level: Grade 4 through college

Kits for rapid vocabulary building designed by Dr. Bergen Evans. The kits use a multimedia approach, with stories, biographies, narratives, filmstrips, and cassette tapes. They include student manual with pretests, scripts, and posttests.

Mathematics programs
Project Mathematics Series

Winston Press
25 Groveland Terrace
Minneapolis, Minn. 55403

Level: Kindergarten through grade 6

Project Mathematics Series is a comprehensive program for developing basic mathematics skills. It is an activity approach, structured into sixteen student books of progressive levels of difficulty, which overlap normal grade levels. The test component of the program is criterion referenced, showing attainment or lack of specific skill objectives.

Smaller kits that accompany the program can be used by themselves, if desired. One such kit is called *Developing Number Experiences Kit*. Designed for kindergarten through second grade, it deals with shapes, colors, and patterns, providing individual work in

ISP CAN HELP YOUR PUPILS, TOO!

Individualized Computational Skills Program

Level One: Grades 1-2; Level Two: Grades 3-4; Level Three: Grades 5-6; Level Four: Grades 7-12   **Bryce R. Shaw • Petronella M. W. Hiehle • Miriam M. Schaefer**

Susan, a fourth-grader in Flint, Michigan, was one of many youngsters whose achievement in math computation fell below grade level. After working with *Individualized Computational Skills Program*, she was performing at grade level, as were other members of her class. Here's how the program helped her …

COMPUTATION TEST (EXCERPT)

First, Susan took the fourth-grade Computation Test (the test consists of eight pages; only one section is shown here) and obtained a grade equivalent score of 3.5 (fifth month of grade 3).

ARITHMETIC SKILLS INVENTORY

Susan then took the appropriate Arithmetic Skills Inventories to discover which computational skill (or skills) she needed to practice. The Inventories revealed weaknesses in whole numbers. (Only the *Whole Numbers: Multiplication* test appears.)

STUDENT ARITHMETIC RECORD CARD

Her teacher recorded these results on Susan's Student Arithmetic Record Card.

DRILL AND PRACTICE SHEET

For ten minutes a day, Susan used Drill and Practice Sheets, working problems and correcting answers to help remedy her computational weaknesses.

TEACHING MODEL

Additional help for Susan came from the Teaching Models, pupil-oriented explanations and examples that give the mechanics of performing each skill.

CLASS PROFILE CHART (EXCERPT)

In just two weeks of practice Susan made significant progress in multiplying, adding, and subtracting whole numbers. This Class Profile Chart shows her mathematical performance in relation to the rest of the class, after she used *ICSP*.

Do your pupils need help with computational skills? *ICSP* can help them, just as it helped Susan and her classmates. Ten minutes a day of this easy-to-administer program detects and corrects computational skills weaknesses.

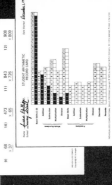
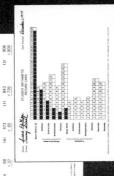

Fig. 22. ICSP program. (Houghton Mifflin Company.)

classifying, structuring, and ordering sets of objects and in matching and building patterns.

A second kit, called *Project Mathematics Activity Kit* (for kindergarten through third grade), provides eighty-four activity cards. These cards stress basic skill development in geometry, measurement, and number. They are color coded and sequenced by level of difficulty. A set of duplicating masters comes with the kit. They provide number lines, exercises, and puzzles. A comprehensive teacher's guide accompanies the materials.

Individualized Computational Skills Program (ICSP)

Houghton Mifflin Co.
Pennington-Hopewell Road
Hopewell, N.J. 08525

Level: Grades 1 through 9

The Individualized Computational Skills Program (ICSP) is a diagnostic-prescriptive program for the development of computational skills. It contains:

1. Sequential skills outline
2. Computation tests
3. Arithmetic skills inventories
4. Student and class record forms
5. Drill and practice sheets
6. Teaching models

The program is organized so that students follow these procedures:

1. Take the computation test to determine grade equivalent.
2. Take the arithmetic skills inventories to identify which skills need practice.
3. Record findings on the student arithmetic record card.
4. Use drill and practice sheets to correct computational difficulty.
5. Use a teaching model. (This is a detailed illustrated explanation of computational procedures, which students follow.)
6. Record efforts on the class profile chart.

Fig. 22 shows examples of the elements included in the ICSP program.

SRA Mathematics Learning System (1974)

Science Research Associates, Inc.
259 East Erie St.
Chicago, Ill. 60611

Level: Kindergarten through grade 8

The SRA Mathematics Learning System is a comprehensive elementary mathematics program. It is built around "resource boxes" that correlate with basic textbooks. Each resource box contains:

1. *Goal sheets* that correspond to textbook chapters. They include survey questions, a student study guide, and space for record keeping.
2. *Personal progress folders*, which include a list of objectives and directions for using the resource box. Objectives are checked off as they are mastered.
3. *Activity masters* that can be duplicated for providing additional practice in skills and concepts.
4. A *tutorboard*, on which students place pins to show where they are working in the program.

Supplementary materials include:

Math Applications Kit, containing 210 activity cards on mathematics involved in various areas, such as social science and sports
Mathematics Involvement Program, a box of activity cards and manipulable objects for math skills and concepts.
Computapes, a cassette tape program for use in practicing basic arithmetic skills
Arithmetic Fact Kit, to develop speed and accuracy in basic facts
Cross-number Puzzle Boxes, with puzzles on whole numbers, fractions, decimals, percent, and story problems
Computational Skills Development Kit, emphasizing addition, subtraction, multiplication, and division
Inquisitive Games Series
The Detect Series

Individualization can allow students to progress at their own rates and follow different sequences. Diagnositc and criterion test materials are included.

Continuous Progress Laboratories: Individualized Mathematics

Educational Progress Corporation
Palo Alto, Cal.

Level: Grades 1 through 8

The CPL mathematics program individualizes instruction through the use of a set of audio tapes, some 350 lesson cards, teacher resource materials, and student progress books. It stresses the use of multiple learning resources, individual work, self pacing, and self testing.

Each lesson card in the lab presents a complete lesson, including learning objectives, learning resources, a challenge test, and a performance test.

The learning objectives are stated behaviorally. Each lesson contains from one to four objectives.

The learning resources are coded by symbols and numbers. Symbols stand for a book or tape. Numbers stand for tape numbers or book page numbers.

The challenge test is one the students take when they believe they are ready for it—that is, when they can reach the learning objectives for the lesson. Students check their own answers.

The performance test must be taken at the conclusion of the lesson. Students check their own work.

Fig. 23 shows the activity sequence students follow in CPL.

Check and Double Check

Scholar's Choice
1051 Clinton St.
Buffalo, N.Y. 14206

Level: Kindergarten through grade 8

Eight levels of materials for basic math. The program is used to supplement the regular math program. Diagnostic and evaluative tests are included. "Return to basics" emphasis.

Mathematics Skills Development

Nystrom
3333 Elston Ave.
Chicago, Ill. 60618

Level: Grade 5 through junior high

A basic program built around thirty key concepts in math. The program consists of thirty auto-tutorial modules with cassette tapes that focus on a single computational concept with accompanying skills. Materials include tests and suggestions for additional instructional activities.

Cassette Activity Books; Cassette Learning Packages

Media Materials, Inc.
2936 Remington Ave.
Baltimore, Md. 21211

Level: Elementary and junior high

Activity books have planned activities, reproducible pages, answer keys, and cassette tapes. Learning Packages have cassette tape lessons, student response booklets, teacher's guide, and posttests.

Special education
Special Education Teacher's Kit

Love Publishing Co.
6635 East Villanova Place
Denver, Co. 80222

A kit for teaching exceptional children in regular classrooms. It includes activities in arithmetic, vocabulary development, science, art, music, and language. Contains spirit masters, learning games, awards, and numerous ideas and suggestions.

Continuous Progress Path

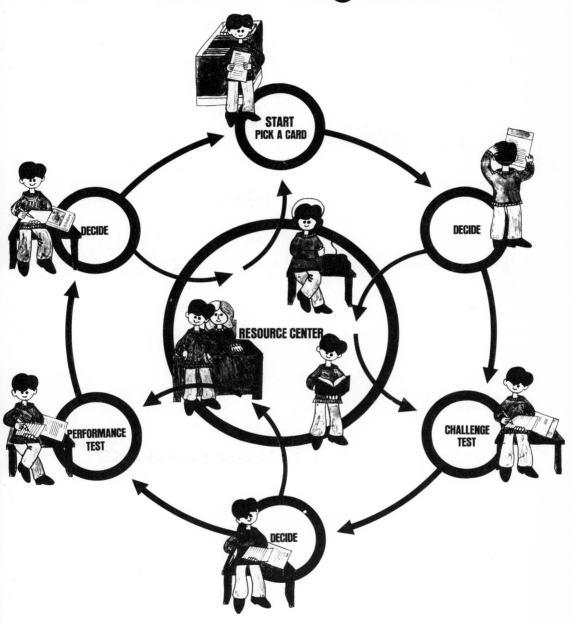

Fig. 23. Activity sequence students follow in CPL. (Educational Progress Corporation.)

Basic skills
SRA Basic Skills Kits

SRA, Inc.
155 North Wacker Drive
Chicago, Ill. 60606

Level: Grade 4 through junior high

Separate kits for teaching Graph and Picture Skills, Organizing and Reporting Skills, and Map and Globe Skills.

Thinking skills
Basic Thinking Skills

Midwest Publications
P.O. Box 129
Troy, Mich. 48099

Level: Grades 4 through 10

Series contains twelve small books, each intended to sharpen thinking skills. The series is available either as booklets or spirit masters.

Materials in machines and laboratories

Somewhere on the scale between kits and large-scale commercial programs are sets of materials intended for use in machines and laboratories. Audio-cassettes and visual displays come into greater play. Many kinds of materials and equipment fit into this category. The following are a few examples.

System 80

Borg-Warner Educational Systems
600 West University Drive
Arlington Heights, Ill. 60004

The System 80 is a machine with display screen and buttons for students to push. It accommodates a large quantity of materials in various curricular areas. The materials are programmed. A visual display appears before the student. It calls for a response, which is made by pushing selected buttons. If the response is correct, the material advances to the next frame. If incorrect, the material is repeated or it branches into a remedial avenue.

Language Master System

Bell and Howell
Audio-Visual Products Division
7100 N. McCormick Road
Chicago, Ill. 60645

The Language Master System consists of a recording-playback unit that uses cards. The cards are printed, with an audio-tape strip on the bottom. The student inserts the card in the machine, listens to what is recorded, and then records a response onto the card. This system is used mainly for language and mathematics.

Holt Databank System

Holt, Rinehart and Winston, Inc.
383 Madison Ave.
New York, N.Y. 10017

The Databank, a system for teaching social studies, is made up of many components that contain information on people, cultures, communities, history, technology, and cities. Materials include cassette recordings, filmstrips, data comix, data foldouts, data masters, games and simulations, data cards, and data packs. A teacher's guide provides background material, objectives, lesson plans, and scope and sequence charts.

SELECTED TEACHER MATERIALS (ANNOTATED)
Thinking and learning skills

Atwood, B.: *Building Independent Learning Skills*, Learning Handbooks, 1974

Activities for students in grade 3 through junior high for developing skills in investigation, organization, analysis, evaluation, and transformation, without the direct supervision of the teacher.

Baratta-Lorton, M.: *Workjobs*, Addison-Wesley Publishing Co., Inc., 1972

Activities for primary children in developing language and math abilities through manipulative activities.

Sharp, E.: *Thinking is Child's Play*, Discus Books, 1970

Easy, enjoyable games for intellectual stimulation based on the ideas of Jean Piaget.

Language/English

California Association of School Librarians: *Library Skills*, Fearon Publishers, 1973

Numerous lessons on developing skills for using the library. For grade 3 through high school.

Chappel, B.: *Independent Language Arts Activities*, Fearon Publishers, 1973

Primary grade, challenging seatwork, reading exercises, comprehension exercises, spelling, phonics, vocabulary development, and language usage.

Goodson, R., and Floyd, B.: *Individualizing Instruction in Spelling*, T. S. Denison, 1974

Practical guide with inventories, word lists, directions.

Hurwitz, A., and Goddard, A.: *Games to Improve Your Child's English*, Simon & Shuster, Inc., 1969

A variety of fascinating games for intermediate grades through high school. Includes rhyming, vocabulary building, alphabetizing, spelling, and grammar.

Kerby, M.: *Independent Language Arts Activities*, Fearon Publishers, 1973

Intermediate grade activities in spelling, dictionary skills, grammar, punctuation, capitalization, sentence structure, composition, poetry, and word usage.

Muncy, P.: *Word Play*, Instructor Publications, 1977

Book A and Book B include duplicating sheets of puzzles, anagrams, and so forth.

Spache, E.: *Puzzlers to Teach Vocabulary* and *Puzzlers to Teach Phonics*, Instructor Curriculum Materials, 1977

Primary and intermediate levels.

Reading

Burie, A., and Heltshe, M.: *Reading With A Smile: 90 Reading Games That Work*, Acropolis Books, 1975

Primary through intermediate games to develop

skills in reading readiness, basic reading, and content reading.

Burmeister, L.: *Words—From Print to Meaning*, Addison-Wesley Publishing Co., Inc., 1975

Classroom activities for building sight vocabulary, context clues, morphology, and phonemes. Good for high school level.

Lee, D., and Van Allen, R.: *Learning to Read Through Experience*, ed. 2, Prentice-Hall, Inc., 1963

The language experience approach to teaching reading.

Otto, W., and Chester, R.: *Objective Based Reading*, Addison-Wesley Publishing Co., Inc., 1976

Building the reading program around behavioral objectives.

Russell, D., Karp, E., and Mueser, A.: *Reading Aids Through The Grades: A Guide to Materials and 440 Activities for Individualizing Reading Instruction*, ed. 2, Teachers College Press, 1975

Primary to junior high.

Strang, R.: *Diagnostic Teaching of Reading*, ed. 2, McGraw-Hill Book Co., 1969

Group and individual methods originating from diagnostic procedures.

Mathematics

Griffin, C.: *Practice in Mathematics: Skill Building Puzzlers*, Instructor Curriculum Materials, 1976

Ditto masters for individualized math programs.

Monster Math, Media for Education, 1976

Grades 1 through 3.

Science

700 Science Experiments for Everyone, Doubleday & Co., Inc., 1962

Activities compiled by UNESCO for intermediate through high school.

Strongin, H.: *Science on a Shoestring*, Addison-Wesley Publishing Co., Inc., 1976

Over 50 activities at primary and intermediate level on scientific method, changes, energy fields, forces.

Involves observation, investigation, and experimentation.

Social studies

Bechtol, W., and Conte, A.: *Individually Guided Social Studies*, Addison-Wesley Publishing Co., Inc., 1976

Includes objectives, assessment techniques, and management.

Special education

Developing Instructional Units: Applications for the Exceptional Child, ed. 2, William C. Brown Co., Publishers, 1976

Guidelines for planning instruction to meet the needs of handicapped students.

Mann, P., and Suiter, P.: *Handbook in Diagnostic Teaching: A Learner Disabilities Approach*, Allyn & Bacon, Inc., 1974

Curriculum and activities for disabled learners.

Learning Centers

Charles, C., editor: *Learning Centers That Teach*, University Press of America, 1977

Twenty exemplary centers, primary through high school, with details on construction and management.

Collier, M., Forte, I., and MacKenzie, J.: *Kids' Stuff*, Incentive Publications, 1969

A large variety of easy-to-use activities in all curriculum areas for young children.

Forte, I., Pangle, M., and Tupa, R.: *Center Stuff for Nooks, Crannies, and Corners*, Incentive Publications, 1973

Contains many good ideas for learning centers.

Petreshene, S.: *The Complete Guide to Learning Centers*, Pendragon House, Inc., 1978

Logistics of centers with management and several sample centers.

Miscellaneous

Aubrey, R.: *Selected Free Materials for Classroom Teachers*, ed. 6, Fearon Publishers, 1978

Indexed guide to free materials for curriculum areas, kindergarten through high school.

Dardig, J., and Hweard, W.: *Sign Here: A Contracting Book for Children and Their Parents*, Behaviordelia, 1976

A device for bringing family involvement into schooling and home behavior.

Educational Structures for Individualized Progress, ed. 2, Helios Individualized Learning, 1976

For secondary education—iverview of a number of established systems for individualizing instruction.

Kohl, H.: *Math, Writing, and Games for the Open Classroom*, New York Review Books, 1974

Open education activities for kindergarten through grade 6.

Pate, G., and Parker, H., Jr.: *Designing Classroom Simulations*, Fearon Publishers, 1973

Techniques for designing simulations for various curriculum areas, kindergarten through high school.

Simon, S., Howe, L., and Kirschenbaum, H.: *Values clarification*, Hart Publishing Co., Inc., 1972

Large number of classroom activities to help students clarify their values.

Willingham, W., Ferrin, R., and Begle, E.: *Career Guidance in Secondary Education*, College Entrance Exam Board Publication, 1972

Career awareness, self awareness, school programs, annotated bibliography.

V

INDIVIDUALIZATION—POWER AND PROMISE

tying together what you have learned about the organization and application of individualized instruction, through

15

Mainstreaming: special education in regular classes

16
Strategies and strategists

15

Mainstreaming

special education in regular classes

If you have been around schools very much you have heard teachers say things like:

"Tommy has an IQ of 73. He ought to be in an EMR class. He can't keep up with the rest of the students, and he just causes trouble."

"Sally is really hyperactive. She's a terror when she doesn't get her medication. They ought to move her to _____ School where she can get special attention. She just ruins things for the rest of us."

"Alex is a nice kid; he never bothers anyone. But I can't get through to him at all. He can't read, can't do math, won't even try. I can't give him the help he needs. I'm trying to get them to put him in a special class."

Teachers who make statements like these are not cranks, complainers, or shirkers. They are speaking their minds honestly. Kids like those mentioned cause them great concern. When teachers say a student belongs in a "special class," they usually mean one or more of the following:

The student is badly disrupting normal class procedures.

The student is showing almost no growth socially or academically.

The teacher's efforts with the student have been frustrated, and he or she is at wits' end in trying to deal with them.

MAINSTREAMING

Until recently students who simply could not succeed in regular classrooms were placed in "special" classrooms. There they received the help they needed from teachers specially trained to deal with physical handicaps or learning disabilities of various kinds. That segregation did not solve all the problems, however. Even though the special classes were small, the teachers specially trained, and the classrooms equipped as necessary, students did not become sufficiently well rounded. Their isolation kept them from associating with the majority of students—the main stream. Their social development and even their academic development often suffered. Neither did their absence do service to students in regular classes. Handicapped and learning disabled students needed to be seen as worthwhile members of society. It was hard for others to see them that way when they were continually kept apart and labeled. For those reasons a push has grown nationwide to "mainstream" special education students. That means they are to participate in regular classes as much as their individual needs and limitations allow.

Public Law 94-142

In 1975 this push received great new national impetus. That year the United States Congress enacted Public Law 94-142—Education for All Handicapped Children Act of 1975. P.L. 94-142 was enacted because it was judged that handicapped students were not receiving educational programs commensurate with their needs and limitations. The law intended to correct that weakness by requiring:

1. Active searching out of handicapped students. (Estimates ran as high as four million handicapped children receiving no special help at all.)
2. Appropriate public education for all children identified as handicapped, from age 3 to 21, to be fully operational by 1980.

The law stipulated that this "appropriate public education" be provided in the form of "individualized education in the least restrictive setting," which meant that schools must:

1. Write an individual educational program for each handicapped child.
2. Educate handicapped children together with nonhandicapped children to the extent possible. (This is what is meant by mainstreaming.)

The law made federal monies available to school districts to help them comply with its requirements.[1]

These requirements portend well for all students, regular and special. But the new direction has brought worry to many regular classroom teachers. They are accepting special education students back into their

---

[1] For a concise listing of the provisions and implications of P.L. 94-142 see Goodman, L.: A Bill of Rights for the Handicapped, American Education **12**(6):6-8, July 1976.

classes. With those students come additional disruptive behavior, withdrawal, and the traditional lack of achievement. The teachers wonder how they will ever be able to cope.

If you are one of these teachers, don't despair. These students can learn and they can control themselves. To bring about such learning and control, teachers will have to learn to use a few techniques they may not be using now. For instance, they will need to know how to use behavior modification and precision teaching. They will need to become much more adept in individualizing instruction—in providing activities and materials best suited to the needs and abilities of every single student in their classrooms.

We will examine some of these techniques for working more effectively with "exceptional" students in the regular classroom. But first, let's see why we have had special education classes, what their results have been, and why so many of them are being abandoned.

Individual differences

Take almost any human trait you can think of and you will see that it shows a wide range of variation. There are a few exceptions, of course. But generally speaking it is "normal" to find great variability in physical, mental, emotional, and verbal traits. These variations show up strongly in the classroom, in areas such as:

Achievement	Self control
Comprehension	Outgoingness
Coordination	Conformity
Motivation	Aggression

The range of variations in these traits, when plotted graphically, often shows the kind of symmetry shown in the illustration on the top of p. 235.

Put simply, many individuals cluster near the "average" for a given trait, while a few fall far above or below that average. The

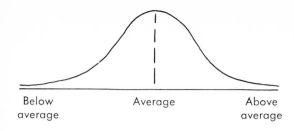

Below average   Average   Above average

curve that graphically shows the shape of variability is called the normal curve, the bell-shaped curve, or the Gaussian curve, after Karl Gauss who first described it. Height, weight, IQ scores, and achievement test scores vary in close correspondence to the Gaussian curve. So, probably, do traits such as self control, aggression, outgoingness, and others.

Classroom teachers can cope with student behaviors that fall within most of the normal curve range. Certain behaviors that fall toward the extremes, however, cause difficulty. Thus it is you find teachers worrying about the student with the very low IQ, the student who is highly aggressive, the student who is frenetically active, the student who is withdrawn and apathetic. These students show two tendencies, both of which trouble teachers very much: They do not progress academically and they continually disrupt normal class activities.

Exceptional students

When speaking of exceptional students, one is sorely tempted to use labels. The labels name groups of characteristics that cause certain students to be considered eligible for special education classes. Labels help us talk more easily, and sometimes they help us talk more precisely. But they have one bad effect. Once placed on students, they stick like glue. You can almost never get them off. So an "educable mentally retarded" student stays EMR thenceforth. A "hyperactive" child vir-

tually has to go into a catatonic state to get rid of his label. The "gifted" stays gifted through hell, high water, and failing grades.

Despite this problem, we need to use three general labels for a moment to indicate students who have been considered different enough to require special classes of their own, that is, those judged unable to profit from instruction taken with other students in regular classes. These general labels are "normal," "gifted," and "handicapped." This grouping is artificial, since the boundary lines between groups are not nearly as clear cut as you might think at first.

Normal students are those whose mental and emotional traits do not differ markedly from the average. Or if they do differ, the difference does not significantly affect their ability to participate profitably in regular classrooms. They comprise most of the students in regular classrooms.

Gifted students are those whose level of intelligence seems markedly higher than the average—so much higher that they profit when placed in learning environments with more difficult levels of work and faster pacing than is customary. These students seldom cause difficulties for teachers in regular classes, however. They learn very well and rarely disrupt learning for others.

Handicapped students are those who possess one or more traits that seriously hinder their doing the work usually provided in regular classrooms. Their traits often hinder other students as well. This label includes many traits besides the physical handicaps we commonly think of. Handicapped students exhibit most of the behavior patterns teachers usually associate with the label "exceptional children."

So it is, then, that we will try to limit our use of the word "handicapped" on these pages. We will also try to avoid such labels as "brain damaged," "emotionally handicapped," "schizophrenic," "autistic," or "hyperactive." Instead, we will give attention to some of the kinds of behavior you might expect to encounter. Later we will examine a few techniques that have proved successful in reducing undesired behavior.

Berkowitz has listed categories of children's difficulties in school that can help teachers attend to behavior problems without labeling their students.[2] Among those categories are:

1. *Learning problems.* The main difficulty has to do with slow learning or failure to learn in one or more subject areas. Behavior problems are inconsequential.
2. *Social adjustment problems.* The main difficulty is withdrawal, isolation, depression, fear, or undue dependency.
3. *Behavior problems.* The main difficulty has to do with behavior that interferes with learning, such as disruptive acts of various kinds, aggression, negativism, hyperactivity, destructiveness, disobedience, and inattention.

When we focus on the difficulty, we have a chance to do something to alleviate it. We need to do more than simply identify the difficulty. We need to identify specific student behaviors. Take depression, for example. What exactly does the student do that causes us to use the term "depression"? We must specify the observable behaviors. Then, perhaps, we can do something to improve them. Or take "aggression." What exactly does the aggressive student do that we can clearly observe? If we can specify his behaviors, there is a good chance we can correct them.

WHITHER SPECIAL EDUCATION?

But why do regular teachers have to worry about such matters? The predominant opinion now is that special education should be a

series of programs and services, not a collection of segregated special classes. Many students still require highly specialized services that regular teachers are not trained to provide. The search, therefore, is to find means to provide those specialized services, but with a minimum of segregation and labeling of students. In a nutshell, this means that a large proportion of exceptional students will be working in regular classrooms for much, most, or all of each school day.

Special education has not long been a part of public education. Students with very obvious disabilities, such as deafness, blindness, and severe cerebral palsy, were of course easily identifiable, and special educational provisions were made for them. Most of the less obvious disabilities, such as mild mental retardation and the host of perceptual and emotional disabilities believed associated with minimal brain damage, have been recognized only recently. This recognition has been made possible by increased sophistication of diagnostic procedures and increased skills of diagnosticians such as psychologists and psychometrists.

Recognition is one thing; providing the best educational programs is another. Students diagnosed as handicapped were placed in special classes on the assumption that they could learn better there. Grouped together, it was believed, they could be isolated from the name calling and the strong competition of the regular classroom. They could receive instruction specially designed for them, and as a result of all this they would learn faster and have better self images. That sounded so possible and reasonable that nobody seriously questioned it for a while.

But you always have your doubting Thomases. In this case some of them had the research skills necessary to ask and answer questions about the value of special education. Investigators began checking to see whether, in fact, students taught in separate

[2]Berkowitz, H.: A preliminary assessment of the extent of interaction between child psychiatric clinics and public schools, Psychology in the Schools **5:**291-295, October 1968.

special education classes really did progress faster and feel better about themselves than did similar students taught in regular classes. By now you can guess what they found. Budoff summarizes it.[3] Segregated students make no better academic gains; being in the regular classroom may increase their incentive to learn and help them develop better self images.

Richard Iano explains the situation well in his article "Shall We Disband Special Classes?"[4] First he points out that exceptional students (in this case, those believed mentally retarded) originally were placed in special classes because they were thought (1) to have learning processes sufficiently different from normal students to require special teaching methods and materials, (2) to require goals and curricula significantly different from normal students, and (3) to be rejected by students in regular classes.

Iano then describes how these ideas have been refuted. For example, as far as mentally retarded students are concerned, it has been found that when retarded students and normal students are matched for *mental* age, they use the same procedures on learning tasks.[5] This conclusion corresponds with findings concerning the progression of individuals through Piaget's stages of intellectual development; that is, all go through the same stages in the same sequence; they enter and exit the stage at different chronological ages, however.

Regarding special goals and curricula, it is probably true that these are needed at the secondary level, where students are beginning to prepare for social and vocational concerns. At the elementary level, however, exceptional students profit from the same range of topics and activities as other students. They are still growing and developing intellectually and should be provided instruction that is in keeping with their interests and levels of ability.

Concerning special students' acceptance by other students, there is no doubt that most of them are early recognized as different in some way. They may be rejected by other students to some extent. On the other hand, Iano points out that various studies have shown minimal or no advantage in social development for students in special classes.

In summary, most handicapped students, including the emotionally disturbed, learning disabled, and physically handicapped, do as well or better in regular classrooms than in segregated classrooms. Teachers will have to make provisions for managing and instructing them. Techniques for doing this are available and easily learned. Special classes will still be required, but only for the severely handicapped, such as the blind, deaf, and trainable mentally retarded.

And what of the classroom teachers? Can they adjust to having exceptional students in their classrooms and can they provide the kind of instruction these students require?

The answer to these questions seems to be yes. Christopolos and her colleagues worked with first grade teachers to help them feel able to teach learning disabled students in their regular classrooms.[6] They proceeded from the basic notion of remaking instruction to fit a wider diversity for the whole class. Specifically, they found ways to do three things:

[3] Budoff, M.: Providing special education without special classes, Journal of School Psychology **10**:199-205, June 1972.

[4] Iano, R.: Shall we disband special classes? The Journal of Special Education **6**:167-177, Summer 1972.

[5] See Denny, M.: Research in learning and performance. In Stevens, H., and Heber, R., editors: Mental retardation: A review of research, Chicago, 1964, University of Chicago Press.

[6] Christopolos, F.: Keeping exceptional children in regular classes, Exceptional Children **39**:569-572, April 1973.

1. Complete task analyses, in which learning tasks were broken into small parts
2. Improve record keeping techniques
3. Use interstudent tutoring, with the more able helping the less able. This developed mutual respect, established one-to-one learning situations, and eased the teacher's adjustment to the great variety among students in the class.

Glass and Meckler report encouraging results from a summer training program for regular classroom teachers who were to have mildly handicapped students in their classrooms.[7] The "mildly handicapped" included those students usually labeled educable mentally retarded, emotionally disturbed, behaviorally disordered, educationally handicapped, and learning disabled.

The workshop was intended to provide these regular classroom teachers the diagnostic, remedial, and behavior management skills necessary to instruct handicapped children in regular classrooms. Interpersonal relation skills were also stressed.

Diagnosis skills included formal and informal testing procedures for determining academic strengths and weaknesses, perceptual characteristics, and preferred learning modalities.

Remediation and management skills included behavior modification, role playing appropriate classroom behaviors, cross-age tutoring, task structuring, and remedial procedures and materials for typical class subjects.

Interpersonal relations skills included using classroom meetings and developing abilities to listen and respond, encourage and accept.

The results of the summer workshop showed that teachers did develop the desired skills and attitudes for working profitably with mildly handicapped students in regular classrooms.

TEACHING ALL CHILDREN

But what, exactly, are teachers to do? After they have become sensitive to the needs of all students and after they have recognized that they will have to confront learning problems and behavior problems, what skills do they bring to bear in carrying out their duties?

Frostig has summarized them well by describing abilities that contribute strongly to teacher success in special education:

1. The ability to diagnose learning needs and remediate them.
2. The ability to individualize instruction.
3. The ability to match teaching to individual students' learning styles.
4. The ability to use paraprofessionals well.[8]

Various portions of this book have focused precisely on how to individualize instruction, on how to diagnose and prescribe, and on how to match instruction to learning style.

Teachers have access to additional techniques that serve very well in solving both learning problems and behavior problems. Among these techniques, three in particular merit attention here. Those techniques are:

1. Success structuring
2. Behavior modification
3. Precision teaching

We will consider each of these three techniques separately. That is not the way they ordinarily occur in practice, however. Success structuring typically is used in conjunction with either behavior modification or precision teaching. Moreover, you will see that behavior modification and precision teaching

---

[7]Glass, R., and Meckler, R.: Preparing elementary teachers to instruct mildly handicapped children in regular classrooms: A summer workshop, Exceptional Children 39:152-156, October 1972.

[8]Frostig, M.: Learning difficulties: Optimism or pessimism, School Psychology Digest, 5(1):5-8, Winter 1976.

have much in common. They simply differ—albeit significantly—in the ways they go about attempting to produce the same kinds of changes in students' behavior.

Success structuring

Success structuring refers to arranging the curriculum so that students experience success most of the time. It is very important that slower learners, particularly, find repeated success in school. They are used to frustration and failure. They come to see themselves as failures, and they lose the motivation to succeed. This failure syndrome can be reversed fairly easily. Success breeds success. If you arrange your learning tasks and materials so they ensure a very low rate of failure, you will be surprised at how much, and how quickly, "slow learners" can learn.

How do we arrange activities and materials to maximize success? Basically, we do these four things: (1) We provide activities whose concepts and procedures are appropriate to a student's stage of intellectual development, as determined, say, by Piagetian tests. (2) We break the activities down into series of small steps, so that each step leads easily into the next. (3) We provide a wealth of support materials, such as objects, pictures, and resource materials, that explain and illustrate the concepts being learned. (4) We provide activities consonant with students' cognitive styles, especially with regard to preferences for structured materials and close teacher support.

Let's look a bit more closely at each of these four conditions.

1. Stages of intellectual development. In Chapter 13 we noted both Piaget's and Montessori's theories of intellectual development. Their work convinced them that students, during their years in school, pass through succeeding, yet quite distinct, stages of mental development. In each stage youngsters have definite ways of thinking, reasoning,

and considering the world. There are limits to what they can do intellectually. It is very important that teachers recognize these stages and the limits they involve, so they can provide activities, concepts, and procedures that are within the capabilities of every student they teach.

Perhaps you remember that Piaget, for example, is convinced that school students pass through three separate stages of intellectual development. The first of these three stages, the intuitive thought stage, occurs roughly between the ages of four and seven for normal children. At this stage the children cannot "conserve" or "reverse" operations. They cannot use logic. They cannot follow lists of rules. They reason mostly on the basis of intuition or hunches, and they probably use mental pictures instead of words for much of their thought.

The second of these three stages, the stage of concrete operations, occupies roughly the ages seven to eleven for normal children. These students can now conserve quantities (they can remember that you still have eight marbles after you separate them into groups, for example), and they can reverse operations mentally (which allows them to test hypotheses, since they see they can "undo" many things they do—that is, can reverse the process). These two abilities allow them to do mathematics with comprehension and perform experimentation. They always think in terms of concrete (tangible) objects, however, so manipulable materials must play a prominent part in instruction. The students can now follow rules, remember steps in sequences, and do logical thinking.

The third of these three stages, the formal operations stage, occupies roughly the ages eleven to fifteen for normal students. By the end of this stage students use adult patterns of thought. They can think about thought, and they can understand and use a great variety of abstractions. They readily make hypotheses and theories about virtually everything that catches their fancy.

One very important thing we must keep in mind is that different students enter and exit these stages at different chronological ages, though they all go through the same sequence. Thus it is not only possible, but probable, that some third grade students (possibly labeled "slow learners") will still be functioning at the intuitive thought stage, unable to conserve, reverse, or follow series of steps, while the other students are functioning at the concrete operations stage. Instead of being called slow learners and given increased drill on the concepts their classmates acquired easily, these students need quality instructional activities and materials suited to their level of intellectual functioning. That will give them a far better chance for continuing progress than will trying to pound concepts into their heads that they cannot yet handle.

Similarly, some eighth grade students, who are supposed to profit from doses of abstractions, may still be functioning at the concrete operations stage, unable to conceptualize and use abstract ideas in thought and speech. Instead of stigmatizing them with labels, however well intended, we do them a service by providing activities and materials they can use to advantage.

2. Small step sequencing. In the middle 1950s, first psychologists and then curriculum writers became intrigued with a new technique for organizing subject matter. That technique was (and is) called "programmed instruction." Programmed instruction did three things. First, it broke the subject matter down into a series of small pieces, each of which led directly and naturally into the next. Second, it required students to make active responses as they moved through the materials. Third, a system of reinforcement, in the form of immediate feedback concerning correct responses, was built into the material, to provide better timed reinforcement than teachers could hope to furnish.

Initially, programmed materials were devised for use in teaching machines. It was soon discovered, however, that the mechanical devices—the machines—had little to do with the effectiveness of the materials. What mattered was the small step sequence and the constant reinforcement.

If you want to provide success experiences most of the time for all your students, you will want to take a page from the programmed material concept, giving attention to small step sequencing. Not all students need this kind of structure. Many, in fact, will find it unnecessarily tedious and boring, preferring to move ahead in leaps rather than small steps. Others, however, will make satisfactory progress through materials only when it is organized so that each new fact, idea, or concept goes only slightly beyond what is already known. Programmed materials provide a model for this kind of organization. Here, for example, is how we could present this information in linear program form. Put a strip of paper over the answers to the right and move it down to check your responses.

The example following shows one way of breaking written information down into small steps, to ensure that students make successful responses to it. You can do the very same thing when you give students information orally. You can intentionally build redundancy (excessive repetition) into what you say, and you can continually check, through questioning, to be sure students understand. This questioning, which can be done with pauses, much as if there were blanks in what you were saying, also cause the students to listen and respond actively to what you are saying.

Yet another place where you can break material down into small steps is in the worksheets you use for giving students practice

Programmed instruction does three things:

First, it breaks learning tasks down into small steps. These small _____ steps help learners avoid making mistakes. That, then, is the first purpose of programmed instruction—to break material into small steps to help learners avoid

making _____. mistakes

Second, programmed instruction requires that students make active responses

while they work. These active re_____ are often made by filling responses in blanks in the programmed material.

Third, as you respond actively by filling in each _____, you can check blank immediately to see whether you made a correct response. This immediate knowledge of correct response is the reinforcement built into the program. When you

see that you gave the correct response, that knowledge is your r_____. reinforcement

with newly learned material. Make your worksheets so they contain few concepts or skills, but present those concepts and skills over and over in slightly varied forms. On a mathematics worksheet, for example, you might have students fill correct answers in the boxes, as shown below.

In summary, small step sequencing is very important in success structuring. It lets students progress with great likelihood of being correct. Each step leads obviously into the next. Repetition is built into the procedure, so students confront new information in several slightly different forms.

3. Support materials. Suppose you wanted to know about Brazilian education—what the school buildings looked like in various parts of the country such as the Amazon jungle, the inland plateaus, and the great cosmopolitan cities like Rio and Sao Paulo; what class-

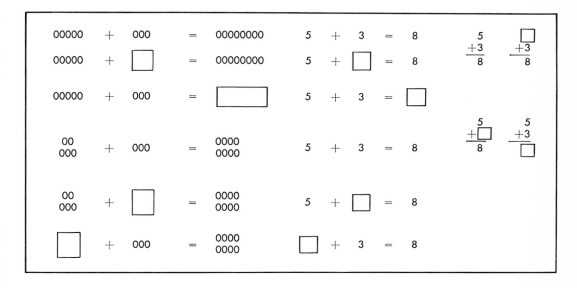

rooms looked like; what instructional materials were used; what teachers did; how work and teaching schedules were organized. You might find someone who could tell you about it. Or you might find a book where you could read about it. Both these sources could help you a great deal. However, just think how much more easily and how much more accurately you could acquire this information if you had access to good audiovisual support materials.

Support materials let you extend the use of your senses. They let you see the buildings, classrooms, materials, students, and so on. They let you hear the sounds of Portuguese, with teachers speaking and students responding. These sensory extensions can greatly enlarge and clarify your concepts of Brazilian education.

So it is with all of us, adults and students alike. We learn better and easier if we not only read and hear teachers talk, but if we can also see pictures, hear sounds, and handle objects.

There's more to the matter than that, however. In the chapter on learning styles, we alluded to the fact that different people seem to learn better through different sense modalities. That is, some learn more through listening and talking; some learn more through reading; some learn more through using media such as still pictures, films, filmstrips, three-dimensional objects, charts, and audio recordings. Teachers should make all these kinds of resources available to students. Generally speaking, support materials, such as pictures and objects, should accompany verbal presentations. Students at the intuitive and concrete operations stages must have objects to manipulate in almost all their learning activities. When students have different kinds of support materials available, you can expect them to naturally select those they enjoy and profit from most.

As you try to structure your classroom for success, you want to keep in mind not only the range of student abilities but their diversity of sense modalities and learning styles as well. Many students may be able to learn well using printed materials such as textbooks, workbooks, and reference books. Others may be unable to learn without the addition of audiovisual support materials. One thing is safe to say, however. Virtually all students learn and remember more when their learning activities permit them to use as many of their senses as possible. Support materials make possible this extended use of the senses.

4. Learning styles. Little purpose would be served by repeating the material on learning styles presented in Chapter 6. Let is suffice to mention once again the fact that students often have noticeably different ways of approaching learning situations. In Chapter 6 we examined the possibility that teachers might find, among their students, three rather distinct learning styles. We called those three styles "Adventurers," "Ponderers," and "Drifters," after the outward behaviors that students exhibit. Each style is as good, as poor, as indifferent as any other. No value levels should be attached to them. They describe what students do and how they behave when they engage in learning. It is our task to provide instruction best suited to the style of each of our students.

What were those styles? Adventurers, you will remember, tend to be spontaneous, eager, and active. They approach new tasks with enthusiasm. They often abandon them with equal enthusiasm for other tasks. It doesn't seem to matter greatly whether the first task is finished or not. It is not hard to get Adventurers started on tasks, but it may be difficult getting them to follow through to the end, once the initial glamor and novelty have worn off. Adventurers tend to be creative and self starting. Providing interesting activities and materials is all you have to do to get them going. They work well on their own, at least for a time.

Ponderers start more slowly, but they have more staying power. They like to think and work tasks through to the end. They pay attention to detail, and they don't shrink from drudgery. They work well using sequenced activities, such as programmed materials, modules, and diagnostic-prescriptive teaching. They usually seek teacher approval for what they are doing, and they respond well to systems of reinforcement.

Drifters have difficulty beginning and following through on activities. They do not start well, and they require rather close teacher presence and supervision. They seem to progress best in "success environments," in which materials and activities are sequenced into small steps, in which they can respond correctly, and in which they can receive high levels of positive reinforcement. They respond well to programs of behavior modification—surprisingly so in many instances. They can learn and will learn. But they must find success and be rewarded for it. Since they tend to be easily distracted from their work, they require frequent changes of activity and direct support, encouragement, and direction from the teacher.

In summary, we have examined four instructional considerations that are important in structuring the classroom for success. Those four considerations were: (1) adapting instruction to each student's stage of intellectual development, (2) sequencing materials into small steps, (3) providing a wealth of support materials, and (4) adapting instruction to different students' learning styles. This success structuring allows—actually almost forces—students to respond actively in their learning tasks, while being correct most of the time.

Now we will see how to apply principles of reinforcement in student learning to bring about significant gains in both academic achievement and general classroom behavior.

Behavior modification

Behavior modification is a technique for shaping student behavior in desirable directions. This behavior includes both academic performance and comportment (good manners) in the classroom. The technique is tried and true. It works.

Behavior modification uses principles of reinforcement for operant conditioning, which have been so thoroughly detailed by B. F. Skinner. Operant conditioning is a beautifully simple phenomenon. What it amounts to is this:

1. An organism performs an act—a movement of some kind, simple or complex.

2. If immediately following that act there occur conditions the organism finds desirable, the tendency for it to repeat the act is strengthened.

This phenomenon seems to hold for almost all kinds of animals—earthworms, pigeons, humans. The incredible acts you have seen trained dogs and sea lions perform were developed through operant conditioning, using food as the reinforcement following desired acts by the animal.

Behavior modification makes practical use of operant conditioning. It, too, is a beautifully simple procedure. When you use it, here's what you do.

1. You let students know which behaviors are desired and which are not.

2. When the student performs a desired act, you immediately supply something you think will reward him—a smile, a compliment, a token, or whatever. If what you supply pleases the student, he becomes more likely to repeat the act.

3. Undesired acts are either ignored, or if serious enough, are followed with mild punishment. Punishment, however, is used only

when considered absolutely necessary. Behavior modification stresses the positive and the pleasurable.

Most behavior modification programs used in the classroom stress three elements:

Expectation

about class conduct, work habits, and achievement

Approval

given when behavior moves in desired directions

Ignoring

inappropriate behavior; it is not acknowledged at all

For most students, the expectation-approval-ignoring model is all you need to use. If you haven't used it yet, you are in for a pleasant surprise. Approval is the key part of the model. You can use several different varieties of approval to shape behavior. Here are some of them.

1. Personal reactions. Personal reactions refer to teacher actions, both verbal and nonverbal, that show acknowledgement, acceptance, and praise. Such actions include:

Nonverbal

Smiles	Hugs
Winks	Pats
Nods	Hand shakes
Okay signs	Thumbs up

Verbal

Okay	You're on the right track.
Right	I'm proud of you.
That's it	You're really improving.
Yes	You should feel good about that.
Super	Keep up the good work.
Well done	
Fine	
All right!	

2. Graphic symbols. Graphic symbols include points, grades, drawings—marks of various kinds that you put on students' work or that you award for desirable behavior. Some teachers obtain rubber stamps of different kinds of symbols—smiling faces, stars, bolts of lightening, and words such as "right on," "super star," "you're my type," and so on. Others use felt tip markers and their imaginations to provide reinforcers of this type.

3. Activity reinforcers. Take not of this generalization:

If students would rather be doing some activity other than that associated with a particular learning task, you can use the preferred activitiy as a reinforcer.

TRANSLATION: Suppose that given their choice, your students would rather write on the chalkboard than do their mathematics worksheets. If they do their worksheets correctly and quickly, you can show approval by allowing them to write on the chalkboard. If they recognize that doing worksheets brings a payoff in chalkboard writing, they will begin to do their worksheets with enthusiasm.

This phenomenon, wherein a more-preferred activity reinforces a less-preferred activity, is called the Premack principle, after its discoverer, David Premack. Used judiciously, you can accomplish great things with the Premack principle. You needn't always resort to using "play" activities to reinforce "work" activities. Less desired learning tasks can be reinforced by preferred learning tasks, such as free reading, project work, or learning games. Too, you can use privileges as reinforcers, so that students work to earn free time, to serve as lab assistant, or whatever privilege activities you have available.

4. Token systems. For many students, receiving, possessing, and accumulating tokens can be very rewarding. Tokens can be almost anything tangible—poker chips, plastic discs, small cards, play money. You only want to be sure that the objects you use are small and harmless. You can assign values to them, so that five red cards, for example, equal one white card, and five white cards equal one blue card.

At first, you will probably want to set up a cash-in system, such as an auction, in which students periodically exchange their tokens for objects such as pencils, erasers, funny buttons, and candy, or for privileges such as taking care of classroom animals or spending extra time working on individual projects.

Later, you may find that the students will work just to earn the tokens, without caring to exchange them for other things.

5. *Prize systems.* Prize systems involve using highly desired objects as reinforcers—objects such as candy, crackers, small toys, and even real money. This type of reinforcement system has produced dramatic results in teaching students who had not progressed in learning situations employing social reinforcers.

Many teachers use inexpensive breakfast cereal, such as Trix and Froot Loops, dispensed one morsel at a time. Others use M & M's, pieces of sugarless chewing gum, and small flavored crackers. Some students respond very well to real money—pennies and nickels—especially when there is a machine where they can spend their coins to get bubble gum, peanuts, or toys.

Prize systems are often used in conjunction with point and token systems. Students who are able to delay gratification can work for longer periods, earning points that they can apply toward winning small trophies, certificates, ribbons, and other such awards.

These five systems, then, are known to be effective and are widely used in programs of behavior modification. Whatever system you use to show approval, you must remember one thing and stick to it:

Approval is given only after students show desired behavior. You must not reward inappropriate or undesired behavior. You must not say "I'm giving you an extra ten minutes' free time. Afterwards, I expect you to work very hard on your geography lesson." Instead, you can say "If you work very hard on

your geography lesson, I will let you have an extra ten minutes' free time afterwards. But you get the free time *only* if you work hard now." And you stick by your guns. If the students goof off, but you relent and give them free time anyway, you will be strengthening the undesired behavior you want to eliminate. Remember then: Reinforce only desired behavior and do so very soon after students have exhibited that behavior.

Behavior modification and exceptional students

The overall effectiveness of behavior modification has been well documented. It works wonderfully with fast, average, and slow learners. Perhaps its most dramatic effects, however, have been seen in its use with exceptional children, especially those who have trouble controlling themselves well enough to participate in regular classrooms.

Let's take note of a few studies that show how behavior modification has produced desirable results in classes with students of different ages and different learning handicaps.

1. Uncontrollable retarded children.[9] Twenty boys, ages eight to fourteen and considered mildly to profoundly retarded, received prolonged instruction in social behaviors needed for attending school. The behaviors included entering the classroom at the right time, going to the right desk, getting necessary materials, going to the rest room, raising hands, talking only when permission was given, following instructions, and giving up activities when it was time to do so.

These boys were, at first, unteachable in the sense of normal schooling. They threw tantrums, would not sit down when told, and

[9]Birnbrauer, J.: Preparing "uncontrollable" retarded children for group instruction (1967). In Becker, W.: An empirical basis for change in education, Chicago, 1971, Science Research Associates Inc., pp. 213-218.

could be counted on to do something other than what they were directed to do.

At first their training procedures involved only social reinforcement (praise) and the opportunity to engage in preferred activities. This strategy produced minimal results.

A new strategy was then adopted, which yielded significant results:

1. The teacher used tangible reinforcers that were edible, such as crackers and candy. They were dispensed along with praise for appropriate behaviors.

2. As students learned to respond to edible reinforcers, tangible but nonedible reinforcers were substituted. Poker chips were given along with praise. The chips could later be exchanged for candy or toys.

3. Later, the poker chips gave way to a checkmark system, where the boys worked to earn marks instead of chips.

After eight months seven of the "unteachable" boys could work in acceptable ways for about three and a half hours per day.

2. A hyperactive child.[10] A nine-year-old boy continually disrupted the class. He showed very high incidence of talking, pushing, hitting, pinching, moving about the room, tapping, and squirming.

An experimenter used a "magic teaching machine," which was explained to the boy. It flashed a light each ten seconds during which the boy was showing appropriate behavior. Each flash meant that he had earned another M & M or penny, which he collected at the end of the lesson. Social reinforcement from peers also came into play. The boy shared the M & M's or pennies earned (from 60 to 100 each lesson) with classmates. Hence, they showed interest in his good behavior, and they congratulated him as he improved.

After several days of conditioning, the boy's behavior had improved to the extent that it did not differ noticeably from that of three other boys selected for comparison.

3. A juvenile delinquent.[11] A bright sixteen-year-old girl was a chronic truant, made very poor grades, and was incorrigible at home. About to be expelled from high school, she agreed to go on a behavior modification program intended to improve her attendance in school.

She had lost allowance and telephone and dating privileges. Dating on weekends and use of the telephone were set up as contingent on school attendance. The attendance officer was to give her a note at the end of each day she attended school. If she could earn four notes during the week, she would be allowed one weekend date night. For five notes she could have two weekend date nights.

The girl began attending school regularly from the outset of the plan. After seven weeks the notes were stopped. During the first three months she had only two illegal absences. For the entire following semester she had no illegal absences. Her grades improved and she began expressing positive attitudes toward her classes.

4. Academically retarded students.[12] Eight students in an elementary school learning disabilities class showed near normal intelligence levels, yet their academic achievement levels were two years or more below grade level. These students were diagnosed as having minimal brain damage with accompanying emotional disturbance. They were all

---

[10]Patterson, G.: An application of conditioning techniques to the control of a hyperactive child. In Ullmann, L., and Krasner, L., editors: Case studies in behavior modification, New York, 1965, Holt, Rinehart and Winston, Inc.

[11]Thorne, G., Tharp, R., and Wensel, R.: Behavior modification techniques: New tools for probation officers. In Becker, W., *op cit.*, pp. 298-309.

[12]McKenzie, H., and others: Behavior modification of children with learning disabilities using grades as tokens and allowances as back up reinforcers, Exceptional Children **34**:745-752, 1968.

highly distractible and prone to engage in disruptive behaviors.

A behavior modification plan was put into effect, which would allow them to earn the following:

1. *Recess,* for completing assigned work
2. *Free time activities,* for early completion of assigned work
3. *Special privileges,* for those who had worked very well or had shown large improvements
4. *Group lunch,* for all who finished the morning's assigned work before noon
5. *Teacher attention,* for good work behavior
6. *Weekly grades,* of A, B, C, or Incomplete, to be taken home and signed by parents
7. *Pay for weekly grades,* to be given by parents, at a suggested rate of 10¢ for A, 5¢ for B, 1¢ for C, and minus 10¢ for Incomplete

As a result of this program, all eight students showed a rapid and lasting increase in academic achievement and in desirable work habits in class.

Precision teaching

Suppose you have a student, Fred, who never completes assigned work in mathematics. On worksheets with twenty problems, Fred does the first three or four. After that, he does almost anything except what he is supposed to do. He daydreams, doodles, talks, goes to the pencil sharpener, bothers other students—you name it. You have tried kindly persuasion and not so kindly scoldings. Neither worked. He still doesn't get his work done. What's more, he's not improving. He may even be getting worse.

A new technique for improving those unhappy circumstances has been developed in the past few years. That technique is called "precision teaching." What it entails is this:

First, you pinpoint and define clearly the behavior(s) you want to change. Your definitions must be stated in terms of movements. That is, you can't define a behavior as "disrupting the class." You have to say what the behavior is in terms of movements, for instance, "walking about the room," "hitting other students," or "shouting out during lessons." Ogden Lindsley, who pioneered precision teaching, stipulated two criteria for movements:[13]

1. They must have clear beginning and end.
2. They must pass the "dead man's test"—if a dead man can do the act, it can't be counted."

Second, you use a precise method of recording and charting data on the student's behaviors (movements) you wish to change. Precision teaching uses a chart developed by Lindsley that shows the frequency of occurrence of a particular behavior and how it changes—accelerates, decelerates, or remains constant—over a period of time.

Let's return to Fred, our unwilling math students, and see how we would use precision teaching to improve his task-completing behavior. What must we consider? First, we must identify the behavior we want to influence. In this case, it is the number of math problems he completes correctly in a given period. Second, we must record and chart the frequency of this behavior over several days. To do these things, we will use a modified version of Lindsley's "Standard Daily Behavior Chart" (Fig. 24).[14]

You use the chart for one student only. It shows individual, not class, behavior. Here's what the various markings on Lindsley's chart mean.

Frequency per minute. This indicates how many times each minute the target behavior occurs.

[13] Bradfield, R.: Precision teaching: A useful technology for special education teachers, Educational Technology **10**:22-26, August 1970.

[14] Lindsley devised a semilogarithmic chart that could serve for recording the frequency of virtually all behaviors, with a frequency of 1000 per minute to one per 1000 minutes. Lindsley's charts must be accurately drawn. The modified form shown here is easily prepared, and it serves well for most purposes.

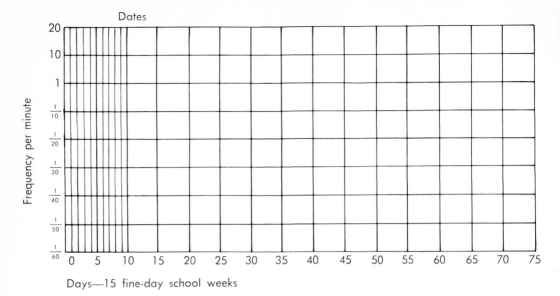

Fig. 24. Modified version of Lindsley's Standard Daily Behavior Chart.

20 = 20 times in 1 minute
10 = 10 times in 1 minute
1 = 1 time in 1 minute
1/10 = 1 time in 10 minutes
1/20 = 1 time in 20 minutes
1/30 = 1 time in 30 minutes

Days. This shows each day the behavior frequency was recorded.

Dates. This can show the dates for beginning and ending a series of observations. You write in the dates above this line to show the beginning and end.

Here's how we could use the chart for Fred and his assigned task behavior. Suppose we begin observing and recording this behavior on Monday, October 14, and we make one entry each day for two weeks—a total of ten entries. Suppose also that Fred is given a math worksheet each day, containing thirty problems, on which he works for twenty minutes.

The first day, October 14, he correctly completes five problems in twenty minutes. To show this on our frequency per minute scale, we divide 5 into 20 to show that he completed one problem every four minutes. We have him place a dot on the scale for the first day 4/10 of the way between 1 and 1/10.

The next day, October 15, he correctly completes seven problems. We have him place a dot for the second day 3/10 of the way between 1 and 1/10. He connects the dots with a line.

His progression continues like this:

Oct. 16   10 in 20:   Mark 2/10 below 1 on scale
Oct. 17   10 in 20:   Mark 2/10 below 1 on scale
Oct. 18   14 in 20:   Mark approximately 1/10 below 1
Oct. 21   20 in 20:   Mark on 1
Oct. 22   30 in 20:   Mark slightly above 1 to show 1½ problems completed each minute
Oct. 23   30 in 10:   Mark 3/10 above 1
Oct. 24   30 in 10:   Mark 3/10 above 1
Oct. 25   30 in 8:   Mark to show almost 4 problems per minute

Fred's chart, expanded to show only the part used, would look like this:

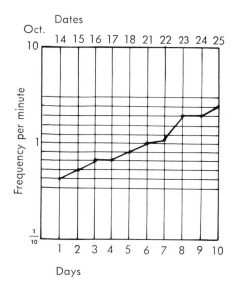

As a success story, this illustration might be slightly overdrawn, though similar results have been commonly reported.

Fred's example illustrated how we would hope to increase the frequency of a given behavior. We could use the exact same procedure in attempting to reduce the frequency of a behavior. Suppose, for example, that Fred had a strong tendency to leave his desk and walk around the room during study periods. We observed for a week or so and noticed that he would continually get out of his chair five or six times during a twenty-minute study period.

We could start keeping track of the number of times Fred did this act during the twenty-minute period each day, and we could have him start keeping a daily behavior chart on which he recorded the frequency of this behavior. Fred would know, of course, that his walking about was considered undesirable. What we would hope to do through the charting would be to reduce the frequency of the occurrence for that behavior.

Perhaps as a result of Fred's keeping track of his behavior, he shows the following frequencies over a two-week period of observation:

Nov. 7	4 times:	Mark 5/10 below 1 to show one occurrence every 5 minutes
Nov. 8	5 times:	Mark 4/10 below 1
Nov. 9	3 times:	Mark 7/10 below 1
Nov. 10	3 times:	Mark 7/10 below 1
Nov. 11	2 times:	Mark on 1/10
Nov. 14	4 times:	Mark 5/10 below 1
Nov. 15	1 time:	Mark on 1/20 to show one occurrence each 20 minutes
Nov. 16	0 times:	Mark bottom of scale
Nov. 17	0 times:	Mark bottom of scale
Nov. 18	0 times:	Mark bottom of scale

The portion of Fred's chart showing his behavior during the two weeks would look like this:

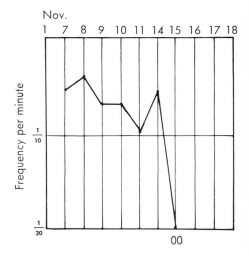

What is precision teaching?

After seeing the fantastic improvements we made in hypothetical Fred's behavior, you are no doubt eager to know more details about precision teaching. Lindsley stresses the following characteristics of precision teaching[15]:

[15] Precision teaching in perspective: An interview with Ogden R. Lindsley, *Teaching Exceptional Children* **3:** 114-119, Spring 1971.

1. Precision teaching is similar to behavior modification except:
   a. Extrinsic reinforcers such as tokens and candy are not used.
   b. Modifications are made in the curriculum to encourage improved behavior.
   c. Extensive records are kept; this can be done by the students themselves.
2. The curriculum—the content, activities, and materials—is changed in a constant attempt to excite and involve the learner. This attempt contrasts with using reinforcers to try to get students to engage in a dull curriculum.
3. The record keeping focuses on the frequency of occurrence of a specified behavior over a certain period. The emphasis is always placed on improvement, on trying to better one's past performance. This procedure has proved to be more fun, more effective, and less expensive than typical behavior modification programs using tangible reinforcement systems.
4. The combination of exciting curriculum and behavior charting encourages and facilitates the preparation of individualized programs for each student. Each is given the opportunity to work at materials in ways he prefers, and each works to improve a behavior identified especially for himself.
5. Precision teaching is not an approach to teaching. Rather, it is a technique for improving student behavior, both academic and social. The improvement is shown through the charts on which frequency of behavior is graphed. Each student works against his own past behavior, not against the behavior of other students.

When considering our make-believe Fred, it was mentioned that he would be instructed to mark and keep his own chart. You may be wondering whether students, especially younger ones, can keep such records accurately. Haughton assures us that they can, reporting that children as young as three and one half years of age can manage their own recording projects and are usually enthusias-

tic about doing so.[16] Haughton believes it is not only possible, but necessary that students chart their behaviors. He thinks each should decide what he wants to change about his behavior and how he wants to make this change. This focusing on behaviors and needed changes help students know themselves better and helps them reach some of their personal goals.[17]

Precision teaching has been touted as an especially effective technique in working with exceptional students. That's why it is discussed here. However, you should be aware that its effectiveness is not limited to handicapped students. It shows graphic evidence of student performance, and through that performance it shows teacher success. It serves well in any program of individualized instruction, whether the students are gifted, average, or slow, because it allows individual students to attend to and keep track of matters of special importance to them alone.[18]

RECAPITULATION

In this chapter we have noted that "exceptional children" will be returning in large numbers to regular classrooms—to the "mainstream" of education. This return has been mandated by P.L. 94-142, which specifies quality education for all handicapped students through individualized programs in the least restrictive environment. It has been found that students do not progress faster either academically or socially in segregated classes and the labeling that accompanies their identification for special classes often does more harm than good. Therefore, segregated special education classes are being abandoned, except for those students whose disabilities are so severe that they cannot participate in regular classes.

---

[16] Haughton, E.: Great gains from small starts, Teaching Exceptional Children **3**:141-146, Spring 1971.

[17] Ibid.
[18] Starlin, C.: Peers and precision, Teaching Exceptional Children **3**:129-140, Spring 1971.

Many of the students heretofore called handicapped will bring "problem" behaviors with them into the regular classroom. These problem behaviors, often associated with minimal brain damage, include slow learning and a variety of acts that tend to disrupt procedures in the regular classroom. For this reason, teachers will need to use certain teaching techniques known to be effective in working with students who exhibit such behaviors.

We considered three of these techniques. They were:

1. *Success structuring*—using ways of maximizing success experiences for students. Four such ways discussed were (a) attending to stages of intellectual development, (b) sequencing information into small steps, (c) using varieties of support materials, and (d) attending to students' cognitive styles.

2. *Behavior modification*—shaping behavior through reinforcement. We noted three parts to this process: (a) expectations—letting students know what is expected, (b) approval—showing acceptance or pleasure, through provision of social and tangible reinforcers, and (c) ignoring—giving no attention at all to inappropriate behaviors.

3. *Precision teaching*—a way of helping students identify and improve behaviors, through charting their progress and working to surpass their own past performances.

These are but three techniques for working with groups of students who show a wide range of abilities and behaviors. There are other important techniques not discussed in this chapter but described in other chapters of this book. They include techniques for improving communication and ways teachers can show warmth, concern, and acceptance for all the students they teach.

16

Strategies and strategists

In Chapter 3 you read the story of Sam Morgan, a first year teacher who stumbled his way to success in a village school. By a fortuitous combination of luck and determination, Sam learned to work with youngsters whose ideas about school differed remarkably from his own. In many ways, those youngsters were like the ones you will teach. Yours, too, will have their individual natures, their inner drives toward growth, their special interests, and their needs for fulfillment and recognition. Like Sam, you must find ways to help them where they need help, encourage them where they need encouragement, and stand aside when your efforts hinder more than help.

Fortunately, you have a lot more going for you than Sam did. He learned to fly by the seat of his pants, as they used to say. You have to do some of that, too. But the advantage you have is that you can choose from philosophies, procedures, and techniques that Sam didn't have available when he began. Sometimes it seems we advance awfully slowly in educational methodology. Yet, looking back across recent years, you can count a number of techniques, such as open education, interaction analysis, behavior modification, inquiry training, classroom

meetings, success environments, questioning strategies, and individualized instruction, that have been refined to the point that their value and ease of use make them commonplace in classrooms everywhere. Those techniques are just a few of the many we could list. Sam didn't have a single one available in refined form twenty years ago. The hot new items in his day were three group instruction in elementary reading and student discussion instead of just reading and listening in other subjects and levels.

But that's enough of Sam. He did the best he could with what he had. We can do better because we have more skills in our bag and we know how to use them.

SYNTHESIS

In this final chapter we will bring together the diverse ideas we have considered heretofore. We will begin, as we did in the first chapters, by noting some important human traits and growth processes. We can follow with a reconsideration of how we intend that education contribute to some of those processes. Then we can show how the techniques we have examined can be used in systematic ways to further the development of human traits in directions we think desirable. In short, we can make useful strategies out of what we know.

Goal: maximum growth

Abraham Maslow and other psychologists have described the human drive toward growth. Provided that lower needs are met, there exists within each of us a compelling urge to unfold, to develop, to become more than we now are. This urge—this need for self actualization—lies within us all, and it remains with us throughout our lives. Education can serve no higher purpose than to facilitate this process of unfolding. It should maximize our human potential by helping each of us develop in ways our inner natures suggest.

Each one of us has a unique set of potentialities and desires, just as we have unique personalities. Still, our potentialities and desires can be placed into a few categories that beckon education with sirens' calls. We have made a point of attending to education's role in enhancing intellectual development, development of self image, and acquisition of knowledge.

Strategy: climate

One of the principal strategies we must develop early is concerned with classroom climate. There is good reason to believe that most desirable human potentialities can best be nurtured in a classroom setting that is open, warm, trusting, and accepting. Let's review what each of these conditions entails.

Open classrooms have student self direction as their prime ingredient. Remember that "open classroom" and "open space" do not mean the same thing. Many people (myself included) have the nagging suspicion that open space buildings—those in which interior walls do not separate one group of students from another—reduce the likelihood of having the kind of psychological openness that characterizes the open classroom. They

don't make openness impossible by any means. But since noisy and quiet activities have to be well coordinated in open space situations, flexibility must of necessity be reduced. You cannot have a boisterous activity in one corner of an open space area while another group of students a few feet away is trying to have a quiet activity. If you want to sing, for example, you will have to wait until all groups within the area are ready for noise. This coordination requires careful planning by the teachers involved.

Open classrooms permit students to plan and select many of the learning activities in which they will engage. They also allow flexibility, so that students can easily change from one activity to another and can engage in a number of different activities at the same time.

Warm climates should prevail in all classrooms, regardless of their degree of openness. Warmth, in this case, refers to interpersonal relationships in the classroom. You can't make all students love each other; they won't all love you; you won't love all of them. But you can be friendly. You can support and praise. You can show concern for students' work, interests, and problems. This attitude on your part will carry over to your students and will affect their behavior toward each other.

Supportive warmth may not be necessary for maximizing academic achievement. You can probably scare your students into learning as much algebra as you can charm them into learning. However, you cannot scare people into having positive attitudes. If you think it important that your students have an abiding interest in and positive feeling for what you are teaching them, you will have to show that you are concerned about them, about what they are learning, and about problems that may be hampering their progress.

Warmth also plays a key role in the development and maintenance of good self images. What we think about ourselves depends in large measure on two things: how well our appearance and behavior match the ideals we hold for ourselves, and what other people say and do to us. What we say and do to our students, then, has strong influence on how they see themselves. If we treat them as important and worth our attention, they will see themselves as more worthy and important.

Trust between teacher and student may seem an odd idea to emphasize. Traditionally, students and teacher played a strange game in which each seemed intent on outsmarting the other. They seemed to be antagonists rather than partners working toward the same goals. Teachers acted as though they expected students to cheat, goof off, antagonize, and behave irresponsibly. Students acted as though teachers were tragic comics, whose demands were not to be taken seriously, or else frightening task masters whose purpose in life was to browbeat students.

Yet, we know that one purpose of education is to develop fully functioning persons. None of us can function fully in an atmosphere of distrust. We must know that it is safe to behave naturally and to try out ideas, without threat of stern disapproval from others. We must know that others have confidence in us and will support us. We cannot work well in an atmosphere of suspicion.

Trust has an interesting way of expanding itself. If you let students know you trust them, they will begin to trust you, and more importantly they will begin to trust themselves. Of course this generalization won't always hold true. If you adopt a trusting stance, you will doubtless be disappointed at times. You will see your trust misplaced, and you may decide that trust is one of those things that sounds good but just doesn't work out. Nevertheless, the value of trust is evident in many public school and university class-

rooms—enough to conclude that if you allow students to help select and plan their learning activities, if you put them in charge of keeping track of their own progress, and if you let them know by your behavior that you will help them as best you can, you can reasonably expect that they will do quality work within reasonable periods of time. You will find, too, that your students begin to trust you. They see you as an interested person who truly wants to help them acquire valuable skills, knowledge, and attitudes.

Acceptance is, let us be honest, one of the hardest parts of the classroom climate to provide consistently. It is very easy to accept the behaviors and contributions of students who do desirable things in the classroom. But it is hard to accept student complaining about assignments. It is hard to accept inferior work. It is hard to accept disruptive acts and defiance of the teacher. In truth, you will find many times when you simply cannot accept such things.

Acceptance, however, comes in degrees rather than absolutes. To establish an accepting atmosphere, you look for things you can accept easily, such as good work and good behavior, and you make a point of complimenting students for them. You also begin accepting, rather than rejecting, student performance that shows effort and concern, even when the results are not laudable. Finally, you learn ways to partly accept performance you would usually reject. When students complain about learning tasks, for example, you may find occasion to say, "I can understand why you might feel this work is too hard. Let's give it a try, though, and I will help you get started." Or when a student shows hostility toward you, you can say something like, "There have been times I have felt like you do now. Let's talk about it for a minute as soon as we get a chance." Or if students turn in work that is inferior for their ability, you can say, "Truthfully, I would have been pleased with this work a month ago. But you have improved so much since then that it just doesn't show what you are capable of now. I would feel much better if this work showed what you really can do."

Such efforts toward accepting bear fruit. Rejection produces fear and avoidance. It depresses work output. Acceptance tends to increase work output, and it improves relationships between teacher and students.

Strategy: facilitation

I have known and worked with hundreds of teachers during the past fifteen years. Of the things that remain strongest in my mind about them, one stands out most clearly: virtually all of those teachers sincerely wanted their students to learn, and they sincerely wanted to do what they could to help that learning occur. Certainly, each teacher had distinct ideas about what students should learn. I haven't agreed with all of them. Every teacher had distinct ideas about how that learning could be brought about. I haven't agreed with all those ideas, either. Still, I remain singularly impressed with teachers' sincerity.

Nowadays we use the term "facilitation" to refer to helping students learn. Offhand I would say we can see three rather different types of facilitation being used today. One type we might call "prepare the feast and make them eat it." The tactics in this type of facilitation are familiar to us all because we have had experience with them in our own schooling. Teachers plan the curriculum, prepare the learning activities and materials, and then require students to proceed through them. I don't want to belittle this approach. It has worked well for many of us, me included (I think). I can be a pleasant approach. Many teachers are remarkably skillful at planning exciting activities and preparing intriguing materials. Often that's all it takes. When more is needed, many teachers are also masters of pleasant persuasion and calm coercion.

This approach begins to labor and gasp when students do not show the willingness teachers expect. Then you get to the "make them eat it" part. When students refuse to work, or when the lessons are so boring or frustrating that they divert energies to such undesirables as daydreaming, disruption, anger, and hostility, teachers reach for aversive controls. Now we have a struggle of wills. Teachers have the more powerful arsenal, and they usually, though not always, win out. Students comply hostilely, but they do poor work and their resentment remains alive and glowing.

A second style of facilitation is one we might call "bring them to the table and hope they will eat." The preparation part of this type is similar to the first one we considered. Teachers plan activities and prepare materials. Again there is every hope that students will eagerly leap in and have at it. There is also the realization that all of them won't. So teachers go to lengths to impress upon students the desirability—the absolute necessity—of completing the assigned activities for today. Then, as the lesson gets under way, they expend quantities of energy good naturedly encouraging students to work.

This approach doesn't ruffle many feathers. But it can be frustrating for teachers. Some students will smilingly not complete their important assignments. They won't be hungry for that particular potion. They won't care to eat. They aren't about to nibble if nobody makes them do it. The end of the period finds them with nothing accomplished. This reluctance to complete assigned work can have undesirable effects on students, too. Self discipline, which we all must acquire sooner or later whether we like it or not, goes right out the window. Slovenly work habits develop. Students begin getting payoffs for not doing their work.

A third type of facilitation is one we might call "let them help cook the meals and lick the bowls." Carl Rogers might fall over in a faint to know this, but I am thinking of his ideas about facilitation when I describe this type. We examined Rogers' ideas about facilitation of learning in Chapter 5, remember? Rogers says facilitation includes these aspects:

1. Helping students clarify what they want to learn
2. Helping students arrange suitable learning activities and materials
3. Helping students find the personal meaning of what they learn
4. Maintaining a psychological climate that nurtures the process of learning

If the first and third of these four aspects are accomplished, the learning will likely be "significant" to the learner. Significance is crucial in facilitation. Rogers says that learning is significant when it is self initiated, involves feelings, makes behavior and attitude differences in the learner, and has meaning for the learner.

The fourth aspect listed—psychological climate that nurtures the learning process—is also very important in facilitation. A suitable climate is maintained when teachers show themselves as real people, without front or facade, when they accept learners by showing they care for them as total persons, when they show nonevaluative understanding of students' desires, behaviors, and problems, and when they show that they trust students to behave intelligently most of the time.

Strategy: communication

Communication refers to exchanges of ideas between people. It is a basic means of acquiring and disseminating information. It is so fundamental to human existence that human society without communication is inconceivable.

When you think of communication as exchanges of ideas between people, you think of an individual being a sender of ideas part of the time. If you look at communication patterns that occur between teachers and students, however, you get a different picture. You find, as Ned Flanders, Marie Hughes, and others interested in verbal interaction have found, that teachers do most of the idea sending and little of the idea receiving. Hughes, for example, found that 80% of teachers were dominative in more than half the acts they performed. The mental activity they most often required of students was memory recall.[1] Flanders, in his studies of verbal interaction patterns, has found that teachers typically do two thirds of the talking that occurs in the classroom.[2]

Highlighted against those patterns is the evidence that people learn and remember what they say much better than what they hear. Verbal exchange plays a strong role in the socialization process, which in turn may be related to intellectual development.[3] Some thinkers have pointed out that man is not a think-then-do creature, but a do-then-think creature. John Chapman wrote that one should practice stating opinions before having them formed in the mind, to allow them to grow in a natural way through discussion. He added ". . . if you are dealing with human nature in any form, you go broke if you reason."[4]

---

[1] Hughes, M.: Utah study of the assessment of teaching. In Ballack, A., editor: Research and theory of teaching, New York, 1963, Teachers College Press.
[2] Flanders, N.: Using interaction analysis in the inservice education of teachers, Journal of Experimental Education **30:**313, 1962.
[3] This idea holds a prominent place in Jean Piaget's theory of intellectual development.
[4] Chapman, J.: John Jay Chapman and his letters. An excerpt included in Curtis, C., and Greenslet, F., editors: The practical cognitator, Boston, 1962, Houghton Mifflin Co., p. 76.

These kinds of observations have prompted the development of several techniques for analyzing and improving verbal exchanges. Especially notable among these techniques are interaction analysis, parent effectiveness training, questioning skills, and congruent communication.

Interaction analysis, pioneered by Ned Flanders and his associates, is a system for coding talk that occurs in the classroom and analyzing it to determine such factors as who does how much of the talking, what kind of talk is occurring, and how much of the time the teacher is using direct influence as opposed to indirect influence.[5] One main purpose of interaction analysis is to increase the amount of indirect influence the teacher uses. Indirect influence involves such behaviors as asking questions, encouraging student talk, and accepting student talk and behavior. Several studies have reported significant correlations between indirect teacher behavior and school achievement. At the same time interaction analysis can be used to decrease the amount of direct influence the teacher uses. Direct influence involves such actions as lecturing, giving directions, and criticizing.

Parent effectiveness training, developed by Thomas Gordon, is designed to improve communication between parents and children.[6] It has been further developed into a program called teacher effectiveness training, which (as you no doubt suspect) emphasizes effective communication between teachers and students.

Prominent in parent and teacher effectiveness training are such techniques as "active listening" and using "I-messages." Active listening is a way of showing a speaker that you are following closely what is being said.

The listener makes nonevaluative comments, such as, "Yes. I can see that's troublesome. I see the point," which draw out the speaker to explain further. I-messages are ways of responding to speakers, to show one's own reactions. The opposite of the I-message is the you-message, where one would make remarks like, "You are wrong to think that. You are a pretty bright person." Instead, the listener might react with comments such as, "It bothers me to hear that. I would rather do this than that. I feel this would have good possibilities for me."

At the same time, parent and teacher effectiveness training teaches communicators to avoid what Gordon calls the "typical twelve." These are kinds of statements that parents and teachers typically make when reacting to students' expressions. They include such counterproductive tacks as moralizing, criticizing, evaluating, and sympathizing—responses that tend to shut off communication rather than facilitate it. The typical twelve are listed in Chapter 5.

Questioning, as a teaching technique, must have started before Socrates, but only recently has attention been given to improving it. Though several writers have contributed, Norris Sanders wrote the most influential work on the subject.[7] He developed a questioning strategy around Bloom's *Taxonomy of Educational Objectives: Cognitive Domain*, which causes students to put together verbal responses that fit into the different areas of Bloom's *Taxonomy*. Along a similar line, I composed a group of model questions based on cognitive/psychomotor acts and categories of information.[8] These questions show how students can be caused to use different cognitive acts when responding to

[5] Flanders, N., *op cit.*

[6] Gordon, T.: Parent effectiveness training, New York, 1970, Peter H. Wyden/Publisher.

[7] Sanders, N.: Classroom questions: What kinds? New York, 1966, Harper & Row, Publishers.

[8] Charles, C.: Educational psychology: The instructional endeavor, St. Louis, 1972, The C. V. Mosby Co.

questions concerning any type of information.

Elsewhere, attention has been given to the distinction between closed questions and open questions. Closed questions require a short answer, such as a date, place, or yes or no, that is presumably the one correct answer. Open questions may have many correct answers, and they encourage students to compose and make longer responses that show organization and meaning.

The art of asking questions has also received attention. Investigators have found that teachers often answer their own questions almost as soon as they ask them. They have found, too, that teachers tend to change a question two or three times in the course of asking it. A third tendency is to repeat questions unnecessarily, often three or four times.

All in all, good questioning can greatly improve classroom communication. It can give students a chance to express themselves more; it can help them pinpoint and organize ideas, and it can cause them to use different kinds of cognitive abilities they possess and need to use. Perhaps as important as anything else, good questioning puts the teacher in the receiving role instead of the sending role, permitting active listening, support, and encouragement of student expression.

Congruent communication is a theme developed by Haim Ginott in his excellent book *Teacher and Child*.[9] He uses the term to mean "communication that harmonious, authentic; where words fit feelings." This type of communication, says Ginott, could transform education if it were diligently applied. It stresses that teachers, when speaking with students, should always endeavor to:

1. Focus on the problem, not the character of the student.

---

[9]Ginott, H.: Teacher and child, New York, 1972, The Macmillan Co.

2. Express genuine anger, but without insult.
3. Avoid commands; invite cooperation.
4. Acknowledge students and their contributions.
5. Avoid labeling students: that disables them.
6. Correct students by showing them how to do it right.
7. Avoid sarcasm.

Ginott's book also deals very practically with such matters as discipline, motivation, homework, and encounters with parents. Look at a copy. *Teacher and Child*—it is one of the most helpful books ever written for teachers.

Strategy: success

All persons, young and old, small and large, blessed and cursed, want one thing in common. They want with all their hearts to be successful—to be adept or skillful or cool at what they do and to have other people recognize it. All right, I know you will want to name an exception or two. I will only reply that those exceptions prove the rule (although I have never really understood exactly why exceptions prove the rule). I think I might be hard to convince that you can show me people who don't cherish success. I will agree that there are a lot of different ideas about what constitutes success, and I will agree that different people seek it in different ways. Still and all, at least 99 44/100 percent of us want to be good at what we do, and we want other people to know we are good.

When this fact of human nature is recognized, it seems strange that we don't go to greater lengths to ensure success for all students in school. They want and need success as much as you and I. Yet, our reward systems in school ordinarily permit only a favored few students to count themselves really successful. The majority—about two thirds according to Glasser—see themselves as falling a cut or more short of success.

Some people don't believe that success should come easily or often. Life is not like that, they say. You have to learn how to face up to hard realities. You can't be successful in everything you do. It would not be good for you even if you could. Failure toughens the spirit and hardens the will.

These things may be true for some people, but not for many. Repeated failure toughens few wills; it deadens many. Failure does not motivate, it dampens the courage to try. When you mention great souls who tried and tried again, you can be sure that it wasn't the experience of failure that spurred them on. It was something else—perhaps the very will to succeed that lies within us all—that made them keep trying despite failure.

I agree that occasional failure can teach lessons, and some good ones at that. Failure doesn't mean the end of the world. It doesn't mean you can't try again. I don't believe, however, that its lessons are so great that we want to be sure to provide daily tonics of failure. Let people know failure only when they have had opportunity, wherewithall, and good chance of success, and despite these conditions still do slipshod work. Occasionally let them try something beyond their ability, where they are bound to fail, but where wrath of tongue or grade will not follow. That's how they learn the length of their reach, without damage to will or ego.

In Chapters 5 and 15 we noted ways that schooling can be structured to maximize success. We saw, for example, that curricular topics could be divided into steps so that students could move easily from one to the next. This presupposes that students have reached a stage of intellectual development that permits their conceptualizing the content and processes being taught. We saw that virtually every student could reach mastery level in the material being learned if given sufficient time and help. We saw that you could use feedback systems that let students know clearly and often that their efforts are good, on the right track, and moving toward mas-

tery. Running through those feedback systems is the concept of positive reinforcement. This reinforcement can come in the form of knowledge of results, peer approval, verbal praise, or token reward systems of various kinds.

We noted, too, that competence is essential to success. You can make incompetents feel successful for a time—maybe forever if they don't get to compare their efforts against good models. Sooner or later, though, the harsh light of reality illuminates lack of competence. When that happens, the charade ends. You can't feel successful when you know you are incompetent. That's why we must help students move toward mastery of content and skills, however we can. This means helping them select learning topics of significance and importance to them. It means helping them identify attainable goals. It means structuring the material to maximize progress. And it means using feedback systems that let students know how fast and how well they are progressing.

Strategy: individualized instruction

The entire thrust of this book has been toward personalizing instruction. We personalize instruction when we begin doing the very best job of teaching each student that we possibly can—when we enhance learning environments, capitalize on interests and needs, maximize success possibilities, minimize threat and fear, and provide instruction matched to ability and cognitive style.

We know that personalized instruction does not always mean individualized instruction. Sometimes the best we can do for individual students is to have them work together in group activities. These activities can be carried out in large groups, as in singing, physical education, and group discussions. They can be carried out in small groups, such as in work groups, teams, and special project groups.

Often, however, the best we can do is to facilitate individualized work, where different students work at different topics in different ways. Perhaps you remember that work becomes individualized as one or more of five elements become different for different students. These five elements are contents, objectives, activities, time, and supervision—COATS. There are times, then, when we will want to individualize instruction—that is, make at least one of these five elements different for different students. In some special cases we may be able to vary all five elements. That is rarely possible in the classroom, however.

Rationales. When you think about individualizing your instruction, one basic consideration underlies all others. That consideration has to do with your philosophy about teaching and learning. Your philosophy reflects first whether you believe instruction should be behavior referenced, experience referenced, or possibly a combination of the two. Behavior-referenced instruction aims at student attainment of prespecified behavioral objectives. Experience-referenced instruction aims at providing the highest quality experiences, which allow students to move in directions their abilities and interests seek. We have previously considered these two approaches at length.

You no doubt remember that behavior-referenced instruction begins with a specific set of behavioral objectives, and the purpose of instruction is to enable students to reach those objectives. This kind of instruction is precise, efficient, and accurately evaluated. You always know where you are going and whether you are getting there.

However, many people don't think that's a proper way to go about instructing students. They think behavioral objectives tend to limit horizons, put a ceiling on student performance, and inhibit students' showing initiative, self direction, self evaluation, and so

forth. They think it is better to provide experience-referenced instruction, in which emphasis rests on the quality of experiences in which students engage. We judge the quality of experience in terms of whether the topics are significant to students; whether the activities allow the use of many different senses, such as sight, hearing, touch, taste, and smell; whether there are quantities of good instructional materials for students to use; and whether students can be responsible in large measure for deciding on the procedures they will follow in moving through the experiences. People who believe in experience-referenced instruction believe that this kind of instruction opens new vistas for students, allows them to move in different directions, and causes them to practice self direction, responsibility, and self evaluation.

The first thing, then, you will want to decide when you individualize instruction for your learners is whether you want to use a behavior-referenced approach or an experience-referenced approach. Or, as many people do, you may prefer a combination of these approaches. Typically, a combination approach will use behavioral objectives for basic knowledge and skills that are necessary to proceed through the materials and do work on one's own. Then the rest of the instruction is left in experience-referenced format so students can branch out as their interests dictate and follow through on their own.

A second fundamental consideration has to do with students' learning styles. Authorities have long written about the different ways students approach intellectual activities, and they have urged teachers to adapt instruction to those differences. In Chapter 6 we considered learning styles, examining the possibility that three rather distinct styles will be evident among students in typical classrooms. Those three styles were labeled Adventurers, Ponderers, and Drifters. Each style is considered equally "good." Yet each style suggests different kinds of instructional activities.

The Adventurers, you will remember, are those students who are very active, alert, bright eyed, eager, and curious. They are anxious to try out every new activity, to explore every new idea. They work well on their own, at least for a while. They are self starters. They do not require much support and encouragement from the teacher. However, they do not pay close attention to detail, and they tend to leave activities incomplete in their eagerness to move on to others.

The Ponderers may not appear as eager as the Adventurers. They start more slowly, but they persevere longer. They like structure. They seek positive feedback. They work through to the end, paying attention to details. They tend to produce high quality work, though it may not be as creative as that done by the Adventurers.

The Drifters neither begin easily nor persevere in their learning activities. They require structure and consistent positive feedback. Too, they usually require the physical presence of the teacher for encouragement, psychological support, and adherence to task.

These differences in learning styles suggest significantly different instructional approaches. Adventurers will likely seek and profit from experience-referenced instruction. Ponderers seek and profit from more structured approaches. Drifters require structure and direct guidance from the teacher. Thus, any single instructional approach will not meet the needs of all learners.

A third consideration in deciding which instructional strategies you will use involves preparation time and available resources. Most individualized approaches require considerable preparation. If you want to use learning centers, for example, you must plan to spend somewhere around fifty hours for organizing and putting together each center.

Once completed, though, you have an instructional device of long and useful life. The module on linear metric measurement, presented in Chapter 10, took about forty hours to prepare. The DPT program in kindergarten phonics, presented in Chapter 9, took about 100 hours to prepare. Both the module and the DPT program can be used for a number of years. Thus, their long-term value easily offsets the time required for preparation. Nevertheless, you should realize that they do take time to prepare.

Available resources, too, play an important role in your strategy selections. For example, you may lean philosophically toward experience-referenced instruction. Unless and until you acquire quantities of good instructional materials, you cannot do justice to this approach. Students must have activity and material options that capture attention and allow them to move in different directions. Fortunately, you can start small in experience-referenced instruction. Kohl, you remember, started with ten minutes per day of open experience. Meanwhile, he and his students began adding quantities of books and materials to the classroom. As they expanded their instructional capabilities, they were able to increase the amount of open experience.

If your inclination lies toward behavior-referenced approaches, you can get off to a good start if you have some commercial materials available. Many schools have kits of materials such as those described in Chapter 14. Most of the kits, such as the SRA materials, are behavior referenced. They aim at specific skill and knowledge attainment, and they can form a core for your individualized program while you prepare or acquire other necessary materials.

Behavior-referenced approaches. Let's go back now and review for a moment some of the different approaches we can use in behavior referenced instruction.

One of the most widely used approaches is

diagnostic-prescriptive teaching (DPT). This highly structured approach is individualized in that it allows students to work directly toward specific objectives identified through diagnostic procedures. It also allows them to work at their own speed. DPT, you remember, starts with comprehensive sets of behavioral objectives, which are instructional intents specified in advance. Diagnostic procedures are then used to determine which of the objectives individual students can already reach and which they cannot. For those they can reach, they receive no further instruction. For those they can't, they are given directions for work. Those directions are called prescriptions. Prescriptions indicate which objectives are to be worked toward and which materials and activities are necessary for working toward them. Later, criterion tests are used to ascertain whether students can reach the objectives toward which they have been working. Teachers keep track of all this on a large master form that shows which objectives each student has reached and, obviously, which objectives each student has not reached.

You might decide to use DPT if you were sure you knew what the students needed to learn, such as skill development in reading and mathematics. You might also use it for students whose cognitive styles seemed to be those of the Ponderer and the Drifter.

As far as preparation is concerned, DPT is not difficult to prepare and use, especially if you have sets of objectives with which to begin. If you have to compose the objectives, preparation time is increased considerably. To prepare a DPT program, you have to formulate or acquire sets of objectives, construct diagnostic and criterion tests (which may be one and the same), prepare prescriptions corresponding to each objective, arrange activities and materials for each prescription, and prepare forms for record keeping. While it does take some time to

prepare a program such as this, once prepared it is easy to use and keep track of. Generally speaking, most students work quite satisfactorily in DPT programs.

A second kind of behavior-referenced approach you might want to consider is modularized instruction. This approach too is quite structured. It uses behavioral objectives, as do all the behavior-referenced approaches. But it differs from DPT in that it provides optional learning activities for students. Like DPT, it uses pre- and post-assessment, but unlike DPT, it does not use specific prescription. In many ways the module is similar to a unit of instruction, a type of organization that has been with us for many years, especially in such subjects as social studies, language, and science. It organizes materials so that objectives, alternative activities, test materials, and directions for using the related materials are brought together in one packet.

Probably the outstanding aspect of modularized instruction is that it provides alternate activities, often as many as three or four different possibilities. Students can select the kind of activity that suits them best. Teachers prepare activities that involve different sensory modalities and suit different cognitive styles. They include some that emphasize reading. They include others that minimize reading while emphasizing other types of learning activities, such as construction projects, games, and audiovisual materials such as filmstrips, audio tapes, graphic materials, and so on. All these activities lead to attainment of the same objectives, but students select the type of activity they prefer.

A third kind of behavior-referenced approach you might use involves learning centers with behavioral objectives. Learning centers are at once the most interesting and the most limiting approach you can use in individualized instruction. They are interesting because they put together in a multisensory display materials and activities that are especially appealing to students. They contain objects, pictures, and examples of student work—the sorts of things that attract student's attention while drawing them into active engagement.

Learning centers are limiting, however, in that they do not easily permit individualization of more than a small part of any basic program. Physical limitations of size and space make it hard, for example, to individualize more than a small part of your mathematics, English, or biology program; you can't get enough materials and activities into a learning center to last very long. Of course you can continually change materials and activities, but when you do, you remove some that slower students still need to use. Another severe limitation of learning centers is that only a few students can work in a center at a given time. Therefore, other students have to be working at activities not included in the center.

All this, then, makes it difficult to build an individualized program entirely around learning centers. Still, it can be done, and some teachers put their entire elementary language arts program into learning centers. They include centers on handwriting, spelling, library reading, phonics, reading games and activities, various kinds of worksheets, and what have you.

Despite their limitations, learning centers are well worth the time and effort involved in putting together and using them. They add a dimension of excitement to the classroom. They display intriguing pictures, objects, and examples of student work. These materials are out for everyone to look at and handle. The centers can be set up in experience-referenced or behavior-referenced format, or in combinations of the two. They do have definite instructional value, and they are motivating to students. They are especially well suited to students whose cognitive styles we called Adventurers. They can also be very attractive to Ponderers, especially when they include objectives, directions, and means of checking work that has been completed.

A fourth kind of behavior-referenced approach is that which we have called nonformal basic programs. These programs are so varied that they resist description. Perhaps they can best be thought of as teachers' attempts to individualize instruction using whatever they have at hand in the way of textbooks, audiovisual materials, and other instructional materials. These programs can be suited to practically any teaching situation.

You can use nonformal basic programs very nicely with both Adventurers and Ponderers. You have to remember, however, that students whose learning styles we have called Drifters need both structure and the presence and encouragement of the teacher. Thus, nonformal basic programs, in which you simply tell students they have a certain amount of math, reading, or whatever to do during the week, do not work well with students who are not self starting and who cannot continue without supervision.

Now that you have a knowledge of other means of individualizing instruction, you will probably want to use nonformal basic programs only temporarily. Meanwhile you can be preparing more interesting and useful programs for your students.

A fifth kind of behavior-referenced program you can use involves commercially available sets of materials and activities. Paradoxically, commercial programs can be among the very best and the very worst individualized programs you can use. This paradox is not because of the way commercial materials are constructed. In some cases a well-prepared program simply will not be appropriate for the students in a given class. It won't suit their levels of ability, their interests, or their learning styles.

One thing you can be sure of with most commercial programs, however, is that technically they are very well organized. They are often put together by people who are experts in different cirricular areas. Usually, they are field tested with different students in different settings to prove their effectiveness.

Commercial programs have a drawback besides their failure to fit the abilities and cognitive styles of some of the students in a given class. They usually cost a good deal of money. The simplest kits cost about $60. Costs range up to hundreds of dollars for more elaborate programs, some of which use computers in instructing and testing. This factor puts many programs out of the reach of all but a few classrooms in which special money might be available.

Most teachers would like to have at least one commercially prepared kit in their classrooms, such as an SRA reading kit or mathematics kit, to use for a sizeable portion of a basic program. Then they design their own approaches, such as learning centers, DPT programs, or nonformal basic programs, for students not suited to the kit. Using commercial programs in this way reduces the preparation time necessary to initiate individualized instruction.

Experience-referenced approaches. As you know, experience-referenced programs place emphasis on the nature of learning experiences rather than on specific objectives to be attained. The philosophical viewpoint that supports the experience-referenced approach includes the belief that we can't specify all the worthwhile objectives we hope students will attain, and even if we could, we wouldn't want to, because specifying objectives puts restraints on students and tends to inhibit their branching out in directions that might be more suitable for them.

We will give brief attention to two experience-referenced approaches that have been treated extensively elsewhere in this book. The first is the open experience approach, in which students are allowed to select from among several different activity options available in the classroom. The other is the learning center approach that does not use behavioral objectives, consisting instead of collections of different kinds of activities and materials for students to explore and work through as their interests suggest.

The open experience approach upsets many teachers who have not tried it. They believe you are asking for trouble when, as they say, you just let students do whatever they please. How, they ask, can you expect students to learn anything at all worthwhile? If they are just going to play and fool around, they would do better to stay at home.

Those fears would be well grounded if teachers made no preparation for open experience sessions and if they reached no understandings with their students. Such is not the case in open experience, however. First, teachers realize that they must provide exciting, significant activities and intriguing materials if they hope to have students engage in and profit from open experience. Second, all students understand from the outset that their freedoms in open experience have limits. They reach only to the point where they begin to interfere with other students' rights. And they do not allow willful destruction of materials.

As was noted in Chapter 13, most teachers who try open experience in their classrooms like it. They find that students not only engage in the activities but that the amount of disruptive behavior often decreases while the amount of purposeful behavior increases.

A second experience-referenced approach involves the use of learning centers without behavioral objectives. Because learning centers are so attractive and compelling, students go to them naturally and explore the various kinds of activities and materials they contain.

This approach provides an excellent first step for teachers who have misgivings about open experience. The center provides outward structure, while allowing students some latitude. The center also appears organized, and you know that students who work there will be engaged in worthwhile activities.

WHAT YOU HAVE LEARNED

Having been a student most of your life, you have probably reached the end of certain instructive books only to ask yourself "What have I learned?" I hope you're not asking yourself that question now. But in case there's the slightest chance, I want to use a ploy I found helpful many years ago. Then, I would have my students recall, before they went home, what they had learned in school that day. That way, if their parents asked, they could say a little more than their usual answer "Nothin'."

The prime purpose of this book was to provide you the knowledge and skills necessary for personalizing instruction. That knowledge and skills include the following:

Chapter 3. The current meaning of humanism and how it influences education, especially in its attention to dignity, freedom, values, morality, feelings and emotions, and concern for others. Implications for schooling include promotion of trust, emphasis on helping students, and elimination of aversive, dehumanizing practices such as competitive grading and caustic discipline. Implications for teachers include warm, humane relations with students, flexibility, supportive facilitation, and provision of exciting, success-oriented learning environments.

Chapter 4. The meaning of self image and its relation to learning. Self image is significantly related to school achievement though the cause is not clear. Self image is also closely related to mental health. Implications for teachers include detection of poor self image, providing activities that enhance the self and providing a warm supportive learning environment for all students.

Chapter 5. Various techniques and practices believed helpful in enhancing self image. Beginning with the truism that self image is learned, the following approaches toward improving self image seem advisable:

Communication, including the facilitative aspects furnished by interaction analysis, parent effectiveness training, and transactional analysis.

Classroom meetings, as suggested by Glasser: social-problem–solving meetings, open-ended meetings, and educational-diagnostic meetings.

Facilitation, as suggested by Rogers, emphasizing learning that is significant, meaningful, self initiated, that involves feelings and intellect, that makes behavior and attitude differences in the learner, and that is evaluated by the learner. Teachers (facilitators) must be real, accepting, understanding, and trusting, while setting the class mood, eliciting and clarifying, and organizing and seeking out resources.

Values development, in which students identify what is important to them, through clarifying procedures, in an atmosphere of psychological safety.

Creativity, wherein students learn to be more flexible, fluent, and productive.

Behavior modification, which is a humane way of shaping desirable behavior while removing undesirable behavior, through use of principles of positive reinforcement and extinction.

Mastery/competence/success, using mastery strategies to help students feel capable and successful.

Chapter 6. The meaning of learning styles, how they are identified, how they relate to instruction and learning, what categories teachers might encounter in the classroom, and what kinds of comfort conditions, feedback systems, and instructional strategies seem most appropriate for different learning styles.

Chapter 8. Individualized instruction—what it means, various ways it is organized, and management details necessary to make different approaches successful. Such instruction falls into two main categories—behavior-referenced instruction and experience-referenced instruction. Specific strategies in behavior-referenced instruction include diagnostic-prescriptive teaching, modularized instruction, learning centers, informal basic programs, and commercial programs. Specific strategies in experience-referenced instruction include open experience and learning centers without behavioral objectives. Management details include room arrangement, instructional materials, schedules, placement and directions, tutoring and instructing, monitoring, assessing performance, conferencing, and record keeping.

Chapter 9. Diagnostic-prescriptive teaching (DPT)—its nature, uses, organization, and implementation, emphasizing the necessity for behavioral objectives, prescriptions, pre- and postassessment devices, attention to management details, and procedures for preparing DPT materials. This is a very precise method for teaching and evaluating.

Chapter 10. Modularized instruction—its nature, uses, organization, and implementation, emphasizing unitized format, optional learning activities, management details, and procedures for preparing modules. This approach maximizes organization and sense of direction.

Chapter 11. Nonformal basic programs—their nature, uses, organization, and implementation, emphasizing their diversity and ease of organization. They are built around whatever materials and conditions characterize a given class of students, and they can range from very simple to very complex.

Chapter 12. Learning centers—their nature, uses, organization, and implementation, emphasizing clustering of activities and materials, components, construction, management, and student reactions to learning centers. This approach lends itself well to both experience-referenced and behavior-referenced formats. Learning centers are attractive to students, and they enhance the overall classroom environment.

Chapter 13. Open experience—its nature, uses, organization, and implementation, emphasizing the rationale of student freedom and self direction, the advance preparation required, the working arrangements necessary, and ways of moving gradually from structured to open approaches in learning. The contributions of many people, including Rousseau, Pestalozzi, Froebel, Montessori, Piaget, Dewey, and Kohl helped shape the movement toward open education.

Chapter 14. Commercial programs—typical types, uses, and organization. Some, such as IPI and PLAN, are complex and costly and beyond the reach of most schools and teachers. Others, such as the various kits in reading, language, mathematics, and social studies, are relatively inexpensive (costing between $50 and $150), which makes them more available to typical classrooms. They are well planned and organized but won't suit all students' ability levels, interests, and learning styles.

Chapter 15. Mainstreaming of special education students, in which students previously assigned at least part of each day to special classes (EH, EMR, and others) are returning for full-day instruction in regular classes. Techniques helpful in facilitating their learning include success structuring, behavior modification, and precision teaching. Attention must also be given to stages of intellectual development, as described by Piaget.

Chapter 16. Instructional strategies, consistent with student abilities, interests, and learning styles and with teachers' philosophical viewpoints about teaching and learning. Many useful strategies are available. Teachers, as facilitative strategists, can select from among several options those that best suit the educational realities within which they function.

With the knowledge and skills detailed in each of these fourteen areas, you can move forward significantly in personalizing instruction for each and all of your students.

You will be successful.

Index